*Oracle Press*™

# PeopleSoft PeopleTools Data Management and Upgrade Handbook

Paula Dean
Jim J. Marion

New York  Chicago  San Francisco
Lisbon  London  Madrid  Mexico City  Milan
New Delhi  San Juan  Seoul  Singapore  Sydney  Toronto

The **McGraw·Hill** Companies

Cataloging-in-Publication Data is on file with the Library of Congress

McGraw-Hill books are available at special quantity discounts to use as premiums and sales promotions, or for use in corporate training programs. To contact a representative, please e-mail us at bulksales@mcgraw-hill.com.

**PeopleSoft PeopleTools Data Management and Upgrade Handbook**

1234567890   QFR QFR   1098765432

ISBN       978-0-07-178792-5
MHID       0-07-178792-5

| | | |
|---|---|---|
| **Sponsoring Editor**<br>Paul Carlstroem | **Acquisitions Coordinator**<br>Ryan Willard | **Production Supervisor**<br>Jean Bodeaux |
| **Editorial Supervisor**<br>Jody McKenzie | **Technical Editor**<br>Scott Schafer | **Composition**<br>Cenveo Publishing Services |
| **Developmental Editor**<br>Sarah K. Marion | **Copy Editor**<br>Lisa Theobald | **Art Director, Cover**<br>Jeff Weeks |
| **Project Editors**<br>Howie Severson and Emilia<br>Thiuri, Fortuitous Publishing<br>Services | **Proofreader**<br>Paul Tyler<br><br>**Indexer**<br>Jack Lewis | **Cover Designer**<br>Pattie Lee |

*This book is dedicated to my husband, Rick,
and two children, Danielle and Maddie.*
—*Paula Dean*


*In loving memory of Dr. Delmar Corrick. "I have
fought the good fight, I have finished the race,
I have kept the faith." II Timothy 4:7*
—*Jim J. Marion*

# About the Authors

**Paula Dean** is a Principal Instructor at Oracle University. She began her career as a PeopleSoft developer in 1996 and worked extensively with the product for the next 11 years. In that period she was involved in the initial implementation of the Financial install of PeopleSoft. Paula was a part of the upgrade team for multiple upgrades of the Financial and HCM products starting with release 6.5 through 8.44. She has first-hand, real-world experience in the field performing the upgrade process. She began teaching the technical PeopleSoft courses at Oracle University in 2007 and currently serves as the Lead Instructor for Upgrade and Data Management, SQR, and PeopleSoft Test Framework courses. She is also a presenter of PeopleTools topics at conferences such as Oracle OpenWorld, HEUG's Alliance, and OAUG's Collaborate.

**Jim J. Marion** is an AICPA Certified Information Technology professional who currently works as a Principal Sales Consultant at Oracle. He is the author of the Oracle Press book *PeopleSoft PeopleTools Tips & Techniques* and runs a popular blog for the PeopleSoft community at http:// jjmpsj.blogspot.com. Jim is also an international presenter of PeopleTools development topics at conferences such as Oracle OpenWorld, UKOUG events, HEUG's Alliance, Quest's IOUG, and OAUG's Collaborate.

## About the Developmental Editor

**Sarah K. Marion** is an English major with more than 20 years of experience working in education and ten years of experience working in the computer and publishing industry. She has a background in curriculum development and public speaking. She is listed in Who's Who of American Women and received the outstanding graduate award, graduating as a member of the honor society. She has an eye for detail, an ability to organize content, and a great sense of humor. Sarah is a wife and mother of three.

## About the Technical Editor

**Scott T. Schafer** has more than 14 years of experience working with PeopleTools and PeopleSoft applications. Over the last five years, Scott has worked as a Product Strategy Manager in the PeopleTools development organization. Prior to working in PeopleTools development, Scott spent six years in the PeopleSoft IT group, implementing and upgrading, and integrating the internal PeopleSoft Financial and CRM applications. Scott has presented PeopleTools topics at Oracle OpenWorld, HEUG's Alliance, Quest's IOUG, and OAUG's Collaborate. Scott graduated from Willamette University with a BS in economics and a master's degree in finance from Golden Gate University.

# Contents

## PART I
## Data Management

## PART II
## Change Management

### PART III
### Upgrades

PART IV
## Appendixes

# Foreword

Paula Dean and Jim Marion have taken their extensive knowledge and background with PeopleSoft implementations and upgrades, and translated it into a well thought out and organized handbook. A member of Oracle University, Paula is a highly respected senior instructor. Likewise, Jim Marion is a well-known, highly respected member of the PeopleSoft development community. Both have real-life and field experience with the technical aspects of the PeopleSoft product line. This book should be a valuable companion to anyone involved with the implementation, administration, customization, and upgrade of PeopleSoft applications and tools.

The PeopleSoft product family is a robust, flexible, extensible, open, and integration-friendly enterprise software line. The content of this book will help you maximize your knowledge of the PeopleSoft PeopleTools Data Management capabilities, allowing you to truly benefit from the deep technical functionality offered by PeopleSoft. Paula Dean and Jim Marion review best practices involving the PeopleSoft Data Management components within PeopleTools, which will help you move, diagnose, audit, and customize your enterprise data.

Greg Parikh
Senior Director
Oracle PeopleSoft Enterprise Information Development

# Acknowledgments

I would like to give special thanks to my husband, Rick. Working my full-time job, traveling, and writing a book in a matter of months in the evenings was the most challenging task I have undertaken to this point. Rick worked as an unsung hero, keeping our home intact and standing. If not for him taking on the additional roles during those months as I wrote, this book would not have been possible.

To my children, Danielle and Maddie, the support you have given and love you have shown from the project's inception through the completion of this book has been unwavering. Thank you for filling in while I was holed up in my office writing until all hours of the night.

I would like to thank Paul Carlstroem, Sheila Cepero, Stephanie Evans, Ryan Willard, and Jeff Picchione for helping me get this book started. To my manager, Jeff Picchione, thank you for your incredible support during this process and encouraging me to write this book. To Paco Aubrejuan, Greg Parikh, John Hall, Rob Green, Scott Stoll, Rob Zic, Chayne Kosloske, and Jeff Picchione, thank you for approving this book. Scott Schafer, thank you for accepting the role as the technical editor for this book; it was a pleasure working with you. Jim Marion, thank you for your contributions to this book; your knowledge and insights were invaluable. It has been a pleasure working with you on this book.

I would like to recognize special people who have contributed to making my life a better place—your love and care are appreciated and cherished. My sister in-law, who is really a sister to me—Cindy Jo Ledington, thank you for your unending love and support; you mean the world to me. I would also like to thank my mother, Lois, always my cheerleader. Great Aunt Ruth, your love and support over the years has meant the world to me. Bill and Janet Dean, my father and mother in-law, thank you for encouragement; you are loved.

My adopted daughter, Madison Caiarelli, the best friend a family could have. To my best friends who have been sisters to me, thank you for always lending an ear when needed—Lora Heaton and Lora Farrell.

The most important thank you is to my personal Lord and Savior Jesus Christ. With God all things are possible.

—Paula Dean

Thank you to my wife, Sarah, for spending the last three months converting my abstract ideas into intelligent documentation. To our children for playing quietly while we worked on this book. Nicolas Gasparotto for ALL of your PeopleSoft system administration blog posts. I wouldn't have a working test environment without your expertise. David Kurtz, the Oracle Data Management expert, for your great gems of wisdom shared online, in presentations, and through your book *PeopleSoft for the Oracle DBA*. Duncan Davies and Steve Elcock from Succeed Consultancy, Ltd., for being ready to test content against your servers. Hakan Biroglu and J. R. Hunter for some very good conversations on the OTN forums.

Thank you to my wonderful managers, Bud Oliver, Michael Boucher, and Michael Rosser, for approving this book and supporting me while writing this text. Paco Aubrejuan, Michael Krajicek, Michael Thompson, and Brent Mohl for their approval and technical expertise. I appreciate your willingness to explain the finer details of PeopleSoft's Life Cycle Management tools.

To siblings and extended family, thank you for your patience with us while we were frequently unavailable during the writing of this book. Our deepest gratitude to Uncle Pedro for your encouragement to "put on your shoes" and take the small steps necessary to accomplish big goals in life. To Marshall for your willingness to stay current in the computer world and your encouragement during this writing adventure; we did agree "How best to turn a phrase" during this book, and, Mike, for your authentic interest in the lives of others and ours especially during this project. Donnie and Kathleen, we appreciate the love and support you give to each and every person around you. Greg and Candy, without the two of you team Marion would not be writing books. Special thanks to Dirk for his assistance during Chapters 10 and 12. Thanks to CAB and BB.

Howie, you are awesome! Thanks to McGraw-Hill, Paul Carlstroem, Jody McKenzie, Ryan Willard, and Paula Dean for inviting us to join this project.

Thanks to all the PeopleSoft customers, consultants, and technical presales consultants who visit my blog, ask me questions at user groups, and communicate with me on a daily basis.

Most important, thank you to my personal Lord and Savior Jesus Christ. Writing a computer programming manual is a monumental effort. To do it in three months, as a second job, requires divine intervention. He is the chief author of all good ideas, the creative force leading all great innovation.

—Jim J. Marion

# Introduction

This book is for developers and system administrators who want to learn more about PeopleTools data and upgrade management. Whether you are looking for more information on Data Mover or PeopleSoft Test Framework or you are trying to implement a secure Environment Management Framework (EMF), this book will assist you in your pursuit of knowledge. By reading this book, you will learn how to manage data, apply routine maintenance, and plan for an upgrade.

## What's Inside

The content of this book is divided into four parts:

- Data Management
- Change Management
- Upgrades
- Appendixes

## Data Management

Functional users often debate which module represents the center of the software universe. Is it the general ledger, the human capital management system, or the customer relationship management system? The truth is, all of them are equally important. What is really at the heart of each of these enterprise systems? Data. In the "Data Management" part of this book, you will learn how to use Application Designer to build and maintain database structures (Chapter 2), Data Mover to maintain and migrate data (Chapter 3), and Data Archive Manager to archive and restore historical data (Chapter 4).

# Change Management

In "Change Management," you will learn how to install, configure, and utilize PeopleTools Change Management applications. In Chapter 6, you will learn how to configure the EMF, which is responsible for collecting information about and applying changes to PeopleSoft installations. Chapter 7 builds upon Chapter 6 by showing you how to use Change Assistant to find and deploy patches, bundles, and maintenance packs through the EMF. In Chapter 7 you will also learn how to create and deploy your own change packages the same way Oracle creates PeopleSoft patches.

When applying changes, it is important that you consider the impact of those changes upon the existing application. In Chapter 8 you will learn how to use Change Impact Analyzer to identify PeopleTools definitions affected by change packages.

Change is part of life. Nevertheless, an organization must control system changes. That *control* may involve locking definitions, auditing history, or versioning changes. In Chapter 9 you will learn how to use PeopleTools Change Control features to secure and audit PeopleTools definitions.

# Upgrades

Sometimes it seems that a fine line separates routine maintenance from an upgrade. Both require many of the same steps. The key difference, however, is size. An upgrade is a significantly larger version of routine maintenance. Because of the similarities, both utilize the same skills and tools. In Part III of this book you will learn about additional tools to help you perform a successful upgrade. In Chapter 11 you will learn how to create and interpret compare reports; in Chapter 12 you will learn how to record and run functional tests using the PeopleSoft Test Framework; and in Chapter 13 you will learn additional tips and techniques for a successful upgrade.

# Appendixes

Appendixes A and B complement the chapters in this book. Appendix A supplements Chapter 7 by showing you how to apply patches, bundles, and maintenance packs without using Change Assistant. Appendix B supplements

Chapter 3 by listing all of the commands and command modifiers that you can use when writing Data Mover scripts.

# PeopleTools Versions and Naming Conventions

All examples from this book use PeopleTools 8.52.03, the latest version of PeopleTools available. The bundle and maintenance pack examples specifically reference Supply Chain version 9.1 Feature Pack 2.

Each custom object described in this book is prefixed with the letters *OP* to help you distinguish your organization's custom objects form the custom objects in this book (unless, of course, your organization also uses the prefix OP). This prefix is an abbreviation for Oracle Press.

# PART
# I

# Data Management

# CHAPTER
## 1

# Understanding Data
# Management

ata management is an integral part of maintaining a healthy PeopleSoft ecosystem. Data management consists of building, moving, archiving, and auditing data to ensure consistency and accuracy. A healthy, well-maintained system offers peak performance.

# PeopleSoft Database Structure

A PeopleSoft database is partitioned into three layers: a database system catalog layer, a PeopleTools layer, and an application data layer (Figure 1-1).

## Database System Catalog Layer

Relational database management systems (RDBMS) maintain a collection of tables known as the *database system catalog* (system catalog for short). These catalog tables, or metadata tables, contain significant amounts of information describing table and column definitions, index specifications, procedure instructions, view definitions, as well as many other types of data. Unlike other tables in the RDBMS, we will not interact directly with the system catalog. Rather, we maintain system tables through RDBMS-supplied tools and application programming interfaces (APIs). For example, to insert a

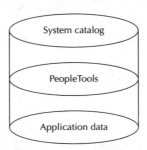

**FIGURE 1-1.** *The three layers of a PeopleSoft database*

new row into the RDBMS system table for storing views, you would execute SQL similar to the following:

```
CREATE VIEW PS_OP_OPR_EMP_MAP (OPRID, EMPLID) AS
SELECT OPR.OPRID
     , EMPL.EMPLID
  FROM PSOPRDEFN OPR
 INNER JOIN PSOPRALIAS EMPL
    ON OPR.OPRID = EMPL.OPRID
 WHERE OPRALIASTYPE = 'EMP'
```

To list all views in your database system catalog, execute the following SQL:

```
-- Oracle
SELECT * FROM DBA_VIEWS

-- Microsoft SQL
SELECT * FROM INFORMATION_SCHEMA.VIEWS
```

**NOTE**
*Although it is possible to maintain a PeopleSoft database using system APIs only, this is not recommended. Instead, Oracle recommends using PeopleSoft-specific maintenance tools. Using the correct tools will simplify your upgrade process and help you maintain a healthy system.*

# PeopleTools Layer

PeopleTools maintains a set of metadata tables very similar, and sometimes redundant, to the system tables. For example, the *PeopleTools layer* includes a table named PSRECDEFN. This table describes record definitions in a manner very similar to Oracle's DBA_TABLES. Why the redundancy? PeopleSoft tables exist first as abstract ideas stored as metadata artifacts and second as physical tables managed by the system layer. This abstraction allows developers to model data structures first as field definitions and then as a collection of fields (aka record definition); finally, it allows developers to construct data structures as physical tables within the system catalog layer.

Another great reason for metadata redundancy is database independence. PeopleSoft applications run on several different database platforms. The PeopleTools abstraction layer allows PeopleSoft applications to run on multiple database platforms without maintaining separate designs.

Although the contents may differ, the structure of the PeopleTools layer is consistent across all PeopleSoft application product lines. Oracle maintains this structure through PeopleTools patches, bundles, and updates.

## Application Data Layer

The *application data layer* forms the persistence architecture for application-specific data. Unlike PeopleTools tables, which stay consistent across PeopleSoft applications, application tables differ among applications. For example, the PS_JRNL_HEADER table within PeopleSoft's Financials module might not make sense in the Human Capital Management (HCM) application, and therefore would not exist in an HCM application data layer.

Part I of this book focuses primarily on the management of this layer, setting aside the PeopleTools layer for Part II, and leaving the system layer to expert DBAs such as David Kurtz.

When reviewing tables with RDBMS-specific tools such as SQL Developer, we can differentiate system, PeopleTools, and application tables by their prefix. All PeopleSoft-managed table names use the prefix PS. Generally speaking, we can distinguish tools tables from application tables by the underscore (_) character; application tables always begin with PS_.

**NOTE**
*Some tables seem to be non-application tables but have the prefix PS_. Because they aren't application tables, you might be tempted to think of them as tools tables. There is, however, another small set of records that belong to a category called common components. These are neither application nor tools tables.*

# Application Data Layer Management Tools

Oracle's PeopleTools suite contains a handful of tools designed for data management: Application Designer, Data Mover, Data Archive Manager, and auditing tools.

## Application Designer

Application Designer is a very important tool for building and maintaining a PeopleSoft database. Oracle's PeopleTools developers use Application Designer to create and modify layer 2, PeopleTools tables. Application developers use it to define and change layer 3, application tables. Chapter 2 covers the data management aspects of Application Designer.

## Data Mover

Data Mover is a tool used for importing and exporting data from PeopleSoft databases. Oracle uses it to deliver important PeopleTools and application updates. System administrators and developers use this program to migrate data between PeopleSoft instances. Chapter 3 will show you how to use this database-independent data management application.

## Data Archive Manager

It is the nature of a database to store data. Even though a database has an unlimited appetite, we often work in an environment with limited resources. When databases grow too big for their storage disks and indexing is not improving performance, you have some decisions to make: archive or add more disk space? In Chapter 4, you will learn how to use Data Archive Manager, a tool that helps you effectively move data out of your main transaction processing tables.

## Data and Configuration Auditing Tools

PeopleTools offers a variety of ways to maintain your data and data model. For example, Application Designer is a program for maintaining both the PeopleTools metadata and system catalog database layers. Other applications, such as database platform's data definition language (DDL) tools, interact only with the database system catalog. In this book, you will learn how to use PeopleSoft's audit features to reconcile the differences that may arise from the improper use of these tools.

# Conclusion

This book is about tools—with emphasis on the plural. Even within the first few pages of this book we have identified several tools for your data management toolbox. Each has its purpose. To ignore one and favor another would be the same as a carpenter who uses only a hammer, ignoring his saw, planer, joiner, and other tools.

Often, the best tool is a new tool crafted by you that combines portions of other tools. Here is an example of a tool that joins *system* metadata and APIs with *tools* metadata to identify all views that reference the table PSOPRDEFN:

```
SELECT R.RECNAME
     , DBMS_METADATA.GET_DDL('VIEW', D.NAME)
  FROM USER_DEPENDENCIES D
 INNER JOIN PSRECDEFN R
    ON DECODE(R.SQLTABLENAME,
              ' ', 'PS_' || R.RECNAME,
              R.SQLTABLENAME) = D.NAME
 WHERE D.TYPE = 'VIEW'
   AND D.REFERENCED_NAME = 'PSOPRDEFN'
```

# CHAPTER
## 2

# Data Management
# with Application
# Designer

pplication Designer is an application development environment for PeopleSoft developers. Don't tell the developers, but Application Designer is really a metadata management tool.

# Abstract Data Modeling

When a user enters information into a PeopleSoft page and then saves that page, where is that information stored? When a user selects a value from a list, from whence did that list originate? The answer to both questions is the *physical implementation of a data model*. The PeopleSoft database is the persistence layer for a PeopleSoft application, and the data model is the blueprint.

Database systems use the term "table" to describe a collection of columns and rows. The term "column" is often synonymous with the term "field." The term "record" refers to a single row within a table. A *record definition* is a collection of fields describing that single row. A collection of records is known as a *table*. Therefore, in this chapter, when you see *record*, it refers to a single row in a table; a *record definition* identifies a record's blueprint, and a *table* is a physical representation of a record definition, which, by definition, is a collection of records.

## Field Definitions

From the database's perspective, a field is an attribute of a table. A field does not exist without its table. As far as the database is concerned, two fields with identical definitions in two different tables have no relationship. The two fields may contain completely different data. If a relationship is supposed to exist between the two fields, the database expects to find some type of relationship definition, such as a foreign key constraint.

PeopleSoft takes a different approach, however. *Field definitions* are independent objects that may be associated with database tables. By convention, two tables containing the same field definition should contain the same data. A field's placement within a table determines the field's relationship to like-named fields in other tables. For example, the PSOPRDEFN, PS_OPR_DEF_TBL_AP, and PS_VOUCHER tables all contain the field named OPRID. In each of these tables, the OPRID field has the exact same definition: character with a length of 30. If you compare the data in the OPRID field among these three tables, you should find similar values. In PSOPRDEFN and PS_OPR_DEF_ TBL_AP, OPRID is identified as a key field. OPRID is not part of the PS_ VOUCHER record's primary index. From this information, we infer that OPRID in PS_VOUCHER is a foreign key to both PS_OPR_DEF_TBL_AP and PSOPRDEFN.

Sometimes a record contains multiple fields with similar meaning but different data. Continuing with the PS_VOUCHER example, this table has OPRID, KK_TTRAN_OVER_OPRID, and OPRID_LAST_UPDT fields. Each of these *OPRID* fields represents a foreign-key relationship to PSOPRDEFN (and potentially some other OPRID table, such as PS_OPR_DEF_TBL_AP).

If two fields in two separate tables have the same name, and both of those tables are included in the same transaction, the PeopleSoft component processor will infer a relationship between those fields. This is important when defining database hierarchies. Hierarchies are common in relational databases. The PeopleSoft Financials and Supply Chain Management application, for example, has several hierarchies. Vouchers, Journal Entries, and Purchase Orders all have header tables and line tables.

Some tables, however, have fields with the same name and same meaning, but no relationship. EFFDT and DESCR are examples of this type of field. The DESCR field is a common fixture of prompt tables. This field serves the same purpose in each table, but no relationship exists between the two fields.

## Creating Field Definitions

As a financial analyst and accountant, my top priority was reporting. The effort required to prepare a report was directly related to database design. Reporting typically requires combining information from a variety of systems with related information. Typically, an analyst has to scrub and reformat data before it can be related. For example, one table may store department ID as a character field while another stores the exact same values in a number field. Because these fields have different types, some database systems won't allow them to be joined together. We can certainly understand two separate systems having different designs. The most frustrating situation, however, is to find one system employing two different designs for the same data. An example of this is a department lookup table that defines department ID as a character, whereas the related transaction tables define department ID as a numeric field.

When they are designing data structures using standard database management tools, database designers find it very easy to create these types of inconsistencies. Database designs often start with a table and relegate fields to the low position of table attributes with no provision for reconciling related attributes between tables. Application Designer protects against this type of inconsistency by defining fields as standalone definitions. Every Application Designer–built table that contains a particular field will define that field using the exact same DDL.

Let's create a field definition to see how it works.

1. In Application Designer, select File | New. Application Designer will respond by displaying the New Definition dialog box, which contains a list of possible object types.

2. From this dialog, choose Field. Application Designer will display the field's editor window (Figure 2-1), where you can specify both data and display attributes.

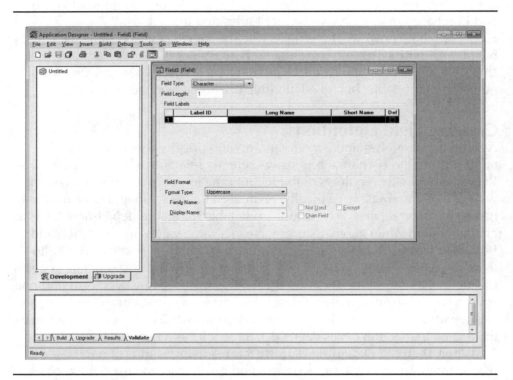

**FIGURE 2-1.**   *Application Designer field definition editor*

3. Set the Field Type to Character (the default value) and set the Field Length to 10. Application Designer will use these values when generating DDL for tables that include this field. For most database platforms, *Character* is a loose term for at least two different field types: CHAR and VARCHAR. Which one will Application Designer choose? We will let Application Designer answer that question later when we build a table from a record definition.

4. Next, Application Designer requires that we specify a Field Label before saving. Enter **OP_DOC_ID** as the Label ID, **Document ID** as the Long Name, and **Doc ID** as the Short Name. Field labels are used by the PeopleSoft application when displaying a field's information. They have nothing to do with the data model. Fields often have multiple labels. The URL field, for example, has nine labels, one for each type of URL stored in the database. By convention, the first Field Label has the same name as the field.

5. Choose File | Save. When prompted, name this field **OP_DOC_ID**.

The finished field definition in Application Designer is shown in Figure 2-2.

# Record Definitions

"Record" is the generic Application Designer term given to any row/column container. Of the seven record definition types, only three will become database-managed definitions: SQL Table, SQL View, and Temporary Table. The other four represent in-memory PeopleSoft-specific row/column containers.

Record definitions require predefined fields. Every field on a record must exist in Application Designer before it can be added to a record. This requires careful planning and design before you construct record definitions.

## Creating Record Definitions

Let's create a record definition to store URL's (bookmarks) of valuable PeopleTools data management pages that exist on the open Internet.

1. Choose File | New.

2. When prompted to select a definition type, choose Record.

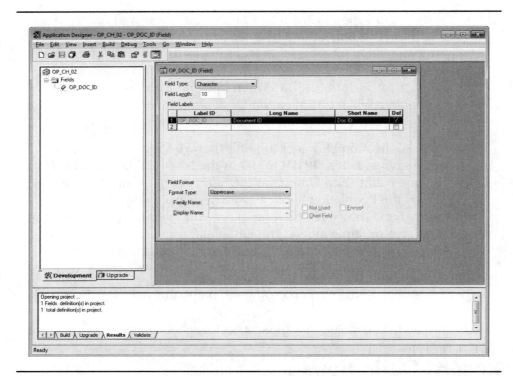

**FIGURE 2-2.** `OP_DOC_ID` *field definition*

3. Application Designer will respond by displaying an empty Record designer. Add fields to this record definition by choosing Insert | Field.

4. In the Insert Field dialog (Figure 2-3), enter the Name as **OP_DOC_ID**.

5. With the Insert Field dialog still open, add the DESCR and URL fields.

6. When finished, close the Insert Field dialog by clicking the Cancel button.

7. Save the record definition as OP_DM_DOCS. This name will appear in the title bar of the edit window, as shown in Figure 2-4.

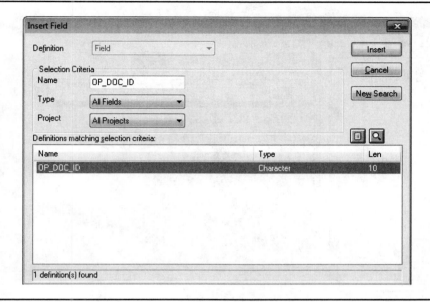

**FIGURE 2-3.** *Insert Field dialog*

Upon saving, depending on your database platform, you may see a Change Space dialog (Figure 2-5). Some database platforms, such as Oracle and DB2, use *tablespaces* to manage data files. The Available Space Name drop-down list shows the available tablespaces within your PeopleSoft database. If your database uses tablespaces to manage storage, select an appropriate tablespace from the drop-down menu. For this example, choose PTTLRG.

**NOTE**
*If the Available Space Name drop-down list is empty, run* setspace.sqr *to update PeopleSoft's tablespace metadata. Running* setspace.sqr *is a database creation step that is very easy to miss because it has no impact until you try to add new record definitions.*

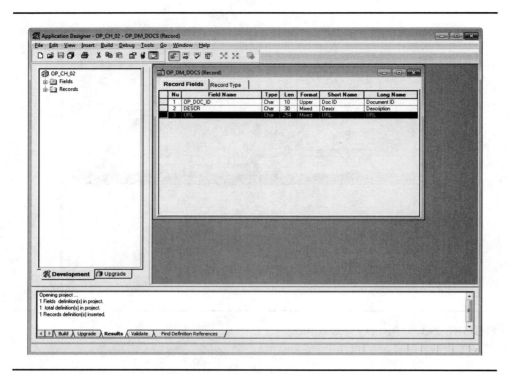

**FIGURE 2-4.** OP_DM_DOCS *record definition*

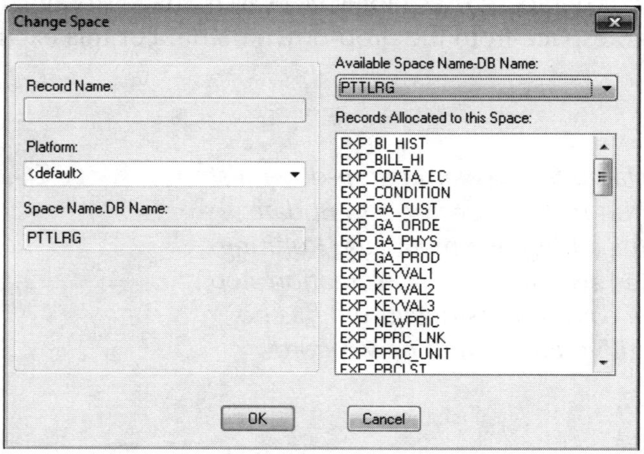

**FIGURE 2-5.** *Change Space dialog*

## Which Tablespace Should I Choose?

Most PeopleSoft modules, such as eProcurement or Absence Management, have APP, LRG, and WORK tablespaces. The general guideline is to place configuration data in APP, transaction data in LRG, and working storage in WORK. Your DBA may have additional recommendations. For example, your DBA might prefer to create a new tablespace for custom tables.

PeopleTools stores the list of available tablespaces in PSTBLSPCCAT. If the tablespace you require isn't displayed in the list, run setspace.sqr to update Application Designer's metadata. The setspace.sqr program inserts rows into PSTBLSPCCAT only for tablespaces that have existing tables. If the tablespace is empty, you can insert a row into PSTBLSPCCAT by cloning an existing row in PSTBLSPCCAT. For example, suppose I create a new tablespace named OPLRG on Oracle using DDL:

```
CREATE TABLESPACE OPLRG
  DATAFILE '/u01/app/oracle/oradata/FSCM912/oplrg'
  SIZE 100M
  EXTENT MANAGEMENT LOCAL AUTOALLOCATE
  SEGMENT SPACE MANAGEMENT AUTO
```

I could insert a row into PSTBLSPCCAT using SQL:

```
-- Copy a row, but give it a different name
INSERT INTO PSTBLSPCCAT (
      DDLSPACENAME
    , DBNAME
    , TSTYPE
    , DBXTSTYPE
    , COMMENTS )
SELECT 'OPLRG'
    , DBNAME
    , TSTYPE
    , DBXTSTYPE
    , NULL
  FROM PSTBLSPCCAT
 WHERE DDLSPACENAME = 'PTTLRG'
```

## Building Record Definitions

We have now defined enough metadata to build a physical table from this record definition.

1. In the Application Designer editor window, choose Build | Current Definition.

2. In the Build dialog box (Figure 2-6), select Create Tables from the Build Options and select Build Script File from the Build Execute Options. This will generate the DDL necessary to construct this physical table, but it won't actually run the DDL against the PeopleSoft database.

3. Click the Build button to generate the DDL.

**NOTE**
Build *is a generic term that refers to any action that alters the design of the PeopleSoft database. This includes creating as well as altering definitions.*

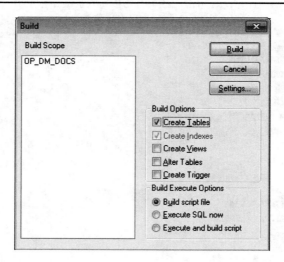

**FIGURE 2-6.** *Build dialog*

The DDL creation step should run quickly. As the process runs, PeopleSoft will log information about the build process to the Build tab displayed at the bottom of Application Designer. The contents should resemble these:

```
SQL Build process began on 6/4/2012 at 11:36:15 PM for database
    FSCM912.


SQL Build process ended on 6/4/2012 at 11:36:15 PM.
1 records processed, 0 errors, 0 warnings.
SQL Build script for all processes written to file
    C:\Temp\PSBUILD.SQL.
SQL Build log file written to C:\Temp\PSBUILD.LOG.
```

In the log output, take note of the line `1 records processed, 0 errors, 0 warnings`. Resolve any errors or warnings before continuing.

The generated DDL should be similar to this:

```
CREATE TABLE PS_OP_DM_DOCS (OP_DOC_ID VARCHAR2(10) NOT NULL,
    DESCR VARCHAR2(30) NOT NULL,
    URL VARCHAR2(254) NOT NULL) TABLESPACE PTTLRG STORAGE (INITIAL
40000 NEXT 100000 MAXEXTENTS UNLIMITED PCTINCREASE 0) PCTFREE 10
PCTUSED 80
```

4. After verifying the generated DDL you can do one of the following:

   ■ Run it directly in your preferred SQL tool (as the database or schema owner).

   ■ Hand it off to your DBA for review and execution.

   ■ Rerun the Application Designer build process and choose Execute SQL Now from the Build Execute Options in the Build dialog.

5. To alter the DDL that the Application Designer generates, choose Tools | Data Administration | Record DDL...

6. From the Maintain Record DDL dialog (Figure 2-7), you can preview the DDL that Application Designer will generate or change DDL parameter values. For example, to change the Oracle MAXEXT parameter, select the parameter in the dialog and then click the Edit Parm button.

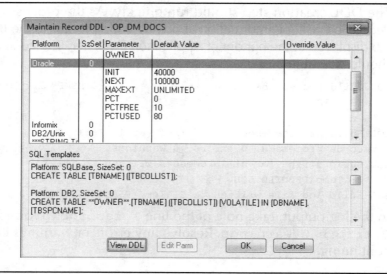

**FIGURE 2-7.** *Maintain Record DDL dialog*

What fun is a table without any data? To make our examples more interesting, insert some of your favorite PeopleSoft data management documents into this table. Here is an SQL script containing a few of my favorites:

```
INSERT INTO PS_OP_DM_DOCS
VALUES ('USEEDIT'
, 'The Mystical USEEDIT - Joe Ngo'
, 'http://xtrahot.chili-mango.net/2005/09/the-mystical-useedit/')
/

INSERT INTO PS_OP_DM_DOCS
VALUES ('PTTBLS'
, 'PeopleTools Table Reference'
, 'http://www.go-faster.co.uk/peopletools/')
/

INSERT INTO PS_OP_DM_DOCS
VALUES ('SETSPCSQR'
, 'Running setspace.sqr'
, 'http://peoplesoft.wikidot.com/no-tablespaces')
/
```

## Altering Tables

Let's add a few common audit fields to our new OP_DM_DOCS record definition. In Application Designer, choose Insert | Field. Insert the fields OPRID_ENTERED_BY, OPRID_MODIFIED_BY, and LAST_DTTM_UPDATE (Figure 2-8). Then save the record.

Recall that Chapter 1 discussed the three layers of a PeopleSoft database. Adding fields to a record definition updates the PeopleTools layer, the set of tables used by the PeopleSoft runtime to display and validate information. To populate these fields, we need to alter the database physically. This ALTER step will update the system layer.

To alter a table, choose Build | Current Definition. Application Designer will display the Build dialog (Figure 2-9). This time, instead of selecting the Create Tables build option, select Alter Tables. When Alter Tables is selected, notice that Application Designer automatically disables the Create Indexes and Create Trigger options.

An ALTER operation can be very destructive, however. Changing field sizes, dropping fields, and other such operations can result in data loss and corruption. Build settings offer us control over these types of operations.

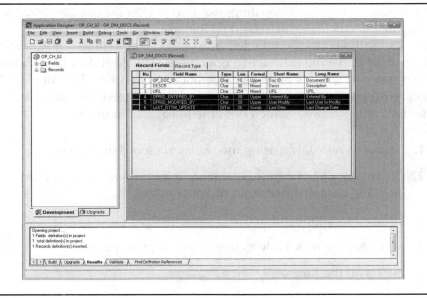

**FIGURE 2-8.** OP_DM_DOCS *with audit fields*

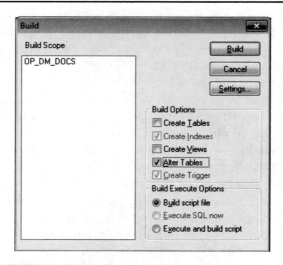

**FIGURE 2-9.** *Build dialog for* OP_DM_DOCS

With the Build dialog open, click the Settings button to open the Build Settings dialog. Figure 2-10 shows the settings we used to alter the OP_DM_DOCS table after adding three fields to the record definition.

The four radio buttons on the left side of the Alter settings tell Application Designer how to handle destructive operations. The Alter Any checkboxes on the right specify the types of ALTER operations to perform. The Alter Table Options group box contains the only setting we changed. The default option is Alter By Table Rename, which does the following, in order:

1. Creates a new table using the updated record definition.

2. Copies data from the original table into the new table (includes inserting default values into the new fields).

3. Drops the original table.

4. Renames the new table to match the original name.

5. Builds all the indexes.

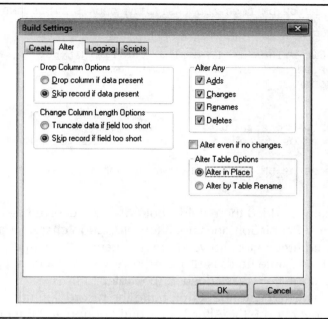

**FIGURE 2-10.**   *Alter build settings*

Alter By Table Rename is a safe way to perform an ALTER, but it may not be the most efficient way. Because our ALTER is not destructive and does not involve data conversions, we can choose either method: Alter In Place or Alter By Table Rename.

When you are satisfied with the ALTER settings, click OK in the Build Settings dialog to return to the Build dialog. When you are altering records, in the Build Execute Options section of the Build dialog, the option Build Script File is selected by default.

It is a good practice to review ALTER scripts before executing them. Ensure that Build Script File is selected and click the Build button. When the process completes, review the Build tab at the bottom of Application Designer. Verify that there are no errors, and then double-click the row containing the generated SQL Build script. The generated script should look similar to the following (comments added for clarity):

```
-- Add the new fields to the table
ALTER TABLE PS_OP_DM_DOCS ADD OPRID_ENTERED_BY VARCHAR2(30)
/
ALTER TABLE PS_OP_DM_DOCS ADD OPRID_MODIFIED_BY VARCHAR2(30)
/
```

```
ALTER TABLE PS_OP_DM_DOCS ADD LAST_DTTM_UPDATE TIMESTAMP
/

-- Set default values as defined by the field types
UPDATE PS_OP_DM_DOCS SET OPRID_ENTERED_BY = ' ',
    OPRID_MODIFIED_BY = ' '
/

-- Add NOT NULL constraints to non-nullable fields
ALTER TABLE PS_OP_DM_DOCS MODIFY OPRID_ENTERED_BY NOT NULL
/
ALTER TABLE PS_OP_DM_DOCS MODIFY OPRID_MODIFIED_BY NOT NULL
/
```

Notice that we added three fields, but only two received default values and constraints. PeopleSoft does not allow NULLs in character and numeric fields. Date and time fields, however, may accept NULL values. The default value for date and time fields is NULL—the very same value supplied by the database when the field was added to the table.

If you are satisfied with the script, build the record definition again. In the Build dialog, choose the Alter Tables build option and the Execute And Build Script option. Click the Build button to complete the ALTER.

When adding fields to tables, data administrator should have a pretty good understanding of the new information those fields will contain. If this is the case, feel free to modify the update section of the generated script. For example, if the new fields are supposed to contain values from other tables within the database, you can modify the updates to include subqueries. Unfortunately, Application Designer will not run your modified script, so you will need to run it with your preferred SQL tool.

# Indexes

PeopleSoft applications use indexes for two purposes: for constraints and performance. A primary key definition is an example of an index-based constraint. Alternate search keys are examples of performance indexes.

## Creating Indexes

Let's add primary and alternate search keys to our new record OP_DM_DOCS.

1. Open the record OP_DM_DOCS in Application Designer.

2. Select the OP_DOC_ID field by clicking anywhere within the first row.

3. Choose Edit | Record Field Properties to open the Record Field Properties dialog.

4. In the Keys column at the left (Figure 2-11), check the boxes Key, Search Key, and List Box Item.

5. Click OK to return to the editor window.

Every field marked as a Key field will become part of a table's primary key. Oracle recommends that all Key fields be listed before other fields and arranged by cardinality, lowest to highest. For example, most transaction tables have a composite key comprising a BUSINESS_UNIT as well as some other key field (VOUCHER_ID, EMPLID, and so on). BUSINESS_UNIT

**FIGURE 2-11.**  OP_DOC_ID *index definition in the Record Field Properties dialog*

has a very low cardinality, whereas the other key field usually has a high cardinality. In delivered record definitions, you will notice that BUSINESS_ UNIT is usually listed first, and the high-cardinality field is listed second.

**NOTE**
*Cardinality refers to the distribution of unique values within a database column. High cardinality means each row contains a unique value. A column with few unique values, such as Business Unit or Set ID, however, has a low cardinality.*

Alternate search keys will become performance-based indexes. In the OP_DM_DOCS record definition in the editor window, select the DESCR field. Then choose Edit I Record Field Properties. In the Record Field Properties dialog, check the boxes for Alternate Search Key and List Box Item. Click OK to save the record definition.

## Building Indexes
Let's build the indexes defined thus far.

1. Choose Build I Current Definition.

2. When the Build dialog appears, select Create Indexes from Build Options and select Build Script File from Build Execute Options. This will generate an SQL script that resembles the following:

```
CREATE UNIQUE  iNDEX PS_OP_DM_DOCS ON PS_OP_DM_DOCS (OP_DOC_ID)
 TABLESPACE PSINDEX STORAGE (INITIAL 40000 NEXT 100000 MAXEXTENTS
 UNLIMITED PCTINCREASE 0) PCTFREE 10 PARALLEL NOLOGGING
/
ALTER INDEX PS_OP_DM_DOCS NOPARALLEL LOGGING
/
CREATE   INDEX PS0OP_DM_DOCS ON PS_OP_DM_DOCS (DESCR,
  OP_DOC_ID) TABLESPACE PSINDEX STORAGE (INITIAL 40000 NEXT 100000
 MAXEXTENTS UNLIMITED PCTINCREASE 0) PCTFREE 10 PARALLEL NOLOGGING
/
ALTER INDEX PS0OP_DM_DOCS NOPARALLEL LOGGING
/
```

3. If your DDL is satisfactory, rerun the build step, but this time, in the Build dialog, choose Execute And Build Script from the Build Execute Options, and then click Build.

Through Application Designer, we can review and change an index's DDL in a manner similar to the way we configure table DDL. To view or modify index definitions, choose Tools | Data Administration | Indexes to open the Change Record Indexes dialog (Figure 2-12).

In the Change Record Indexes dialog, we can add new indexes, edit existing indexes, and even change the DDL for a particular index. Later, we will add more fields to this record and then use this dialog to create new indexes. Notice the first index definition is of type Key and contains one field. This is the primary key and will share the same name as the base table: PS_OP_DM_DOCS.

Index 0 (zero) in the second entry represents the search and alternate search keys. These fields are grouped into a single index because they are typically used together on PeopleSoft search pages.

Select the index 0 line and click the Edit DDL button. The Maintain Index DDL dialog opens (Figure 2-13). The top portion of this dialog contains platform-specific DDL parameters and default values. You can override these default values by selecting a parameter and clicking the Edit Parm button.

For example, scroll down the list to the Oracle Platform and select the BITMAP parameter. Since this parameter has no default value, the BITMAP keyword will be left off the index, creating a B-tree index. To create a

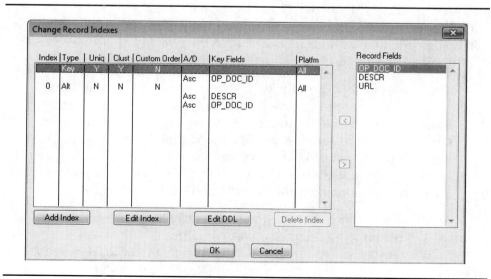

**FIGURE 2-12.**  OP_DM_DOCS *indexes*

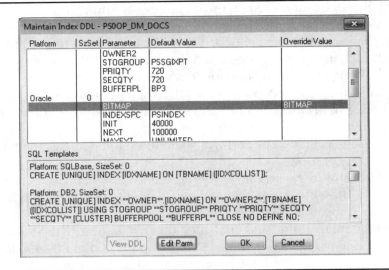

**FIGURE 2-13.** *Maintain Index DDL dialog with a* `BITMAP` *override*

## Index Tablespace

The default PeopleSoft index DDL places all indexes in the same tablespace: `PSINDEX`. Placing all indexes in the same tablespace is not recommended. In his book, *PeopleSoft for the Oracle DBA* (Apress, 2012) David Kurtz says:

> You can typically expect the total volume of index segments to be greater than the total volume of table segments in a PeopleSoft database. So, the index tablespace can be larger than all the table tablespaces put together. As such, a monolithic index tablespace can produce administrative problems and risks. For example, if you have a file corruption to a database in this tablespace, the scope of the recovery operation is much wider and more complex.

> David's book shows how to update the DDL templates to insert indexes into tablespaces named after their tables. Using David's approach, our `OP_DM_DOC` indexes would go in a tablespace named `PTTLRG_IDX`. We will discuss modifying the DDL templates later in this chapter in the section, "Managing DDL Models."

Bitmap index instead of a B-tree index, click the Edit Parm button and, in the Override Column, enter an Override Value of BITMAP and then click OK to return to the Maintain Index DDL dialog. You'll see the parameter appear for the Oracle platform in the dialog (Figure 2-13).

## Adding Custom Indexes

DBAs are often tasked with identifying database performance issues. A proactive DBA will review a list of common, long-running SQL statements and look for ways to optimize performance. Adding indexes is a common optimization technique. Generating these indexes outside of PeopleTools has unfortunate side effects, however, because any Application Designer maintenance involving that same record definition will delete the externally generated index. Often, this deletion is transparent, causing performance to degrade and requiring the DBA to repeat his or her analysis and resolution steps.

**TIP**
*Be sure to add indexes to your projects. The only way to see a custom index is through a dialog buried in the Data Administration menu. Custom indexes are very easy to miss during project migration.*

An alternative is to make PeopleTools aware of custom indexes by adding them to a record's metadata within Application Designer. OPRID_ ENTERED_BY and OPRID_MODIFIED_BY will contain a PeopleSoft user ID. They are foreign keys to the OPRID field of record PSOPRDEFN.

Let's create custom indexes for these fields as well as the LAST_DTTM_ UPDATE field. (Secure Enterprise Search incremental build queries use LAST_DTTM_UPDATE to identify changes.)

1. In Application Designer, choose Tools | Data Administration | Indexes.

2. Click the Add Index button to create a new index. Application Designer will display the Add Index dialog (Figure 2-14).

3. Select options appropriate for your index and enter some comments. For this example, accept the defaults.

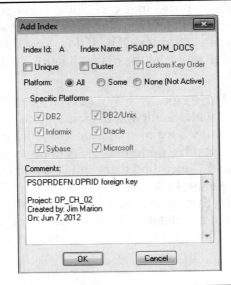

**FIGURE 2-14.** *Add Index dialog for the* `OPRID_ENTERED_BY` *field*

4. Click OK to close the dialog and add fields to the index.

5. From the Record Fields list, select the `OPRID_ENTERED_BY` field and use the < (less than symbol) shuttle button to add the field to the index.

6. Repeat the same steps for the `LAST_DTTM_UPDATE` field. Figure 2-15 shows how the Change Record Indexes dialog should appear after adding these indexes.

**NOTE**
*Notice that we didn't create an index for* `OPRID_MODIFIED_BY`. *Proper indexing is critical to database performance, and too much indexing can be just as detrimental as too little indexing. Most database platforms are smart enough to use partial indexes, so it may be appropriate to create a single, composite index for both* `OPRID_ENTERED_BY` *and* `OPRID_MODIFIED_BY`.

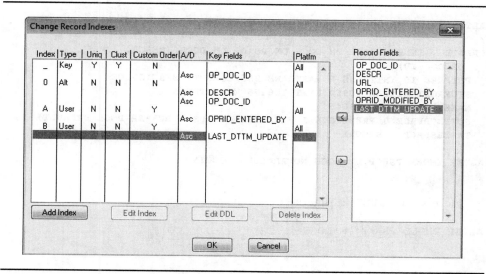

**FIGURE 2-15.**   *Change Record Indexes dialog*

## Altering Tables with Indexes

Earlier in the chapter, we reviewed table ALTER options with an emphasis
on the table's structure. But what happens when altering tables with
indexes? Here are the same ALTER statements presented early, but with
indexes added (indexes are in boldface).

Here's an ALTER by table rename:

```
CREATE TABLE PSYOP_DM_DOCS
. . .
/
INSERT INTO PSYOP_DM_DOCS
. . .
/
DROP TABLE PS_OP_DM_DOCS
/
RENAME PSYOP_DM_DOCS TO PS_OP_DM_DOCS
/
CREATE UNIQUE  iNDEX PS_OP_DM_DOCS ON PS_OP_DM_DOCS (OP_DOC_ID)
   PCTFREE 10 INITRANS 2 MAXTRANS 255 COMPUTE STATISTICS
   STORAGE(INITIAL 40960 NEXT 106496 MINEXTENTS 1 MAXEXTENTS 2147483645
   PCTINCREASE 0 FREELISTS 1 FREELIST GROUPS 1 BUFFER_POOL DEFAULT)
   TABLESPACE "PSINDEX"
```

```
/
ALTER INDEX PS_OP_DM_DOCS NOPARALLEL LOGGING
/
CREATE   INDEX PS0OP_DM_DOCS ON PS_OP_DM_DOCS (DESCR,
   OP_DOC_ID)
  PCTFREE 10 INITRANS 2 MAXTRANS 255 COMPUTE STATISTICS
  STORAGE(INITIAL 40960 NEXT 106496 MINEXTENTS 1
  MAXEXTENTS 2147483645
  PCTINCREASE 0 FREELISTS 1 FREELIST GROUPS 1 BUFFER_POOL DEFAULT)
  TABLESPACE "PSINDEX"
/
ALTER INDEX PS0OP_DM_DOCS NOPARALLEL LOGGING
/
```

Here's an ALTER in place:

```
ALTER TABLE PS_OP_DM_DOCS
. . .

DROP INDEX PS_OP_DM_DOCS
/
DROP INDEX PS0OP_DM_DOCS
/
CREATE UNIQUE  iNDEX PS_OP_DM_DOCS ON PS_OP_DM_DOCS (OP_DOC_ID)
 TABLESPACE PSINDEX STORAGE (INITIAL 40000 NEXT 100000 MAXEXTENTS
 UNLIMITED PCTINCREASE 0) PCTFREE 10 PARALLEL NOLOGGING
/
ALTER INDEX PS_OP_DM_DOCS NOPARALLEL LOGGING
/
CREATE   INDEX PS0OP_DM_DOCS ON PS_OP_DM_DOCS (DESCR,
  OP_DOC_ID) TABLESPACE PSINDEX STORAGE (INITIAL 40000 NEXT 100000
 MAXEXTENTS UNLIMITED PCTINCREASE 0) PCTFREE 10 PARALLEL NOLOGGING
/
ALTER INDEX PS0OP_DM_DOCS NOPARALLEL LOGGING
/
```

Indexes are an important consideration when you're altering tables. Notice that the Alter By Table Rename option does not create indexes until after dropping the original table. If your ALTER reduces the length of a key field, and that truncation results in duplicate rows, you won't find out about it until the script attempts to build the unique index—after the script drops the original table!

Indexes can also have an impact on ALTER performance. An ALTER often involves inserts, updates, data conversions, and data validations. Sometimes a bulk update or insert will execute faster if you first drop a field's index and then re-create the index when the operation completes.

# Views

A data administration discussion would be incomplete without a mention of database views. To create a view with Application Designer, do the following:

1. Create a new record definition.

2. Change the Record Type to SQL Table.

3. Enter the appropriate SQL text.

The columns from the view's SQL select list must match the fields in the record's field list. The SELECT field names and types do not have to match, but the number in the field does. Selected field types should be compatible with the record's field metadata. In Chapter 4 we will create views whose SELECT field names don't match the record's field names.

Application Designer's view metadata allows a developer to specify key structures—but do not confuse them with real database keys. Application Designer won't actually build database keys for these views. Rather, PeopleTools uses them to build search pages, identify relationships, and so on.

# Managing DDL Models

Application Designer uses parameterized templates called *models* to generate DDL. Administrators can access and modify these templates online by navigating to PeopleTools | Utilities | Administration | DDL Model Defaults. PeopleSoft maintains a separate set of models for each supported database platform. From this page, you can add parameters, change parameter defaults, and modify the overall DDL template. Keep in mind that PeopleTools patches and upgrades may overwrite your DDL changes.

**TIP**
*You can hide DDL parameters from your RDBMS by wrapping them with inline comments.*

# Data and System Audits

The PeopleSoft-delivered audit programs identify inconsistencies within PeopleTools definitions as well as between metadata layers (PeopleTools and database). Essentially, a PeopleSoft audit helps you identify trash in your system and then offers suggestions for cleaning up the mess.

## DDDAUDIT

The DDDAUDIT program identifies discrepancies between the PeopleTools and database metadata layers. Table 2-1 shows the relationship between PeopleTools metadata tables and database system tables. The relationship mapping in Table 2-1 is not perfect, however. For example, PSSQLDEFN contains all SQL definition types, not just SQL for views. Likewise, PSRECFIELD contains field definitions as standalone definitions; databases do not use this concept.

To run the DDDAUDIT report, do the following:

1. Log into your PeopleSoft application and navigate to PeopleTools | Process Scheduler | System Process Request.

2. Add a new run control named something meaningful—such as DDDAUDIT.

| PeopleSoft Table | DB2 | Sybase/ Microsoft SQL Server | Oracle | Informix |
|---|---|---|---|---|
| PSRECDEFN | systables | sysobjects | DBA_TABLES | systables |
| PSRECFIELD/ PSRECFIELDDB | syscolumns | syscolumns | DBA_TAB_ COLUMNS | syscolumns |
| PSSQLDEFN/ PSSQLTEXTDEFN | sysviews | syscomments | DBA_VIEWS | sysviews |
| PSINDEXDEFN | sysindexes | sysindexes | DBA_INDEXES | sysindexes |
| PSKEYDEFN | syskeys | sysindexes | DBA_IND_ COLUMNS | N/A |

**TABLE 2-1.** *PeopleTools/System Table Relationships*

3. Click the Run button and select the process that has the description Data Designer/Database Audit. Click OK to continue.

4. When the process completes, look in the process output for the file named dddaudit%.sqr (the real filename will contain your process instance).

The DDDAUDIT report lists database and PeopleTools definitions that don't conform to PeopleSoft development best practices. Just because an item is listed in the audit report, however, does not mean it is wrong. For example, the report section named TABLE-2 contains tables defined in Application Designer that were not built—that is, they don't exist in the database. In a production system, you would expect all Application Designer SQL tables to exist in the database, but intentionally choosing not to build a record is not an error.

Use good judgment when interpreting the DDDAUDIT report. Generally speaking, to remove an item from the report, open Application Designer and either build, alter, or delete the definition. Tables and views that exist in the database but not in Application Designer need to exist in Application Designer only if you plan to use PeopleTools metadata features (Meta-SQL, PeopleCode, and so on). An SQL Table defined in Application Designer that does not exist in the database needs to be built only if it will actually store data. If you don't plan to use the table to store data, you may want to consider using the Record Type tab to change the type to Derived/Work. To resolve the issue of tables that have an SQL table name that differs from the record definition name, either save the record definition using the same name shown in the Non-Standard SQL Table Name property of the Record Type tab or change the Non-Standard SQL Table Name property to match the record definition name. It is best to reconcile differences between record definitions that exist in both metadata stores. Otherwise, patches and upgrades may overwrite the database version.

# SYSAUDIT and SYSAUD01

The SYSAUDIT reports are similar to the DDDAUDIT report in that they check for inconsistencies within a PeopleSoft application. Unlike DDDAUDIT, which compares PeopleTools metadata to database metadata, the SYSAUDIT reports focus strictly on PeopleTools metadata. Use the SYSAUDIT reports to identify a variety of inconsistencies including Application Engine programs without sections, fields with multiple default labels, rowset-based messages that reference nonexistent record definitions, and similar issues.

To run the SYSAUDIT report, navigate to PeopleTools | Utilities | Audit | Perform System Audit. Create a new run control and select the definition types to audit. Resolve any issues identified by the SYSAUDIT report.

**NOTE**
*The PeopleBook* "PeopleTools Data Management: Ensuring Data Integrity" *contains resolution suggestions for each exception. If you do not have PeopleBooks installed at your site, you can find an Oracle-hosted version online within the PeopleTools PeopleBook at http:// www.oracle.com/pls/psft/homepage.*

The SYSAUD01 report is part two of SYSAUDIT. To run SYSAUD01, navigate to PeopleTools | Process Scheduler | System Process Requests and run the SYSAUD01 report. For exceptions noted in the report, follow the same resolution recommendations offered for the SYSAUDIT report.

# Conclusion

Proper database design has a significant impact on system performance and user productivity. Even though several tools are available for database design and administration, using PeopleSoft's Application Designer will help you keep your PeopleTools and system metadata in sync.

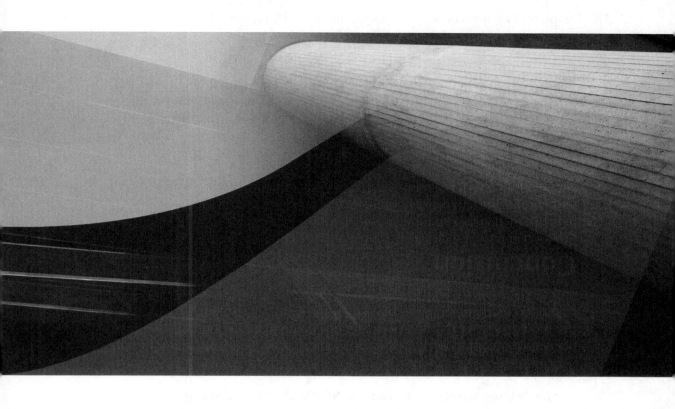

# CHAPTER
## 3

## Understanding PeopleSoft Data Mover

 hat is PeopleSoft Data Mover? How can it efficiently and effectively work for me in conjunction with the PeopleSoft product? We will answer these questions as we explore the topic of Data Mover.

# What Is Data Mover?

Data Mover is a platform-independent database tool that administrators and developers use to perform the following tasks:

- Load databases after creation
- Execute data definition language (DDL) and data manipulation language (DML) statements
- Transfer data between databases
- Convert between database platforms

Data Mover scripts often combine SQL with Data Mover–specific commands to import, export, and process data.

Most database platforms include their own data migration facilities. One of the key differences between Data Mover and other database-specific tools is Data Mover's database-independent file format. This feature allows administrators to move data between databases regardless of platform or operating system. For example, you often need to transfer data from a production environment to a test environment to test with data that closely mimics current production. In addition, Oracle uses Data Mover to deliver important platform-independent PeopleTools and application updates.

PeopleSoft Data Mover is a standalone, two-tier program. On Microsoft Windows, it can run in graphical or command line mode. This allows developers and administrators to create, edit, and run scripts within a graphical environment and then transfer them to a server for batch processing. On other supported operating systems, it runs only in command line mode.

Data Mover plays a critical role in lifecycle management. It is required at PeopleSoft install to populate your application database. Likewise, upgrades and bundles include Data Mover scripts to convert existing data and import new data.

# Installing Data Mover

Data Mover is part of a standard PeopleTools installation. The client-side version is available in two varieties:

- **psdmt.exe**   Graphical client

- **psdmtx.exe**   Command line client

Because the graphical version runs only on Microsoft Windows, make sure you have access to a PeopleTools installation for Windows. If these files do not exist on your network, you can download them from the Oracle Software Delivery Cloud (currently at http://edelivery.oracle.com) and follow the installation instructions included in the Oracle Software Delivery Cloud README file.

# Configuration Manager

After gaining access to a Windows PS_HOME directory, do the following:

1. Launch PS_HOME\bin\client\winx86\pscfg.exe (Configuration Manager).

2. Switch to the Client Setup tab.

3. Select the Configuration Manager, Data Mover, and Install Workstation options.

4. Click the Apply button to install Data Mover. Figure 3-1 displays Configuration Manager's Data Mover installation options.

You should now have a PeopleSoft application group in your Windows Start menu that contains Configuration Manager and Data Mover.

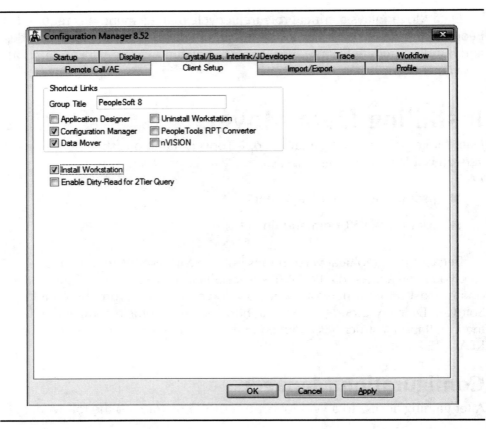

**FIGURE 3-1.** *Installing Data Mover through Configuration Manager*

If Configuration Manager is not running, launch it, and then do the following

1. Open the Profile tab. A standard installation includes a Profile named Default.

2. Ensure that this profile is selected, and then click the Edit button.

3. In the Edit Profile dialog (Figure 3-2), switch to the Common tab and enter values for the Input Directory, Output Directory, and Log Directory. Generally speaking, you set the Input Directory and Output Directory values to your PS_HOME\data directory and the Log Directory to PS_HOME\log. The PS_HOME\data directory is where upgrade scripts look for upgrade data.

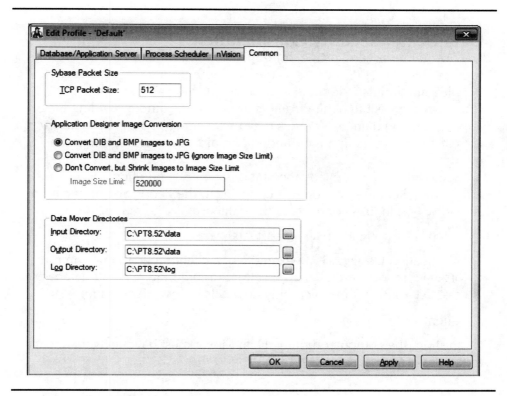

**FIGURE 3-2.** *Data Mover profile options*

# Security

Data Mover is an extremely powerful tool and therefore requires special security clearance. Before running Data Mover scripts, log into your PeopleSoft system and verify that at least one of your permission lists grants access to Data Mover. You must have security access to Data Mover prior to using the tool. Data Mover access is granted through the Permission List PeopleTools page.

**NOTE**
*PTPT1200 is a delivered PeopleTools permission list that grants access to most client-side tools including Data Mover and Application Designer.*

### Data Center Security Consideration

For normal, everyday usage, a PeopleSoft client needs only a web browser and HTTP(S) access to the PeopleSoft web server. Some PeopleSoft administration and security teams hide as many network resources as possible behind routers or firewalls. Although hiding the application and database servers may be an effective security measure for self-service users, it might hinder administration and development efforts.

Some PeopleTools client applications run in "three-tier" mode. This means the client application first connects to the PeopleSoft application server, which in turn connects to the database:

Client → Application Server → Database

Application Designer is an example of a client program that can run in three-tier mode. Three-tier applications do not require direct database access. Data Mover, however, only connects in "two-tier" mode:

Client → Database

In short, the computer running Data Mover must have network access to the database.

# Writing and Running Data Mover Scripts

With Data Mover installed and configured, let's learn how to write and run some scripts.

Effective communication involves *syntax* and *semantics*. More or less, syntax refers to grammar, or sentence structure. In Data Mover, "syntax" is the term we use to describe a valid command. When coding Data Mover scripts, you must follow certain syntax rules to ensure successful execution:

- Text contained in a string constant is case-sensitive and needs to be surrounded by single quotation marks.

- Every command must end with a terminating semicolon (;) or slash (/). If using a slash, the slash must be on its own line immediately following the command statement.

■ SQL commands used in Data Mover accept only physical table names.

■ Comments begin with --, REM, or REMARK and end at line termination. They do not require a terminating semicolon.

Semantics refers to *meaning*. When writing any code, you should always be cognizant of other programmers who will have to read and maintain your code. Just because you can write a syntactically correct, yet incomprehensible command doesn't mean you should. The following list contains some of the semantic rules for Data Mover:

■ Data Mover commands accept both record and physical table names. You may use either.

■ Text in a command is not case-sensitive.

■ A command may contain any amount of white space (including new lines).

■ Commands may span multiple lines.

## Can I Run Data Mover Scripts?

As a PeopleSoft application user, you'll find that your profile likely contains dozens of permission lists. If you have database access, you can skip the exasperating effort of opening each permission list by running the following SQL:

```
SELECT DISTINCT PERM.CLASSID
     , AUTH.MENUNAME
  FROM PSOPRDEFN OPR
INNER JOIN PSROLEUSER ROL
    ON OPR.OPRID = ROL.ROLEUSER
INNER JOIN PSROLECLASS PERM
    ON ROL.ROLENAME = PERM.ROLENAME
INNER JOIN PSAUTHITEM AUTH
    ON PERM.CLASSID = AUTH.CLASSID
WHERE AUTH.MENUNAME = 'DATA_MOVER'
  AND OPRID = :1 — REPLACE WITH YOUR OPRID
```

## Your First Data Mover Script

Launch Data Mover and log in with your standard PeopleSoft credentials. The Data Mover user interface looks very much like that of a normal text editor and represents a standard Windows single-document interface, with a menu at the top, a toolbar, and a main text editing area. The lower region of the UI, the output panel, is reserved for command output. Data Mover will fill this area with feedback while running scripts. Figure 3-3 shows an example of an empty Data Mover application window.

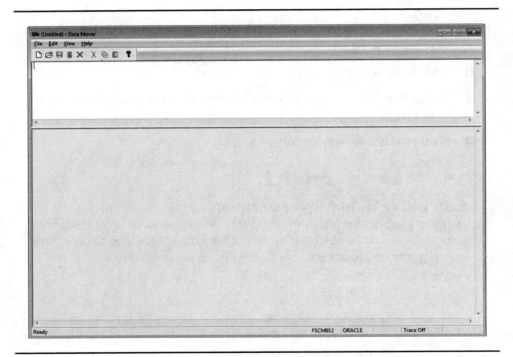

**FIGURE 3-3.**  *Data Mover application window*

**CAUTION**
*Be sure that you connect in two-tier mode (any connection type except Application Server). Do not connect to Data Mover through the application server. Even though Data Mover allows you to log in using a three-tier connection, doing so will result in Data Mover displaying the error "Data Mover can be run in Two Tier mode only." Data Mover will then exit and you will have to log in again using the appropriate database type.*

The following examples show how to use Data Mover to export and import data, starting with a full table export and progressing to targeted subquery selection exports and imports.

## Exporting Data

In Data Mover's text editor, enter the following text:

```
SET LOG C:\TEMP\MYFIRST.LOG;
SET OUTPUT C:\TEMP\MYFIRST.DAT;

EXPORT INSTALLATION;
```

The first two lines tell Data Mover where to save exported data as well as log statements. In this example we used *absolute* file paths. Earlier we ran Configuration Manager to set Data Mover's default log, input, and output directories. These first two lines override the default log and output directories. Later we will use the INPUT parameter to override the default input directory.

The three parameters LOG, INPUT, and OUTPUT make up the three laws for Data Mover: location, location, location. If your default directories point to valid locations, you may omit the path portion of the file location, leaving just the filename. When you're generating scripts to share, omitting the file path allows recipients to choose log, input, and output locations. This is especially important when you're transferring scripts between computers with entirely different path structures.

**NOTE**
*When writing scripts for my own consumption, I often use SET statements to send log and exported data to a location other than the default, reserving the default locations for maintenance.*

The final line exports all of the data in the PS_INSTALLATION table. Notice that the Data Mover script lists the Application Designer record definition name, not the database physical table name. For Data Mover commands, either will work just as well.

Inside Data Mover, you can run this script in one of three ways:

- From the Data Mover menu bar, choose File | Run Script.

- Press the key combination CTRL-R.

- Click the green go traffic signal in the toolbar (fourth icon from the left).

Run the script and watch Data Mover write the results to the output panel. Because the INSTALLATION record contains only one row, you should see the text "Export INSTALLATION 1". The number following the record name signifies the total number of rows exported from the INSTALLATION record. Figure 3-4 shows the Data Mover window after exporting the INSTALLATION record.

## Looking for Data Mover Syntax Highlighting?

Many general-purpose text editors offer syntax highlighting for a variety of structured languages. You can find a listing of the most common text editors used by PeopleSoft developers on this site: http://peoplesoft.wikidot.com/text-editors. Although some of them offer out-of-the-box syntax highlighting support for many common PeopleSoft languages (COBOL, SQR, and SQL), I haven't found any with support for Data Mover scripts. Being a fan of jEdit, I wrote my own jEdit syntax file for Data Mover. You can download my jEdit syntax files and read tips about installing syntax files on my blog at http://jjmpsj.blogspot.com/2009/08/using-jedit-to-edit-peoplesoft-files.html.

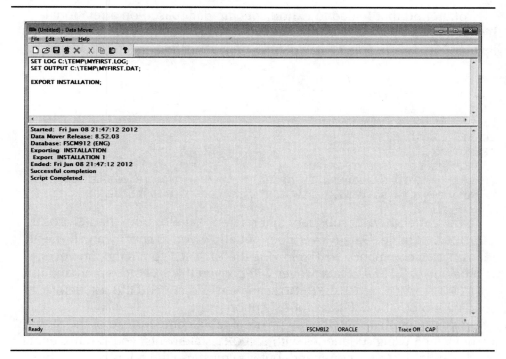

**FIGURE 3-4.** *Data Mover after exporting the INSTALLATION record*

Let's try another export example, but this time we will add some criteria to our export. Choose File | New. Enter the following into the Data Mover text editor:

```
SET LOG C:\TEMP\MYSECOND.LOG;
SET OUTPUT C:\TEMP\MYSECOND.DAT;

EXPORT EOIU_SOPUBDEFN
  WHERE IB_OPERATIONNAME = 'JOBCODE_FULLSYNC';
```

This example exports the JOBCODE_FULLSYNC batch publish rule. This rule exists in PeopleSoft's Financials/Supply Chain and Human Capital Management systems (including Campus 9.0), but it might not exist in other PeopleSoft applications. Just as our first Data Mover script, running this export will create a .DAT file containing one row.

I often find that I need to export specific data based on a relational hierarchy. The following example exports all batch publish rules (header rows) that have a corresponding batch publish program definition (child rows):

```
SET LOG C:\TEMP\MYTHIRD.LOG;
SET OUTPUT C:\TEMP\MYTHIRD.DAT;

EXPORT PS_EOIU_SOPUBDEFN
 WHERE EXISTS (
SELECT 'X'
  FROM PS_EOIU_SOBATPGM PGM
 WHERE PS_EOIU_SOPUBDEFN.IB_OPERATIONNAME = PGM.IB_OPERATIONNAME
   AND PS_EOIU_SOPUBDEFN.PUBLISH_RULE_ID = PGM.PUBLISH_RULE_ID);
```

Notice the EXISTS subquery that references fields from the PS_EOIU_SOPUBDEFN table. Data Mover does not allow you to specify an alias with the EXPORT command. Text following the EXPORT command, however, can be any valid SQL. Data Mover will convert the EXPORT command into a SELECT * FROM TABLENAME statement and append the rest before sending it off to the database for execution.

In this example I used the full physical table name instead of the record name. When using subqueries with EXPORT statements, you can use either for the initial EXPORT command, but you must use the full physical table name in the subquery. In this case, I used the full table name to avoid any confusion.

**TIP**

*As a general rule, I use table names rather than the shorter record names when referring to data structures. This eliminates any confusion that might arise from seeing a record name in the initial export and then a physical table name in the subquery. Even though Data Mover represents my initial audience, odds are very high that someone else is going to have to read my code, and I want it to be easy for someone else to comprehend.*

File attachment records are binary file repositories for the PeopleCode File Attachment API. File attachment records do not contain transaction fields. To ensure uniqueness, the ATTACHSYSFILENAME field may contain concatenated transaction keys, but this is not required. Likewise, concatenated transaction keys are not helpful when attempting to export all files related to a particular transaction. Each attachment record usually has one or more transaction *mapping* records that associate transaction keys with the `ATTACHSYSFILENAME` field. Transaction mapping records contain transaction keys as well as the subrecord `FILE_ATTACH_SBR` (or at least the fields from `FILE_ATTACH_SBR`). `PSFILE_ATTDET`, for example, has several transaction mapping records. The following example exports transaction specific file attachments from the generic `PSFILE_ATTDET` attachment record.

```
SET LOG C:\TEMP\LOAD_JRNL_REQ-EXPORT.LOG;
SET OUTPUT C:\TEMP\LOAD_JRNL_REQ.DAT;

EXPORT PSFILE_ATTDET
 WHERE EXISTS (
SELECT 'X'
  FROM PS_LOAD_JRNL_REQ JRNL
 WHERE PSFILE_ATTDET.ATTACHSYSFILENAME = JRNL.ATTACHSYSFILENAME
   AND JRNL.OPRID = 'SAMPLE'
   AND JRNL.RUN_CNTL_ID = 'GL1' );

EXPORT PS_LOAD_JRNL_REQ
 WHERE OPRID = 'SAMPLE'
   AND RUN_CNTL_ID = 'GL1';
```

**CAUTION**
*When deleting transactions and associated file attachments, you must delete from the file attachment table first. If you delete from the transaction tables before the attachment table, you won't have any transaction keys for identifying associated file attachments.*

## Importing Data
Generally speaking, we export data with a future intent to import that same data somewhere else. Importing can be extremely simple. The exported .DAT file contains all of the metadata required to import the data. Here is a basic

import template you can use when you know the exported information does not exist in the target database:

```
SET LOG C:\TEMP\IMPORT-SOMETHING.LOG;
SET INPUT C:\TEMP\MYDATA.DAT;

IMPORT *;
```

The `IMPORT` command tells Data Mover to identify record definitions in the `INPUT` file, create tables that don't exist in the target database, and then copy data from the `INPUT` file into the target database.

What if the target database already contains the same record definitions with data? If the data in the .DAT file differs from data in the target database and does not violate any constraints, Data Mover will successfully import the new rows. If the same rows already exist, Data Mover will fail, throwing a unique constraint exception. How you proceed depends on whether you require a destructive or nondestructive import.

**NOTE**
*Because Data Mover is copying data from a text file into the database, all import methods use a row-by-row insert. Index changes from these uncommitted inserts may have a significant effect on undo space, and so on.*

**Destructive Imports**   Data Mover contains two destructive variants of `IMPORT`:

- `REPLACE_DATA`

- `REPLACE_ALL`

The `REPLACE_DATA` command will delete existing rows from like tables in the target database prior to import. Unlike `IMPORT`, the `REPLACE_DATA` command won't create tables if they don't exist in the target database.

Here is an example using `REPLACE_DATA`:

```
SET LOG C:\TEMP\IMPORT-SOMETHING.LOG;
SET INPUT C:\TEMP\MYDATA.DAT;

REPLACE_DATA *;
```

The REPLACE_DATA command issues a database TRUNCATE DDL statement. On some database platforms (such as Oracle), DDL statements automatically commit all database changes. Keep this in mind if you have operations in your DMS script that you want to execute as a transaction. Performing a REPLACE_DATA in the middle of those operations may leave your information in an indeterminate state.

The REPLACE_ALL command is the most destructive. Prior to import, REPLACE_ALL drops the target table along with all related indexes, triggers, and so on. Keep this in mind if you have custom database procedures that use these tables. Dropping tables may invalidate custom procedures. Nevertheless, of the two destructive methods, REPLACE_ALL might be more efficient. On my Oracle database, when I perform a REPLACE_DATA operation, the trace file shows a TRUNCATE and then a row-by-row insert, wreaking all kinds of havoc on my indexes. A REPLACE_ALL, on the other hand, drops the table along with its indexes, re-creates the table, performs the same row-by-row insert, and then builds the record's indexes.

Here is an example using REPLACE_ALL:

```
SET LOG C:\TEMP\IMPORT-SOMETHING.LOG;
SET INPUT C:\TEMP\MYDATA.DAT;

REPLACE_ALL *;
```

**Nondestructive Imports**    The least destructive way to import data into existing tables is first to delete potential duplicate rows. Oftentimes the DELETE statement looks very similar to the initial EXPORT statement. Here is an example import for our file attachment export:

```
SET LOG C:\TEMP\LOAD_JRNL_REQ-IMPORT.LOG;
SET INPUT C:\TEMP\LOAD_JRNL_REQ.DAT;

DELETE FROM PSFILE_ATTDET
 WHERE EXISTS (
SELECT 'X'
  FROM PS_LOAD_JRNL_REQ JRNL
 WHERE PSFILE_ATTDET.ATTACHSYSFILENAME = JRNL.ATTACHSYSFILENAME
   AND JRNL.OPRID = 'SAMPLE'
   AND JRNL.RUN_CNTL_ID = 'GL1' );

DELETE FROM PS_LOAD_JRNL_REQ
 WHERE OPRID = 'SAMPLE'
   AND RUN_CNTL_ID = 'GL1';

IMPORT *;
```

Each of the import commands—IMPORT, REPLACE_DATA, and REPLACE_ALL—support modifiers allowing you to specify which records to import. If a .DAT file contains multiple tables, it would be possible for you to (destructively) load one table, re-create another, and then import only new rows from a third table using syntax similar to this:

```
SET LOG C:\TEMP\IMPORT-SOMETHING.LOG;
SET INPUT C:\TEMP\SOME_DATA.DAT;

REPLACE_DATA TABLE1;
REPLACE_ALL TABLE2;

DELETE FROM TABLE3
 WHERE KEY1 = 'VALUE'
   AND KEY2 = 'VALUE2';

IMPORT TABLE3;
```

These modifiers also allow you to specify which rows to import. Using the WHERE clause, you can selectively import rows from a .DAT file:

```
SET LOG C:\TEMP\IMPORT-SOMETHING.LOG;
SET INPUT C:\TEMP\SOME_DATA.DAT;

IMPORT TABLE3
 WHERE KEY1 = 'VALUE'
   AND KEY2 = 'VALUE2';
```

## Dates in Data Mover

Date functions vary widely among database platforms. Data Mover implements the following date and time-specific Meta-SQL abstractions, making it possible to run scripts against multiple database platforms:

- CURRENTDATEOUT
- CURRENTTIMEOUT
- CURRENTDATETIMEOUT
- DATEIN
- TIMEIN

Use the *OUT Meta-SQL statements in SELECT clauses and the *IN functions in WHERE and UPDATE clauses. Here are a couple of examples:

```
-- Lock stale accounts (last login more than 1 year ago)
UPDATE PSOPRDEFN
   SET ACCTLOCK = 1
 WHERE LASTSIGNONDTTM < %DATEIN('2011-12-31');

-- Insert/Select, but use current date:
INSERT INTO PS_OPR_COPY (OPRID, OPRDEFNDESC, LASTUPDDTTM)
SELECT OPRID, OPRDEFNDESC, %CURRENTDATETIMEOUT
  FROM PSOPRDEFN;

-- Update a date/time field using Meta-SQL:
UPDATE PS_OPR_COPY
   SET LASTUPDDTTM = %CURRENTDATETIMEOUT;
```

# Running Scripts at the Command Line

The IMPORT and EXPORT commands transfer data from a database to the computer running Data Mover. The Data Mover graphical client is great for running scripts that operate on minimal amounts of data. Large data transfers, however, might be more efficient when run on a server residing closer to the database. For example, when I run a Data Mover export from my workstation, that data travels a few thousand miles from a database through a handful of routers to a virtual private network (VPN) gateway, and then finally through an encrypted connection to my laptop. Encryption, routers, bandwidth, and distance can have a significant impact on export and import speeds. Another important consideration is disk IO. A well-tuned server with disk caching and large buffers will read and write data a lot faster than my little Dell with a 5400 RPM disk drive. If that server uses solid state, well... there is no comparison.

Data Mover's command line interface was designed for those situations when you need to move lots of data and would prefer a more efficient transfer mechanism (or you just don't want to tie up your workstation; how can you take your laptop home at the end of the day when it is deeply entrenched in a full database export?).

On Microsoft Windows, the Data Mover command line utility (psdmtx.exe) is located at %PS_HOME%\bin\client\winx86. For other operating systems, you will find psdmtx in $PS_HOME/bin.

Let's run a script from the command line just to get the hang of it. Open a command prompt and run the following:

```
SET PS_HOME=c:\pt8.52
%PS_HOME%\bin\client\winx86\psdmtx -CD FSCM912 -CO VP1 -CP VP1
-FP %PS_HOME%\scripts\userexport.dms
```

To override the database type, connect identifier, and so on, run the following:

```
SET PS_HOME=c:\pt8.52
%PS_HOME%\bin\client\winx86\psdmtx -CT ORACLE -CS FSCM912DB
-CD FSCM912 -CO VP1 -CP VP1 -CI people -CW people
-FP %PS_HOME%\scripts\userexport.dms
```

On a non-Windows operating system, run this Data Mover script with the following command:

```
. /path/to/ps_home/psconfig.sh
psdmtx -CT ORACLE -CS FSCM912DB -CD FSCM912 -CO VP1 -CP VP1 \
-CI people -CW people -FP $PS_HOME/scripts/userexport.dms
```

When run from a Windows workstation, this command creates the Data Mover export in `C:\pt8.52\data` and the log file in `C:\pt8.52\log`, the location I previously specified in Configuration Manager. On a Linux server, running this same command produces an export file in `~/PS_DM/data` and a log file in `~/PS_DM/log`.

**CAUTION**
*Data Mover export files may contain sensitive information. This example just exported all the users from the system, including usernames, passwords, and roles. Make sure you secure your export files in the same manner as any other sensitive information.*

Here is the full `psdmtx` call specification:

```
Usage:  psdmtx  [-CT DB2|DB2ODBC|DB2UNIX|INFORMIX|MICROSFT|
                 ORACLE|SYBASE]
                [-CS server name]
                [-CD database name]
                [-CO user id]
                [-CP user pswd]
```

```
            [-CI connect id]
            [-CW connect id pswd]
            [-I  process instance]
            [-FP filename]
    or
psdmtx  [parmfile]
```

Table 3-1 shows a summary of the parameters used by psdmtx.

| Parameter | Description | Comments |
|-----------|-------------|----------|
| CT | Database type | Valid values: DB2ODBC, INFORMIX, DB2UNIX, MICROSFT, ORACLE, and SYBASE. |
| CS | Database server | Required for INFORMIX and SYBASE; optional for all other platforms. |
| CD | Database | Database identifier (SID for Oracle) |
| CO | PeopleSoft user ID | Your PeopleSoft user ID (for Bootstrap mode [discussed next], use the database schema owner's user ID). |
| CP | PeopleSoft password | Your PeopleSoft password (for Bootstrap mode, use the database schema owner's password). |
| CI | Connect ID | The database user ID PeopleSoft uses to connect and validate your PeopleSoft credentials. This is the same ID you specified in Configuration Manager during the initial Data Mover install. Not used with Bootstrap mode. |
| CW | Connect password | The password for the Connect ID (database user's password); not used with Bootstrap mode. |
| I | Process Scheduler instance | Required if run from the process scheduler; optional otherwise. |
| FP | File path | The data mover script's filename. |

**TABLE 3-1.** *Data Mover (psdmtx) command line parameters*

When executing Data Mover from shell scripts, a non-zero return value represents a failure, and a zero (0) return value means success. Here is a simple bash script example

```bash
#!/bin/bash

$PS_HOME/psdmtx -CT ORACLE -CS FSCM912DB -CD FSCM912 \
    -CO VP1 -CP VP1 -CI people -CW people \
    -FP $PS_HOME/scripts/userexport.dms

if [ $? == 0 ]
then
    echo ':D script succeeded! Now do something to celebrate.'
else
    echo ':( script failed'
fi
```

## Bootstrap Mode

Data Mover allows an alternative connection mode called *Bootstrap mode*. This mode allows you to connect using your database username and password rather than your PeopleSoft username and password. This is critical when you're creating a new PeopleSoft database, because the connect identifier, symbolic IDs, and operator IDs don't exist at database creation time. Many of Data Mover's commands are not valid in Bootstrap mode.

# Data Mover in the Upgrade Process

Oracle often includes Data Mover scripts with patches and upgrades. These scripts contain data conversion routines, new application data, and unmanaged PeopleTools definitions. For example, upgrade scripts often contain new message catalog entries—PeopleTools definitions that can't be migrated with Application Designer projects. Having a working knowledge of Data Mover can help you troubleshoot and even enhance these delivered scripts.

## Creating Your Own Upgrade Data Mover Scripts

Oracle builds PeopleSoft applications with extensibility in mind. Odds are high that your implementation already includes custom application and configuration tables. As you change these custom tables, you may need to write your own transformation programs. Likewise, you may need to import new custom configuration options as you move from test to production. Here are a few guidelines to help you write better scripts:

- Perform as much data manipulation on the database as possible.

- Watch out for implicit commits from DDL statements.

- Consider the performance and rollback/undo impact of existing indexes.

- Test, test, test, and test some more. Data Mover is a very powerful program. It is very easy to delete or overwrite the wrong data accidentally.

Far too many times I have run a delete, executed a command with an implicit commit, and then seen the import fail. Before running any custom Data Mover script, I first run an export of each table affected by the script, and then I run the script.

# Conclusion

In this chapter, we looked into installation and setup of the Data Mover tool. We demonstrated PeopleSoft Data Mover. We also reviewed command line execution in relation to UNIX and Windows. We continued our discussion with syntax and common coding examples regarding the construction of the script for execution.

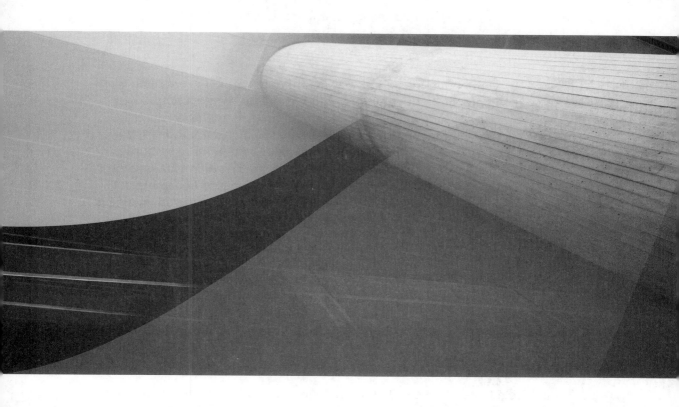

# CHAPTER
## 4

## Data Archive
## Manager

E ven though a database has an unlimited appetite, we often work in an environment with limited resources. Large amounts of data can have a significant impact on disk, memory, and CPU utilization. When your tables grow too big for their disks, you have some decisions to make: archive or add more resources?

Data Archive Manager is a tool you can use for moving online transaction data into online history tables. The point of this migration is to free important online transaction processing (OLTP) resources while continuously maintaining access to historical data.

In this chapter, you will learn how to use Data Archive Manager to move data from transaction tables into *history* tables. We will first run through an archive and restore process using a delivered Data Archive Manager definition and then we will build our own.

# Running a Delivered Data Archive Manager Process

To archive a transaction effectively, an analyst must identify the full ancestry of a transaction (parent/child relationships) as well as any outstanding related transactions. For example, archiving vendor information involves identifying the vendor address, tax information, and so on, as well as identifying any open purchase orders, requisitions, and such against that vendor. Considering, for example, that my Financials/Supply Chain system has more than 65,000 tables, properly identifying these relationships is a daunting task. Fortunately, several PeopleSoft modules include their own Data Archive Manager definitions.

Let's review the vendor Data Archive Manager configuration to get a better understanding of Data Archive Manager, and then run it to see what happens.

A Data Archive Manager definition consists of the following:

■ History tables

■ Archive objects

■ Application engine programs (optional)

■ Archive queries

■ Archive templates

We will get a taste of history tables now, but I'll save a more detailed discussion until we build them (later in this chapter).

PeopleTools includes a Data Archive Manager Homepage (Figure 4-1). To use this homepage, log into your PeopleSoft online application as a PeopleTools user (a user with the PTPT1200 permission list). If your PeopleSoft installation is using the older 8.4+ left-hand navigation menu, then use the menu to expand the nodes PeopleTools | Data Archive Manager and then select Homepage. Otherwise, from the upper left-hand corner, select Main Menu | PeopleTools | Data Archive Manager | Homepage.

## Archive Objects

From the Data Archive Manager Homepage, click the Manage Archive Objects link. Figure 4-2 shows a partial screenshot of the Vendor archive object. An *archive object* contains a collection of mappings that identify

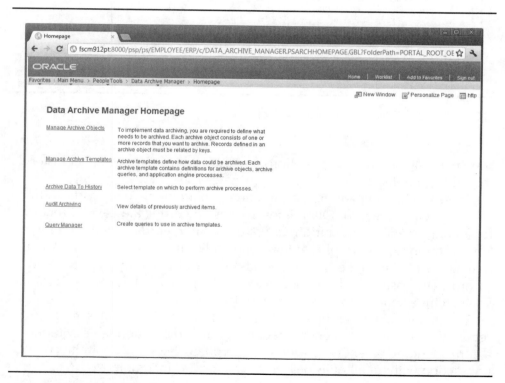

**FIGURE 4-1.** *Data Archive Manager Homepage*

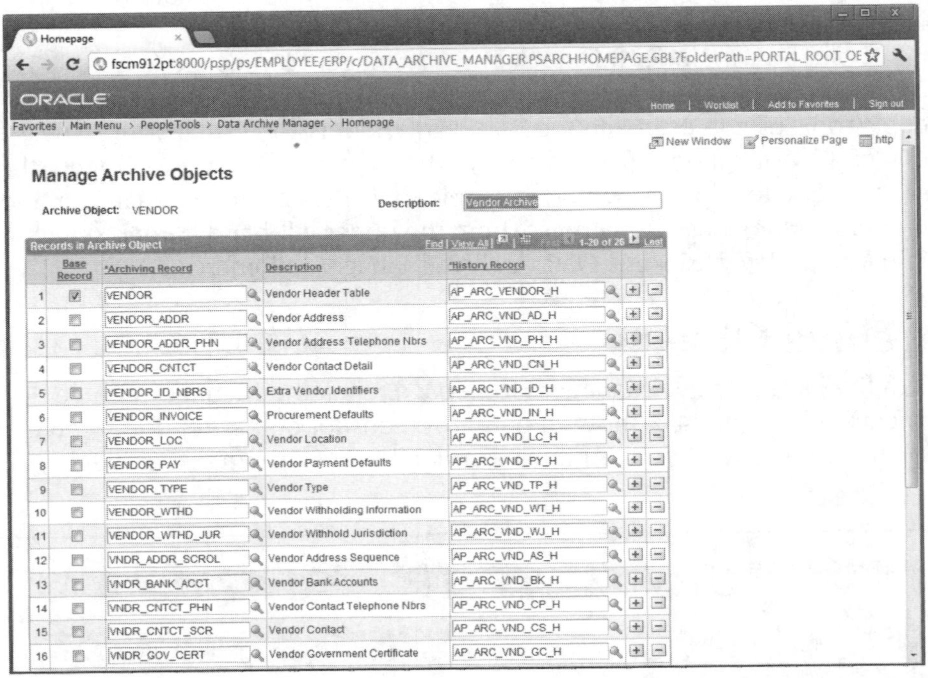

**FIGURE 4-2.** *Vendor archive object*

source transaction record definitions and their corresponding target history record definitions.

To ensure a complete transaction archive, archiving data starts with a *base*, or header, record. Oftentimes the base record is the Level 0 record for a component. By definition, *child*, or detail, records contain the same keys as the base record plus at least one additional key field. Data Archive Manager will use the keys from the base record to identify rows in child records. The base record in an archive object represents that Level 0 record. Each archive object can have only one base record.

When defining an archive object, be sure to include all descendant record definitions. A descendant record left in a transaction table without a corresponding parent is considered an orphan. Likewise, an archived transaction without all of its descendant records is incomplete.

# Archive Templates

Return to the Data Archive Manager Homepage by selecting the Homepage link in the header menu breadcrumb trail. After arriving on the homepage, select the Manage Archive Templates link. Figure 4-3 shows the `AP_VNDR` archive template.

Archive templates describe how to archive data. They associate archive objects with selection queries as well as specify pre- and post-processing programs. Notice that this vendor archive template includes five selection queries. When we run this template, we will use only one of those queries. Each query offers a different mechanism for identifying rows to archive. Archive template queries are PeopleSoft queries that were saved as query type Archive.

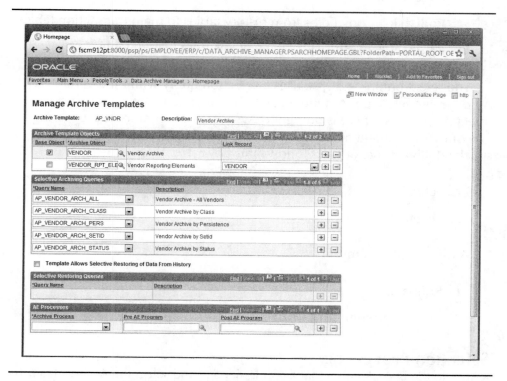

**FIGURE 4-3.**    `AP_VNDR` *archive template*

**TIP**
*When searching for archive queries in Query Manager, switch to Advanced Search and change the Query Type field to Archive. The basic name search does not return Archive queries.*

# Archive Processing

There are four types of archive processes:

- **Selection**    Copy items to history tables.
- **Delete**    Delete items from main transaction tables.
- **Rollback**    Copy items from history tables to main transaction tables.
- **Remove from History**    Delete items from history tables.

The selection process type uses a selection query with bind variables. All other process types require a batch identifier generated from a prior selection process. There is no right or wrong order for archive processing. The only requirement is that you start with selection processing. Generally speaking, an archive process follows this flow:

1. Selection
2. Delete

A restore follows this flow:

1. Rollback
2. Remove from history

## Selection Processing

Return to the Data Archive Manager Homepage and select the Archive Data To History link. Create a new run control for your archive process. I recommend using a naming convention that identifies your archive template, selection method, and selection parameters followed by the process type. In Figure 4-4,

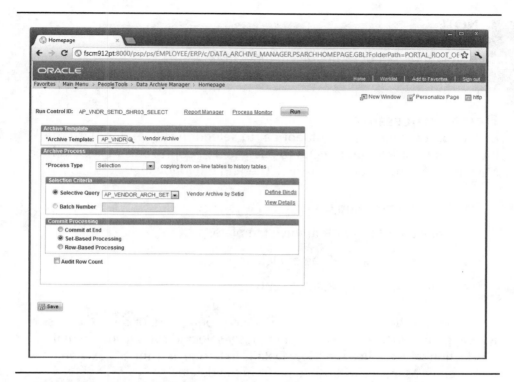

**FIGURE 4-4.** `AP_VNDR_SETID_SHR03_SELECT` *run control*

I created a run control named `AP_VNDR_SETID_SHR03_SELECT` to identify that I am running the `AP_VNDR` template that selects SetID of `SHR03`.

On the run control page, click the Define Binds link to enter query criteria. The View Details link displays a list of each record to be archived as well as the selection SQL and the number of affected rows.

After running the archive process, you can query the corresponding history tables to view copied data. When I ran this process in my Financials and Supply Chain Management (FSCM) 9.1 demo database, Data Archive Manager added three rows to the `PS_AP_ARC_VENDOR_H` table with the batch number 1. My database actually includes four vendors with a SetID of `SHR03`, but only three were selected. This is because one of the vendors has open, related transactions. It would not be wise to archive and delete a vendor required to finalize a related transaction. Keep this in mind when you're writing your own selection queries.

**NOTE**
*Selection processing only copies rows into history tables. It does not delete them from the main transaction tables.*

## Delete Processing

Delete processing is nearly identical to selection processing. Use the breadcrumb (or left-hand) menu to navigate to PeopleTools | Data Archive Manager | Archive Data to History. Then do the following:

1. Create a new Run Control ID.

2. Select the AP_VNDR archive template.

3. Choose a Process Type of Delete.

4. Select an existing Batch Number.

Figure 4-5 shows the AP_VNDR template configured for delete processing. Running this process will delete previously selected rows from the main transaction tables. Click the View Details link to review the SQL statements that Archive Manager will use to perform the deletes.

Running this process on my FSCM 9.1 demo database deleted three rows from the PS_VENDOR table.

## Rollback Processing

Rollback processing copies rows from history tables back into transaction tables. The only difference between a rollback run control and a delete run control is the process type. For the rollback run control, select a Process Type of Rollback. Figure 4-6 shows my Rollback run control.

When I ran this process against my FSCM 9.1 demo database, it copied three rows from the PS_AP_ARC_VENDOR_H table back into the PS_VENDOR table. I could then navigate to Vendors | Vendor Information | Add/Update | Vendor to see all four vendors from SetID SHR03.

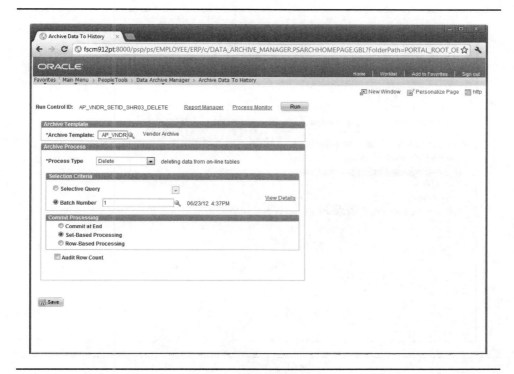

**FIGURE 4-5.**   *Data Archive Manager delete processing*

At this point, both my history tables and my transaction tables contain copies of the same data. What happens next depends on what I need:

■ If my intention for restoring is just to review the data, but not update it, I may choose to leave the historical data alone for now. Later, I can rerun the delete process to remove the rows from the transaction tables.

■ If I intend to begin using the restored data like any other live data, I can either consider the historical data as versioned history or delete the historical data.

■ If I choose to keep the historical data as a type of versioned history, however, it is important that I recognize that any rollback of that versioned history will overwrite the current transaction data.

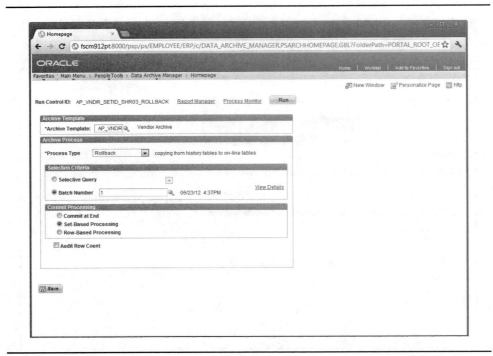

**FIGURE 4-6.** *Rollback processing*

Depending on the selection schemes, keeping versioned history in this manner can get messy.

**CAUTION**
*Delete processing* must *precede rollback processing. Rollback processing performs inserts. Failure to perform delete processing will result in unique constraint violations. Prior to running a rollback, make sure you run a delete. Running a delete twice has no negative impact. Once the rows are deleted, they don't exist. Successive deletes will just result in zero rows processed.*

# Remove From History Processing

If you decide to copy rows from history tables back into transaction tables, it is a good idea to purge those rows from the history tables. This helps you avoid the potential scenario in which someone restores a prior history batch over updated transaction data. Figure 4-7 shows the Remove From History process type. It is the same interface used in delete and rollback processing, except the Process Type field was changed to Remove From History.

**CAUTION**
*Running Remove From History deletes all data associated with that batch. The only way to re-create that batch is to rerun the selection process with the same criteria. Considering that most selection criteria involve a point in time, re-creating that exact batch may be very difficult, if not impossible.*

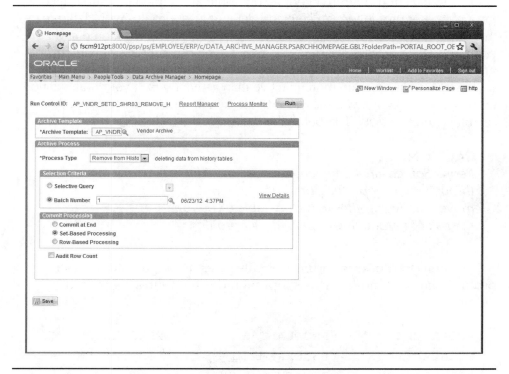

**FIGURE 4-7.** *Remove From History processing*

### Auditing Archives

On the Data Archive Manager Homepage, you will see the Audit Archiving link. If you click this link, the Audit Archive page displays every table touched by archive processing including the template, date/time, process, batch number, operator ID, run control ID, process instance, and SQL.

# Creating Your Own Archives

The remainder of this chapter will show you how to create your own archive processes. Creating an archive process requires that you have exceptional knowledge of the target transaction as well as all related transactions. For example, archiving personal data records without archiving related job records would result in orphaned job data.

## Archiving User Profiles

The *user profile* is a critical component of PeopleSoft transactional systems. Several transactions within a PeopleSoft application maintain audit history through a user profile foreign key, and deleting user profiles would eliminate this audit history. If your company has a relatively stable workforce and changes to user profiles are rare, you may have no need for archiving user profiles. On the other hand, if your workforce fluctuates drastically, your user profile tables may contain more inactive than active users. If your organization fits this latter category, you may be interested in finding a way to move this seemingly unnecessary data out of the main security tables.

**CAUTION**
*PeopleSoft ensures uniqueness of user profiles through the user profile primary key. If you move inactive profiles to history tables, you run the risk of introducing duplicate user profiles.*

The delivered `userexport.dms` file gives us insight into the user profile relational model. This script includes the following record definitions:

| | | |
|---|---|---|
| PSOPRDEFN | PSOPRALIAS | PSROLEUSER |
| PSUSERATTR | PSUSEREMAIL | PSUSERPRSNLOPTN |
| ROLEXLATOPR | RTE_CNTL_RUSER | |

Most of the records follow the standard parent/child relational design pattern, with `PSOPRDEFN` being the clear ancestor of the user profile hierarchy. Unfortunately, few transaction relational models follow a perfect ancestral design pattern with only one forefather. The user profile data model is no exception. Consider `PSOPERDEFN` and `PSUSERATTR`, for example. Both records `PSOPRDEFN` and `PSUSERATTR` have the same key structure: `OPRID`. Since `PSUSERATTR` would not exist without `PSOPRDEFN`, we can clearly consider `PSUSERATTR` a dependent of `PSOPRDEFN`. Data Archive Manager doesn't see it this way, however. It expects to start with a single record, known as the base record, and work downward. Here is Data Archive Manager's relational rule: *Every record in a data archive object must include the same key structure as the base record plus at least one additional key field.*

Data Archive Manager does not accept sibling relationships. When adding new rows to a data archive object, PeopleCode will test the key structure of each record to ensure that the keys conform to this relational rule.

Data Archive Manager just needs "law-abiding" metadata. Whether or not the metadata matches the database's version of the relational model is irrelevant. To work around this rule, we can create updateable views and register those views as the *archiving records*. Before building our history tables, let's create the required archive record metadata.

## Creating Conforming Metadata

As mentioned, the records `PSUSERATTR` and `PSROLEUSER` do not conform to the Data Archive Manager base record relational rule. `PSUSERATTR` does not have enough keys and the `PSROLEUSER` key has the wrong field name. We will satisfy Data Archive Manager by creating views for each of these nonconforming record definitions.

1. In Application Designer, open the `PSUSERATTR` record definition.

2. From the Application Designer menu bar, choose File | Save As.

3. Name the new record `OP_USERATTR_V`.

4. When prompted to copy the record's PeopleCode, select the No button.

5. Double-click the `HINT_QUESTION` field and mark it as a key field. No, `HINT_QUESTION` won't become a key field within the database. This is just metadata and exists solely for PeopleTools' benefit. It will have no impact on the way the `PSUSERATTR` table operates.

6. Switch to the Record Type tab and change the Record Type to SQL View.

7. Select the Click To Open SQL Editor button and enter the following SQL:

```
SELECT %subrec(PSUSERATTR, A)
  FROM PSUSERATTR A
```

Figure 4-8 shows the new `OP_USERATTR_V` record definition.

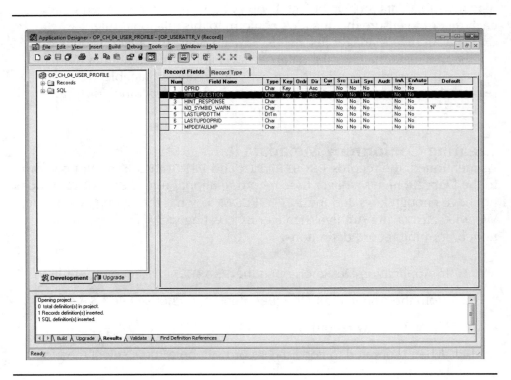

**FIGURE 4-8.** `OP_USERATTR_V` *record definition*

8. In similar manner, open the record definition PSROLEUSER and save it as OP_ROLEUSER_V. The key structure for this record is valid, but the first field name does not match the base record's key field name.

9. From the Application Designer menu bar, select Insert | Field.

10. In the selection criteria name field, enter **OPRID**.

11. Select the Insert button once to populate the search results list, and then double-click the OPRID field in the search results list. This will insert the OPRID field into the OP_ROLEUSER_V record definition.

12. From the record's field list, now four fields long, move the OPRID field to the number one position.

13. Double-click the field to view its properties and mark the field as a Key field.

14. After configuring the OPRID field, select the ROLEUSER field and remove it from the OP_ROLEUSER_V record definition. Figure 4-9 shows how this record definition should appear after making these field changes.

15. Switch to the Record Type tab and change the type to SQL View.

16. Open the view's SQL editor and enter the following SQL:

```
SELECT %subrec(PSROLEUSER, A)
   FROM PSROLEUSER A
```

The userexport.dms file lists one more nonconforming table: PS_ROLEXLATOPR. This table is not directly used by the User Profile component because the key structure does not conform to the User Profile component's key structure. The User Profile component uses the PSROLEXLATOPRVW view instead.

17. Open the record definition PSROLEXLATOPRVW and save it as OP_ROLEXLATOP_V.

18. Mark the ROLEUSER field as a key and save the definition. Figure 4-10 shows the OP_ROLEXLATOP_V record definition.

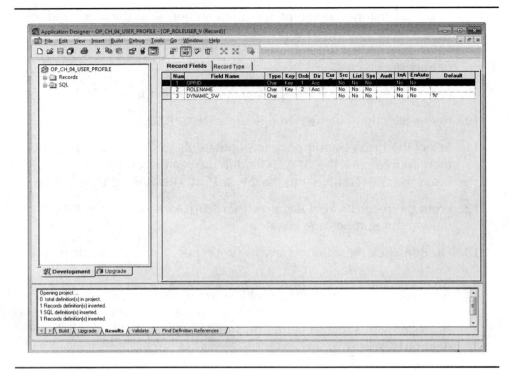

**FIGURE 4-9.** `OP_ROLEUSER_V` *record definition*

## Building History Tables

History tables are clones of regular transaction tables that include the
`PSARCHIVE_SBR` subrecord. To create a history table for the `PSOPRDEFN`
transaction table, follow these steps:

1. In Application Designer, open the record definition `PSOPRDEFN`.

2. From the Application Designer menu bar, choose File | Save As.
   Name the record `OP_OPRDEFN_H`.

3. Choose Insert | Subrecord. Select the subrecord `PSARCHIVE_SBR`.

4. Move the `PSARCHIVE_SBR` subrecord to the beginning of the field
   list (position number 1).

5. Save the new record definition.

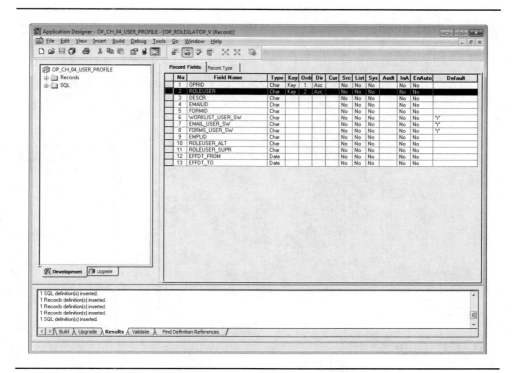

**FIGURE 4-10.** OP_ROLEXLATOP_V *record definition*

Figure 4-11 shows this new record definition.

Repeat this same process for the record definitions listed in the following table, naming each according to the table below. When prompted to copy a record's PeopleCode, choose No. The records with names ending in _V and VW are views, not tables. When cloning them, be sure to change the Record Type to SQL Table.

| Source Record | History Record |
|---|---|
| PSOPRALIAS | OP_OPRALIAS_H |
| OP_ROLEUSER_V | OP_ROLEUSER_H |
| OP_USERATTR_V | OP_USERATTR_H |
| PSUSEREMAIL | OP_USEREMAIL_H |
| PSUSERPRSNLOPTN | OP_USERPRSNLO_H |
| OP_ROLEXLATOP_V | OP_ROLEXLATOP_H |
| RTE_CNTL_USERVW | OP_RTE_CNTL_U_H |

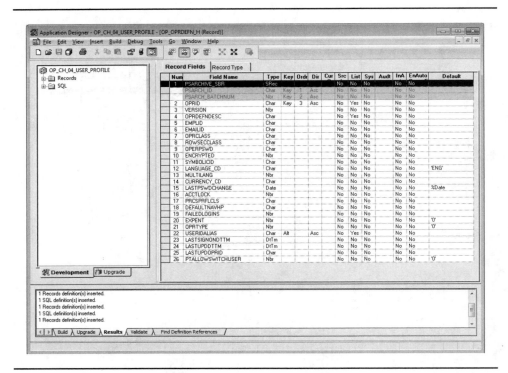

**FIGURE 4-11.** `OP_OPRDEFN_H` *record definition*

After defining these records (views and history tables), assuming you added them all to the same project, build the project by selecting Build | Project from the Application Designer menu bar. Choose the build options Create Tables and Create Views.

**NOTE**
*Some companies require DBA approval before you can build record definitions. If you find yourself in this category, choose the Build Execute Option of Build Script File. Otherwise, choose Execute And Build Script.*

## Archive Object Metadata

With our history tables defined, we can create an archive object to map each source table to a history table.

1. Log into your online PeopleSoft application and use the PeopleSoft navigation menu to open PeopleTools | Data Archive Manager | Manage Archive Objects.

2. Add the new value **OP_USER_PROFILE**.

3. Set the description to User Profiles and add the following record mappings, being sure to mark PSOPRDEFN as the Base Record:

| Archive Record | History Record |
| --- | --- |
| PSOPRDEFN | OP_OPRDEFN_H |
| PSOPRALIAS | OP_OPRALIAS_H |
| OP_ROLEUSER_V | OP_ROLEUSER_H |
| OP_USERATTR_V | OP_USERATTR_H |
| PSUSEREMAIL | OP_USEREMAIL_H |
| PSUSERPRSNLOPTN | OP_USERPRSNLO_H |
| OP_ROLEXLATOP_V | OP_ROLEXLATOP_H |
| RTE_CNTL_USERVW | OP_RTE_CNTL_U_H |

Figure 4-12 shows the new archive object.

## Create an Archive Query

The archive object maps the movement of data from transaction tables into history tables. Next we create a query to tell Data Archive Manager which rows to move from the transaction tables into the history tables. Our example will use the LASTSIGNONDTTM field to archive rows for all users that haven't logged in since a specified date.

**NOTE**
*The example criterion is very simplistic and ignores important facts, such as legitimate medical leave, suspension, and so on. We recommend that you add more criteria based on your organization's business requirements.*

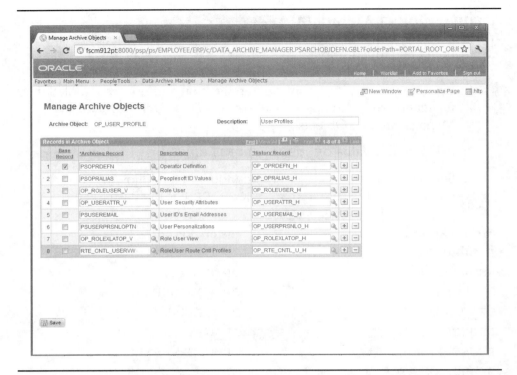

**FIGURE 4-12.**   OP_USER_PROFILE *archive object*

1. Log into your PeopleSoft application and navigate to Reporting Tools | Query | Query Manager.

2. Create a new query. Add the record **PSOPRDEFN**.

3. On the query tab, select the field OPRID.

4. Add the following criteria to the query: **LASTSIGNONDTTM <** prompt. The prompt should have a Date type and a format of None.

   The query's SQL should resemble this:

```
SELECT A.OPRID
  FROM PSOPRDEFN A
  WHERE ( A.LASTSIGNONDTTM < TO_DATE(:1,'YYYY-MM-DD') )
```

5. Save the query. Name it **OP_USER_PROFILE_ARCH_ALL**.

6. Set the Query Type to Archive.

7. Set the Owner to Public.

The Query Type and Owner attributes are critical. Figure 4-13 shows the query's attributes.

## Archive Template Metadata

The archive template unites the various pieces of archive metadata to tell Data Archive Manager exactly how to run an archive or restore process. The template associates the transaction/history table mapping (archive object) with our new selection query.

Now, create a new archive template and name it OP_USERP. Set the Archive Object to OP_USER_PROFILE and select the Base Object checkbox. Figure 4-14 shows the new archive template.

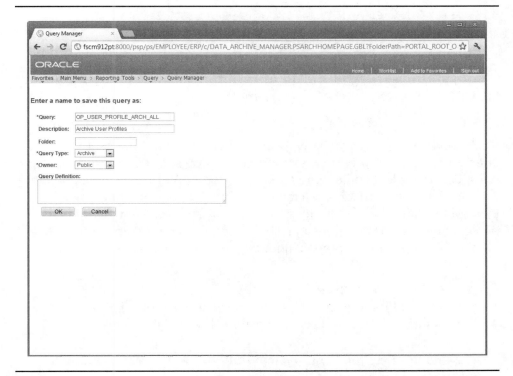

**FIGURE 4-13.** *Query* OP_USER_PROFILE_ARCH_ALL *save properties*

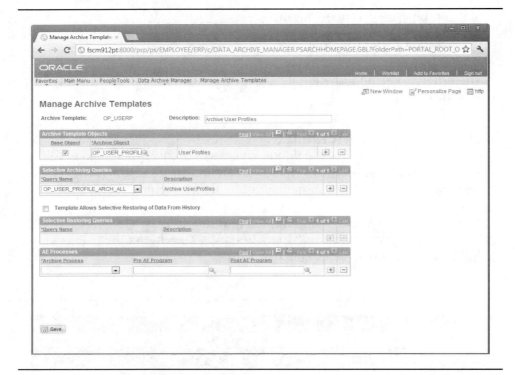

**FIGURE 4-14.** OP_USERP *archive template*

Archive templates also allow for per-process pre- and post-application engine programs. A preprocessing program allows for complex selection rules. For example, I could write a multiple-step Application Engine program that writes base record keys to a table. The archive selection query would then join to this table, determining the rows to archive. After the archive process finishes, a post-processing Application Engine program would clear out the selection table to prepare it for the next archive process.

## Run the Archive Process
To run the User Profile Archive process, navigate to PeopleTools | Data Archive Manager | Archive Data To History. Then do the following:

1. Create a new run control named **OP_USER_PROFILE_SELECT**.

2. Select the Archive Template OP_USERP.

3.  Choose the Selective Query OP_USER_PROFILE_ARCH_ALL
    (the only one in the list).

4.  Click the Define Binds hyperlink within the Selection Criteria
    section of the run control page.

5.  Within the Define Binds dialog, click the Reset Query Bind Variables
    button. This will allow you to specify a value for the Last Signon Date
    query prompt field.

My demo database contains profiles for users who haven't logged in since
October 2001. To archive all users who haven't logged in since December
31, 2002, I select a Last Signon Date of 01/01/2003. Figure 4-15 shows this
new run control.
    After running the selection process, both my transaction and history tables
now contain the same selected user profiles. At this point, as long as a user

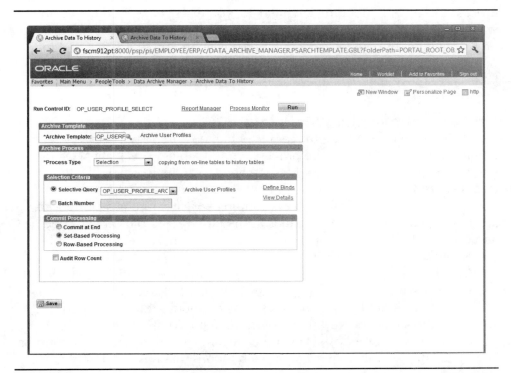

**FIGURE 4-15.**   OP_USER_PROFILE_SELECT *run control definition*

profile is not locked, I can still use it to gain access to my system. To remove the selected rows from the transaction tables, I will rerun the archive process, but this time I'll select the delete process type.

Delete processing does not use the selection query. This means I can actually log in as one of the archived users, updating the last sign-on time, and then run the delete process to delete that previously archived user. Of course, any changes made to the user between archive and deletion would be lost. Instead of a selection query, delete processing requires the selection batch number. You can find the batch number in the process scheduler message log for the selection process.

# Archiving Process Scheduler Data

The process scheduler polls the primary process request table on interval to identify queued processes. Keeping the process scheduler tables lean generally improves process scheduler performance. The problem with purging process scheduler information is that many batch processes log the process instance. If, upon reviewing data, you discover a discrepancy and want to review the batch parameters, message log, and so on, chances are pretty high that the process scheduler data is gone. An alternative that may offer the same performance improvement as purging process scheduler tables is to move that data into history tables.

## Creating Conforming Metadata

PeopleTools delivers a Data Mover script named `prcsclr.dms` that administrators use to purge the process request tables. This Data Mover script contains a list of all the tables we need to archive. Much like the prior user profile example, some of the process scheduler tables contain nonconforming key structures. A conforming key structure is a composite key that contains the same key fields as the base record plus at least one additional field. Before creating history tables, we must create updatable views for these nonconforming records.

We will use `PSPRCSRQST` as our base record. Most of the records listed in `prcsclr.dms` contain the same key field as `PSPRCSRQST`: the `PRCSINSTANCE` field. Some, however, use the field `PROCESS_INSTANCE`, whereas others have no key at all. Of those that have the same key field, some don't have a composite key. Once again, we will generate conforming key metadata by creating views for each record that has a different key structure.

To create the first view, do the following:

1. Open the record definition PSPRCSRQSTTEXT in Application Designer.

2. Choose File | Save As and name the new record **OP_PRCSRQSTXT_V**.

3. Double-click the PRCSINSTANCE field to view the field's properties and mark it as a key field.

4. Do the same for field RQSTTEXTTYPE. In Figure 4-16, the OP_PRCSRQSTXT_V record definition shows both fields marked as keys.

5. Switch to the Record Type tab and change the type to SQL View.

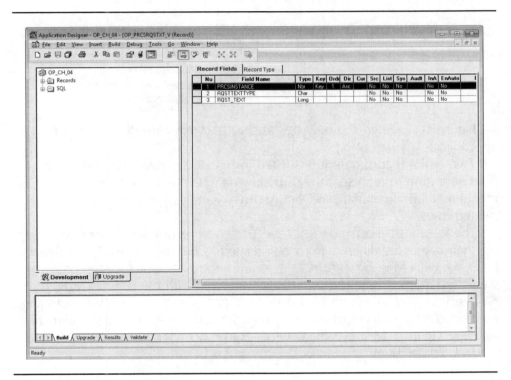

**FIGURE 4-16.** OP_PRCSRQSTXT_V *record definition*

6. Select the Click To Open SQL Editor button and enter the following SQL:

```
SELECT %subrec(PSPRCSRQSTTEXT, A)
  FROM PSPRCSRQSTTEXT A
```

7. Do the same for each record in the following table:

   a. Save it under the name given in column two.

   b. Mark field 2 as a key field.

   c. Change the Record Type to SQL View.

   d. Set the SQL using the value in column three.

| Source Record | New View | SQL |
| --- | --- | --- |
| PSPRCSQUE | OP_PRCSQUE_VW | SELECT %subrec(PSPRCSQUE, A) FROM PSPRCSQUE A |
| PSPRCSCHLDINFO | OP_PRCSCHLDIN_V | SELECT %subrec(PSPRCSCHLDINFO, A) FROM PSPRCSCHLDINFO A |
| PSPRCSPARMS | OP_PRCSPARMS_VW | SELECT %subrec(PSPRCSPARMS, A) FROM PSPRCSPARMS A |
| PRCSRQSTNOTIFY | OP_PRCSRQSTNO_V | SELECT %subrec(PRCSRQSTNOTIFY, A) FROM PRCSRQSTNOTIFY A |

Figure 4-17 shows the new OP_PRCSQUE_VW record definition with appropriate key definitions.

Two of the record definitions listed in prcsclr.dms use a different field definition to represent the same key data. We will use SQL views to create matching metadata so Data Archive Manager can correctly select related rows.

The MESSAGE_LOG and MESSAGE_LOGPARM record definitions have keys, but their names are different from their related record definitions. To resolve this issue, we will clone the MESSAGE_LOG and MESSAGE_LOGPARM records into views and replace the PROCESS_INSTANCE field with PRCSINSTANCE. The process is very similar to creating the OP_PRCSRQSTXT_V view. When adding the PRCSINSTANCE field, be sure to make it the first field in the list and mark it as a key. Figure 4-18 shows the new OP_MSG_LOG_VW clone of the MESSAGE_LOG record definition.

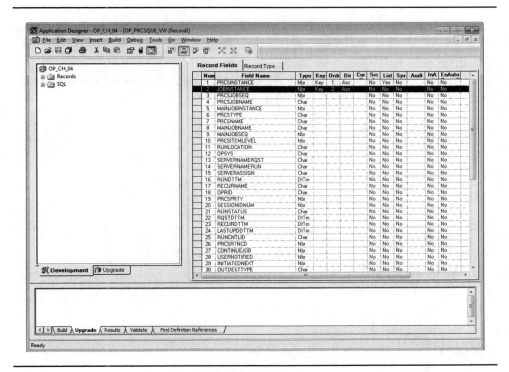

**FIGURE 4-17.** `OP_PRCSQUE_VW` *record definition*

Change the Record Type of `OP_MSG_LOG_VW` to SQL View and insert the following SQL:

```
SELECT %subrec(MESSAGE_LOG, A)
   FROM PS_MESSAGE_LOG A
```

Follow the same steps we used to clone `MESSAGE_LOGPARM` into `OP_MSGLOG_P_VW`, replacing the `PROCESS_INSTANCE` field with `PRCSINSTANCE`. Then add the following SQL to the view definition:

```
SELECT %subrec(MESSAGE_LOGPARM, A)
   FROM PS_MESSAGE_LOGPARM A
```

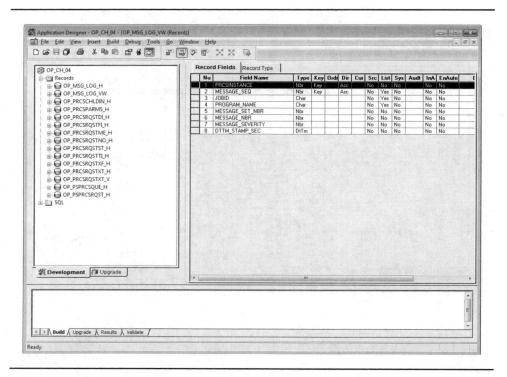

**FIGURE 4-18.** `OP_MSG_LOG_VW` *record definition*

## Building History Tables

To configure the Data Archive Object properly, we must create a history table for each record listed in the `prcsclr.dms` script. Open Application Designer and follow these steps:

1. Open the record definition `PSPRCSRQST`.

2. Choose File | Save As. Name the record **OP_PSPRCSRQST_H**.

3. Choose Insert | Subrecord. Select the subrecord `PSARCHIVE_SBR`.

4. Move the `PSARCHIVE_SBR` subrecord to the beginning of the field list (position number 1).

5. Save the new record definition.

Figure 4-19 shows this new record definition.

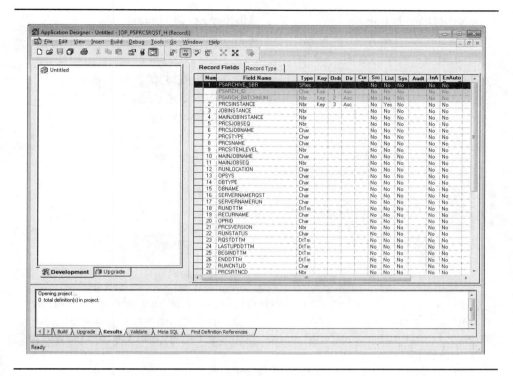

**FIGURE 4-19.**   `OP_PSPRCSRQST_H` *history record definition*

Repeat this same process for the record definitions listed in the following table, naming each according to names in the table. When prompted to copy a record's PeopleCode, choose No.

| Source Record Name | History Record Name |
|---|---|
| PSPRCSRQST | OP_PSPRCSRQST_H |
| PSPRCSQUE | OP_PSPRCSQUE_H |
| PSPRCSCHLDINFO | OP_PRCSCHLDIN_H |
| PSPRCSPARMS | OP_PRCSPARMS_H |
| PSPRCSRQSTXFER | OP_PRCSRQSTXF_H |
| PRCSRQSTDIST | OP_PRCSRQSTDI_H |
| PSPRCSRQSTFILE | OP_PRCSRQSTFI_H |

| Source Record Name | History Record Name |
|---|---|
| PSPRCSRQSTMETA | OP_PRCSRQSTME_H |
| PSPRCSRQSTSTRNG | OP_PRCSRQSTST_H |
| PSPRCSRQSTTIME | OP_PRCSRQSTTI_H |
| PRCSRQSTNOTIFY | OP_PRCSRQSTNO_H |
| OP_PRCSRQSTXT_V | OP_PRCSRQSTXT_H |
| OP_MSG_LOG_VW | OP_MSG_LOG_H |
| OP_MSGLOG_P_VW | OP_MSGLOG_P_H |

**NOTE**
*The last three definitions were views. When you're creating history tables for these views, be sure to change the history table's Record Type to SQL Table.*

After you've defined these records (views and history tables), assuming you added them all to the same project, build the project. Choose Build | Project. Then choose the build options Create Tables and Create Views.

## Archive Object Metadata

With our history tables defined, we can create an archive object containing each definition. Log into your online PeopleSoft application and use the PeopleSoft menu to navigate to PeopleTools | Data Archive Manager | Manage Archive Objects. Add the new value **OP_PRCS_SCHED**. Enter the description **Process Scheduler Requests** and create the following record mappings. Be sure to mark PSPSPRCSRQST as the base record.

| Archiving Record | History Record |
|---|---|
| PSPRCSRQST | OP_PSPRCSRQST_H |
| OP_MSGLOG_P_VW | OP_MSGLOG_P_H |
| OP_PRCSCHLDIN_V | OP_PRCSCHLDIN_H |
| OP_PRCSPARMS_VW | OP_PRCSPARMS_H |
| OP_PRCSQUE_VW | OP_PSPRCSQUE_H |
| OP_PRCSRQSTNO_V | OP_PRCSRQSTNO_H |
| OP_PRCSRQSTXT_V | OP_PRCSRQSTXT_H |

| Archiving Record | History Record |
|---|---|
| PRCSRQSTDIST | OP_PRCSRQSTDI_H |
| OP_MSG_LOG_VW | OP_MSG_LOG_H |
| PSPRCSRQSTFILE | OP_PRCSRQSTFI_H |
| PSPRCSRQSTMETA | OP_PRCSRQSTME_H |
| PSPRCSRQSTSTRNG | OP_PRCSRQSTST_H |
| PSPRCSRQSTTIME | OP_PRCSRQSTTI_H |
| PSPRCSRQSTXFER | OP_PRCSRQSTXF_H |

Figure 4-20 shows the configured archive object.

## Create an Archive Query

Log into your online PeopleSoft application and navigate to Reporting Tools | Query | Query Manager. Then do the following:

1. Create a new query and add the record **PSPRCSRQST**.

2. Select the field PRCSINSTANCE.

3. In the Criteria tab, add Not In List criteria to field RUNSTATUS using the list values 5, 6, 7, 16. These are process statuses that we do *not* want to archive.

4. Add Less Than criteria to field RUNDTTM.

5. Choose Prompt for expression 2.

6. Create the new prompt with a Type of Date and a Format of None. After configuring the query, its SQL should resemble this:

```
SELECT A.PRCSINSTANCE
  FROM PSPRCSRQST A
  WHERE ( A.RUNSTATUS NOT IN ('5','6','7','16')
    AND A.RUNDTTM < TO_DATE(:1,'YYYY-MM-DD') )
```

7. Save the query as Type Archive and set the Owner to Public. Name the new query **OP_PSPRCSRQST_ARCH_ALL**.

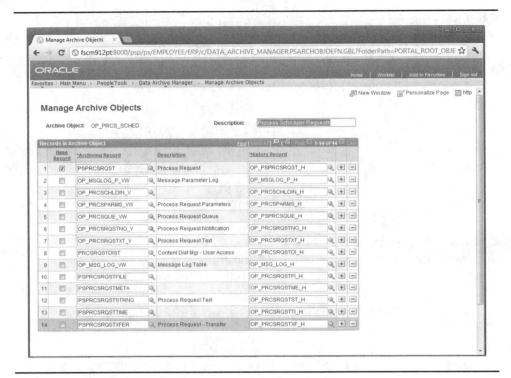

**FIGURE 4-20.** OP_PRCS_SCHED *archive object*

## Create an Archive Template

In your PeopleSoft application online, navigate to PeopleTools | Data Archive Manager | Manage Archive Templates, and then do the following:

1. Create a new Archive Template named **OP_PRCS**.

2. Choose the archive object OP_PRCS_SCHED and mark it as the base object.

3. Select the query OP_PSPRCSRQST_ARCH_ALL. Figure 4-21 shows the new OP_PRCS archive template.

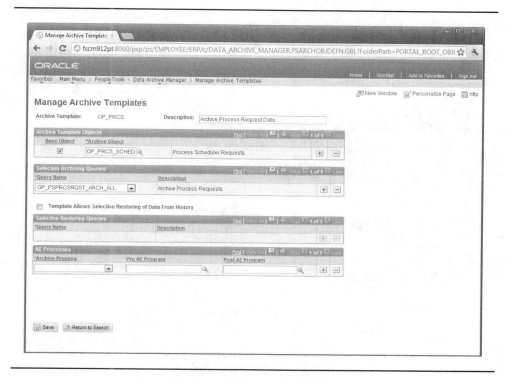

**FIGURE 4-21.** OP_PRCS *archive template*

## Run the Archive Process

To run the Process Scheduler archive process, navigate to PeopleTools |
Data Archive Manager | Archive Data to History; then do the following:

1. Create a new run control named **OP_PSPRCSRQST_SELECT**.

2. Select the Archive Template OP_PRCS.

3. Choose the Selective Query OP_PSPRCSRQST_ARCH_ALL (the only
   one in the list).

4. Click the Define Binds hyperlink and then the Reset Query Bind
   Variables button. This will allow you to specify a value for the Run
   Date query prompt. For testing purposes, I selected today as my Run
   Date. This archives all completed or canceled requests older than
   today. Figure 4-22 shows this new run control.

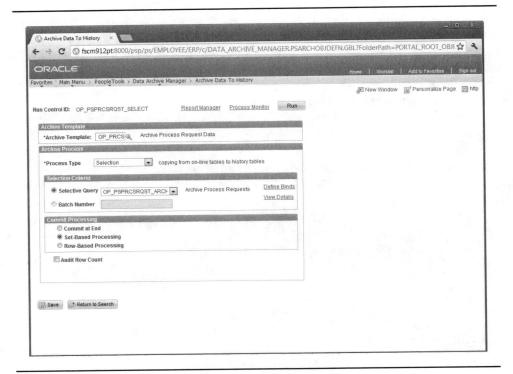

**FIGURE 4-22.** OP_PRCS *selection processing run control*

# Extending Delivered Archive Definitions

It is quite common to extend delivered transactions by creating sibling records that share a common key structure. When archiving delivered transactions, you will likely want to include these custom records in the archive batch. To ensure batch consistency, create history tables (and possibly views) to match your sibling records and then add them to the delivered archive object definitions. This approach, however, may create additional work at upgrade time. Delivered archive definitions are owned by Oracle and will likely be overwritten at upgrade. Be sure to note your changes.

In the last chapter we learned how to use Data Mover to import and export data. One method to persist archive definition customizations across upgrades is to export all custom rows from PSARCHOBJREC prior to upgrade. You may then import those rows back into PSARCHOBJREC post upgrade. Following a consistent, unique record naming convention will help you identify custom record definitions.

# Conclusion

In this chapter you learned how to use Data Archive Manager to keep transaction tables lean and well performing. When creating your own archive definitions, be sure to consider the related transaction impact of moving transactions into history tables. It would not be appropriate to archive a transaction that has open related transactions. For example, archiving a vendor that has open vouchers would make generating payments extremely difficult!

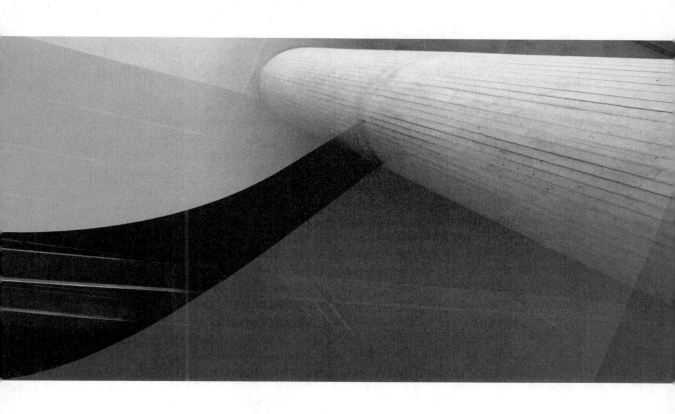

# PART
# II

# Change Management

# CHAPTER
## 5

# Change Management
## Overview

 e can divide PeopleSoft Change Management into two segments: updates and upgrades. An *upgrade* involves moving from one software release to the next, whereas an *update* offers improvements within the same version. We usually associate upgrades with new features and significant enhancements. More recently, however, Oracle has made new features available to existing releases through off-cycle feature packs.

Generally speaking, updates involve routine maintenance: installing bug fixes and regulatory updates, also known as *patches*. Oracle releases updates quite regularly. If your organization runs multiple PeopleSoft modules, then in any given month you may easily identify multiple bundles available for download.

# PeopleSoft Update Package Types

Oracle releases three types of PeopleSoft maintenance packages: updates, bundles, and maintenance packs. These three types make up a hierarchy:

- Update
- Bundle
- Maintenance pack

Oracle initially releases bug fixes as updates. Periodically, these bug fixes are rolled into bundles. After bundle release, the updates included in the bundle are removed from Oracle's download center. To acquire a specific update's resolution after bundle release, an organization must apply the entire bundle. Maintenance packs are periodic collections of bundles. Maintenance packs come in two varieties: *cumulative* and *delta*. Application bundles are never cumulative. Another difference between maintenance packs and bundles is that maintenance packs are application-specific, containing bundles from all modules. Bundles, on the other hand, are module-specific.

# Patching Strategies

How often should an organization apply patches? What patches should an organization apply? Common patching strategies include the following:

- Never

- As required

- Regulatory patching (a derivative of "as required")

- Maintenance packs

- Bundles

The *never* patching strategy means exactly that: no patching, ever. This patching strategy is rarely recommended and is used by organizations with PeopleSoft versions that have long since moved past the regular support window. To say these organizations never patch is not entirely accurate. A more accurate description would perhaps be internally patched, meaning the organization generates its own patches.

The *as required* patching strategy is unfortunately frequent. In this strategy, an organization discovers a problem for which Oracle has released a fix. The customer uses this opportunity to apply just enough maintenance to resolve the problem. This is a reactive approach that often requires more effort than you might expect. Patches usually contain prerequisites. I remember a time when I was so far behind on patching that I had to apply ten bundles to implement a resolution.

*Regulatory patching* is also a reactive response similar to *as required* patching. Periodically, Oracle releases important tax, payroll, and other regulatory updates. The *regulatory patching* strategy applies these patches along with any prerequisites. This strategy is often used in relation to other patching strategies.

The *maintenance pack* strategy is a proactive approach. Organizations that use this approach typically budget maintenance around maintenance pack release cycles. By keeping current on maintenance through maintenance packs, they are in a better position to apply updates and receive support should problems arise.

The *bundle* strategy is a proactive strategy that is similar to the maintenance pack strategy, but more frequent and smaller in scope. Bundles are released more often but cover fewer issues than a maintenance pack. The smaller scope of a bundle makes it easier to identify and resolve issues that might arise from the application of this maintenance. An organization with a team devoted to change management may opt for the bundle strategy.

With Oracle releasing patches on a regular basis, sometimes as often as one bundle per module per month, an organization requires an effective patching strategy. Typically a site chooses either maintenance packs or bundles, but not both. Updates often include data conversion routines that should run only one time. Since maintenance packs include bundles, applying maintenance packs over bundles will likely cause data conversion routines to run multiple times: once for the bundle and once for the maintenance pack. The route chosen by your site will depend on resources and change management philosophy. A common approach is to start with the maintenance pack route. If a site then discovers a bug and can't wait for the next maintenance pack, the customer may switch to the bundle route. Once on the bundle route, however, switching back to maintenance packs may prove difficult—possible, but difficult.

# Change Management Tools

Several tools are available to help manage change with regards to PeopleSoft applications.

## Environment Management Framework

The *Environment Management Framework (EMF)* forms the base for PeopleSoft change management tools. The EMF examines database and file systems to determine the current patch level of an application. PeopleSoft's change management tools use this baseline information to identify patches, bundles, and maintenance packs available for installation. After determining the necessary changes, PeopleSoft's change management tools use the EMF to propagate changes to servers participating in the installation. In Chapter 6 you will learn how to configure the EMF.

## Change Assistant

Change Assistant is an upgrade project management utility. Change Assistant handles pretty much everything, from identifying available patches to pushing changes out to remote systems. In Chapter 7 you will learn how to use Change Assistant to apply application updates and create new change packages.

Change Assistant's change packages assist with segregation of duties. Rather than creating projects, scripts, and lengthy documentation, a change package allows a developer to identify each resource required to migrate an enhancement. PeopleSoft's change packaging tools use this information to generate all of the documentation and steps required to migrate the change. A developer can then perform a proper handoff to the administrator responsible for the destination system.

For example, a Pagelet Wizard–generated pagelet includes both application-specific metadata and PeopleTools metadata (Portal Registry Structures). A developer can package and migrate PeopleTools metadata using an Application Designer project, but Pagelet Wizard application-specific metadata requires a different approach. Pagelet Wizard provides a Data Mover script creation process for moving the application-specific metadata. Without a Change Assistant change package, a developer would document the project details, Data Mover script, and exported data. The developer would then pass this documentation to an administrator. With Change Assistant, a developer adds this information to a change project within Application Designer, generates a change package, and then sends the change package to an administrator for migration.

# Change Impact Analyzer

By definition, a change package modifies the target system. Ever been curious what a change package will alter? A change to a page layout may require updates to user manuals. Likewise, a change to a record definition may necessitate site-specific report and query alterations. In Chapter 8 you will learn how to use PeopleSoft's Change Impact Analyzer to visualize the change package's ripple effect.

# Change Control

Recent regulations require certain organizations to maintain tight control over application code. Regulators often require organizations to keep application change audit records and demonstrate a clear separation of duties between employees within IT. Regardless of regulations, companies often find it prudent to maintain a version of change history to allow for a sort of "undo" for application code changes. Even developers desire some form of change control. Two developers working on entirely different projects may both require a change to a common definition. It is too easy for unrelated developers to interfere with each other's changes. In Chapter 9 we will explore PeopleSoft's mechanisms for managing this aspect of change. We will then explore the various third-party applications available for managing PeopleSoft applications.

# Conclusion

Change is inevitable. How an organization manages change has a significant impact on total cost of ownership. In the chapters that follow, you will learn how to make the most of the tools Oracle delivers for managing change. The tools introduced in this section of the book relate equally to updates and upgrades. This section focuses on updates, saving upgrades for Part III.

# CHAPTER
## 6

# Environment
# Management
# Framework

he Environment Management Framework (EMF) is an essential
component of upgrade management. It consists of an EMF *hub*
and EMF *agents.* Agents running in each tier of a PeopleSoft
installation gather information about the tier and relay that
information to the hub. The hub receives and stores agent
information for Change Assistant, which uploads this information to the Update
Gateway to determine available updates. When applying updates, Change
Assistant sends commands to the EMF hub, which dispatches these instructions
to EMF agents. In this chapter, you will learn how to configure the EMF hub and
EMF agents, a prerequisite for next chapter's discussion of Change Assistant.

**NOTE**
*In other documentation you may see the EMF
hub and EMF agent referred to as PSEMHub
and PSEMAgent. PeopleSoft's documentation
uses both the EMF and PSEM prefixes when
referring to the hub and agents.*

# The EMF Hub

The EMF hub is a PeopleSoft Internet Architecture (PIA) servlet installed in
your PeopleSoft web servlets directory. On WebLogic, this is located at
`$PS_CFG_HOME/webserv/peoplesoft/applications/peoplesoft/`
`PSEMHUB.war`. On WebSphere, look in `$PS_CFG_HOME/webserv/<cell_`
`node_server>/<domain>.ear/PSEMHUB.war/`.

You can view the status of registered agents from your browser by
accessing the URL http://hub_host: port/PSEMHUB/hub. On my Oracle VM
instance, the EMF hub is currently running at the URL http://fscm912pt:8000/
PSEMHUB/hub. (Later, we will move it to a standalone web server.)

## Configuration

The EMF Hub `configuration.properties` file is in the `envmetadata/`
`config` subdirectory of the `PSEMHUB` servlet. The hub is preconfigured at
install to inspect (crawl) agents every 24 hours and revalidate agents every
6 hours. An administrator can change the crawl interval by setting a new
value for `recrawlinterval`. Likewise, to revalidate on a different interval,
change the `revalidateinterval` property. If these values are acceptable
to your organization, you do not need to make any configuration changes to
the EMF hub.

# Logging

The EMF hub uses log4j, a Java logging framework that supports a variety of targets (called *appenders*) and formats. You can find full documentation for `log4j` on the Apache log4j web site at http://logging.apache.org/log4j/. The EMF hub log4j configuration is in the `envmetadata/config/Logconfig.properties` file. From this file, you can change the log file name and location, logging format, rotation schedule, and other information.

The default EMF hub log configuration uses the log4j RollingFileAppender. The RollingFileAppender rotates the log file when it reaches a certain size. The EMF hub log is configured to role when it reaches a maximum size of 1024 KB. An administrator can change the log size by setting a new value for `log4j.appender.R.MaxFileSize`. The maximum number of rotated logs is specified by the `log4j.appender.R.MaxBackupIndex` property. Alternatively, you could switch to the related DailyRollingFileAppender by changing the `log4j.appender.R` property as follows:

```
#log4j.appender.R.MaxFileSize=1024KB log4j.appender.R=
org.apache.log4j.DailyRollingFileAppender
```

# Clearing the EMF Hub Cache

If you clone, move, or change the architecture of a hub or its agents, you may want to clear the hub's cache. When crawled, agents will repopulate the cache with current, relevant information. To clear the hub cache, follow these steps:

1. Stop the `PSEMHUB` servlet container (web server).

2. In the `PSEMHUB/envmetadata` web application directory, delete the following files and folders:

   - `PersistentStorage`
   - `scratchpad`
   - `data/environment`
   - `data/proxies`
   - `data/state.dat`

The following is a transcript from the latest purge of my EMF hub cache:

```
# purge the EMF Hub cache
[psadm2@fscm912pt ~]$ cd ~/psft/pt/8.52/FSCM912/webserv/\
peoplesoft/applications/peoplesoft/PSEMHUB.war/envmetadata/

[psadm2@fscm912pt envmetadata]$ rm -R PersistentStorage
[psadm2@fscm912pt envmetadata]$ rm -R scratchpad
[psadm2@fscm912pt envmetadata]$ rm -R data/environment
[psadm2@fscm912pt envmetadata]$ rm -R data/proxies
[psadm2@fscm912pt envmetadata]$ rm data/state.dat
```

## Configuring a Standalone EMF Hub

Even though the EMF hub is preconfigured to run in PIA, there are a few reasons to run it outside of PIA:

- The EMF hub does not support clustering. If you have a clustered web server, you will need to run the EMF hub somewhere else.

- The EMF hub and agents may share large amounts of information, placing a significant load on production servers.

- For security, running the EMF hub on a standalone, lightweight servlet container offers an administrator a significant amount of flexibility.

To run the EMF hub in a standalone servlet container, first download and install a servlet container. A few of the more popular servlet containers include Apache Tomcat, Jetty, Glassfish, WebLogic, and JBoss (the latter three being full-blown Java 2 Enterprise Edition [J2EE] servers). After installing a servlet container, copy all of the files from a PIA server's PSEMHUB.war file into the servlet container's web application directory. Even though the PSEMHUB web application uses log4j, it doesn't actually include the log4j jar file in its lib directory. Before starting up the PSEMHUB, download the Apache log4j 1.2.17 jar file into the PSEMHUB/WEB-INF/lib directory. You can obtain a copy of log4j from the Apache log4j download site at http://logging.apache.org/log4j/1.2/download.html. Be sure to verify the checksum and expand the archive.

The following listing is a transcript of the steps I used to migrate my PSEMHUB web application from a PIA instance to a standalone Tomcat instance:

```
# Create an installation directory for tomcat
[psadm1@fscm912pt ~]$ mkdir ~/tomcat
[psadm1@fscm912pt ~]$ cd ~/tomcat/

# download and install tomcat
[psadm1@fscm912pt tomcat]$ wget http://www.carfab.com/\
apachesoftware/tomcat/tomcat-7/v7.0.28/bin/\
apache-tomcat-7.0.28.tar.gz
--2012-07-06 22:51:28--  http://www.carfab.com/apachesoftware/
    tomcat/tomcat-7/v7.0.28/bin/apache-tomcat-7.0.28.tar.gz
Resolving www.carfab.com... 205.186.175.60
Connecting to www.carfab.com|205.186.175.60|:80... connected.
HTTP request sent, awaiting response... 200 OK
Length: 7674156 (7.3M) [application/x-gzip]
Saving to: `apache-tomcat-7.0.28.tar.gz'

100%[========================================>]
    7,674,156   2.26M/s    in 3.4s

2012-07-06 22:51:32 (2.17 MB/s) - `apache-tomcat-7.0.28.tar.gz'
    saved [7674156/7674156]

[psadm1@fscm912pt tomcat]$ md5sum apache-tomcat-7.0.28.tar.gz
cfcd5b624df6aa94e9c91cd1fb4d0c71  apache-tomcat-7.0.28.tar.gz
[psadm1@fscm912pt tomcat]$ tar -xzf apache-tomcat-7.0.28.tar.gz
[psadm1@fscm912pt tomcat]$ rm apache-tomcat-7.0.28.tar.gz

# Create links to the start/stop scripts for easy access
[psadm1@fscm912pt tomcat]$ mkdir ~/scripts
[psadm1@fscm912pt tomcat]$ ln -s /home/psadm1/tomcat/\
apache-tomcat-7.0.28/bin/startup.sh ~/scripts/tomcat-startup.sh
[psadm1@fscm912pt tomcat]$ ln -s /home/psadm1/tomcat/\
apache-tomcat-7.0.28/bin/shutdown.sh ~/scripts/tomcat-shutdown.sh
[psadm1@fscm912pt tomcat]$ cd apache-tomcat-7.0.28/webapps

# Copy the PIA PSEMHUB.war into a standalone tomcat instance
[psadm1@fscm912pt webapps]$ cp -R /home/psadm2/psft/pt/8.52/\
FSCM912/webserv/peoplesoft/applications/peoplesoft/PSEMHUB.war\
 PSEMHUB
```

```
[psadm1@fscm912pt webapps]$ cd PSEMHUB/

# download and deploy log4j
[psadm1@fscm912pt PSEMHUB]$ wget -O /tmp/log4j-1.2.17.tar.gz \
http://mirror.nexcess.net/apache/logging/log4j/1.2.17/\
log4j-1.2.17.tar.gz
--2012-07-07 00:10:56--  http://mirror.nexcess.net/apache/
logging/log4j/1.2.17/log4j-1.2.17.tar.gz
Resolving mirror.nexcess.net... 208.69.120.55
Connecting to mirror.nexcess.net|208.69.120.55|:80... connected.
HTTP request sent, awaiting response... 200 OK
Length: 2864448 (2.7M) [application/x-gzip]
Saving to: `/tmp/log4j-1.2.17.tar.gz'

100%[=======================================>]
    2,864,448    134K/s   in 8.9s

2012-07-07 00:11:05 (315 KB/s) - `/tmp/log4j-1.2.17.tar.gz' saved
[2864448/2864448]

[psadm1@fscm912pt PSEMHUB]$ md5sum /tmp/log4j-1.2.17.tar.gz
8218714e41ee0c6509dcfeafa2e1f53f  /tmp/log4j-1.2.17.tar.gz

[psadm1@fscm912pt PSEMHUB]$ tar -xzf /tmp/log4j-1.2.17.tar.gz \
-C /tmp
[psadm1@fscm912pt PSEMHUB]$ cp /tmp/apache-log4j-1.2.17/\
log4j-1.2.17.jar WEB-INF/lib

# purge the EMF Hub cache
[psadm1@fscm912pt PSEMHUB]$ cd envmetadata/
[psadm1@fscm912pt envmetadata]$ rm -R PersistentStorage
[psadm1@fscm912pt envmetadata]$ rm -R scratchpad
[psadm1@fscm912pt envmetadata]$ rm -R data/environment
[psadm1@fscm912pt envmetadata]$ rm -R data/proxies
[psadm1@fscm912pt envmetadata]$ rm data/state.dat

# Startup tomcat and test
[psadm1@fscm912pt envmetadata]$ ~/scripts/tomcat-startup.sh

# Reconfigure and start agents (see next section)
```

**NOTE**
*For security reasons, the EMF Viewer application connects only to the localhost. If you move the EMF hub to a server without a PeopleTools install, then either reverse-proxy the EMF hub URL into a PeopleTools install localhost domain or copy the appropriate EMF Viewer files to the standalone EMF hub server.*

# EMF Agents

An EMF agent is a background process that runs on each server tier of a PeopleSoft application. On startup, these agents register themselves with the EMF hub and wait for the hub to issue commands. Unlike the EMF hub, EMF agents are not preconfigured and do not automatically start. To give the EMF hub a complete picture of a PeopleSoft installation, an administrator should configure and launch one EMF agent for each server host that has a PeopleTools installation. This includes file servers, application servers, process scheduler servers, and web servers.

## Configuration

To configure an EMF agent, edit the `configuration.properties` file located in the `$PS_HOME/PSEMAgent/envmetadata/config` directory. Update the `hubURL` property to the URL of the instance's web server URL. A few lines down, update the `windowsdrivestocrawl` for Microsoft Windows operating systems or `unixdrivestocrawl` for all other operating systems. The following is a partial listing of my EMF agent:

```
hubURL=http://localhost:8000/PSEMHUB/hub
agentport=5283

#ping interval in milliseconds for the peer to contact the hub...
pinginterval=10000

#Windows directories need to use the forward slash ('/')...
windowsdrivestocrawl=c:|d:
unixdrivestocrawl=/opt/oracle/psft/pt/tools|
    /home/psadm2/psft/pt/8.52/FSCM912
```

**NOTE**
*Drives are pipe (|) delimited and should all be listed on a single line. Regardless of operating system, use the slash (/) file path delimiter.*

My installation is a standard Oracle VM two-host demo system installation consisting of a database host and a middle (PeopleTools) tier. My `hubURL` points to the localhost/loopback address because my web server, application server, and process scheduler server all exist on the same middle-tier host.

The term *drive* in the context of EMF is not a physical disk drive, but rather a file system starting point. As you can see from my `unixdrivestocrawl` example, I listed two directories: my `PS_HOME` directory and my `PS_CFG_HOME` directory. The agent will crawl these directories in search of PeopleSoft-specific metadata, identifying web servers, process scheduler servers, application servers, file servers, and even the `PS_APP_HOME`.

## Decoupled Home Configuration

PeopleTools 8.50 introduced the `PS_CFG_HOME` decoupled configuration directory. PeopleTools 8.52 included a new `PS_APP_HOME` decoupled application installation directory. These new directory structures allow an administrator to *decouple* PeopleSoft's installation files. Prior releases commingle PeopleTools, application, and configuration files within the same directory structure. The primary benefits of a decoupled home include these:

- **Security**  A decoupled implementation allows a lesser privileged user to run the applications while still writing to configuration and log files. Proper `HOME` ownership allows for the security principle of *least privilege*.

- **Sharing**  An implementation team can share a `PS_HOME` and/or a `PS_APP_HOME` across multiple PeopleSoft applications or instances, relying on the underlying hardware to provide redundancy and failover.

- **Upgrade**  Decoupling `PS_HOME`, `PS_APP_HOME`, and `PS_CFG_HOME` allows an administrator to replace a `PS_HOME` or `PS_APP_HOME` file system mount point with a new file system, thereby performing an instant middle-tier upgrade. You can read more about this upgrade option in Part III of this book.

If the `PS_HOME` and `PS_APP_HOME` are owned by separate users, you may have trouble performing upgrades with Change Assistant through the EMF hub and agents. Since an EMF agent creates and changes files in the `$PS_HOME/PSEMAgent` directory, the user running the EMF agent must have write access to the `PSEMAgent` directory. Likewise, the EMF agent user must have write access to the `PS_APP_HOME` directory to deploy files successfully. Changing user and group permissions on `PS_HOME` or `PS_APP_HOME` contents violates either the least privilege or compartmentalization principles and quite possibly both principles.

There are several solutions to this problem. One that maintains compartmentalization and least privilege is simply to copy the `$PS_HOME/PSEMAgent` directory into `$PS_APP_HOME/PSEMAgent` and then run the agent as the `PS_APP_HOME` owner. To perform an application upgrade for a host using Change Assistant, a site needs to run only one agent per `PS_APP_HOME` owner.

**NOTE**
*When running multiple EMF agents on the same host, be sure to configure each agent to use a different* `agentport`*.*

# Logging

The EMF agent log settings are very similar to the EMF hub settings, allowing for the same log4j flexible configuration. Unless your organization requires an alternate log file management strategy or prefers to centralize log management, an administrator should not have to make changes to the log file settings. On the other hand, if the EMF agent isn't sending system details to the EMF hub, then changing the log level will provide the administrator with a significant amount of detail. To change the log level, edit `$PS_HOME/PSEMAgent/envmetadata/config/Logconfig.properties`. Search for the line `log4j.rootLogger=info, stdout, R`. Then replace `info` with `all` and restart the agent:

```
log4j.rootLogger=all, stdout, R
```

The log4j logging framework supports the log levels all, trace, debug, info, warn, error, fatal, and off. All is on the verbose extreme, whereas off will stop logging altogether. The other levels are additive. The info level will log info, warn, error, and fatal messages whereas the error level will log only error and fatal messages. When I increased my log level to all, I saw everything from `tnsping` output to `org.apache.commons.httpclient` requests. An administrator can fine-tune logging levels and statements by logger name. Use the following configuration to log all EMF statements and only errors and warnings from other Java classes within the EMF agent:

```
log4j.rootLogger=error, stdout, R
log4j.logger.EMF_CATEGORY=all, stdout, R
```

# Running the Agent

To launch an agent, run the operating system–specific batch file within the `PS_HOME\PSEMAgent` directory. For Microsoft Windows–based agents, run the following:

```
C:>%PS_HOME%\PSEMAgent\StartAgent.bat
```

All other operating systems use the following:

```
$PS_HOME/PSEMAgent/StartAgent.sh
```

As mentioned, the operating system user running the agent must have read/write access to the `PSEMAgent` directory as well as the `$PS_APP_HOME` (or `$PS_HOME`) directory. The operating system user also requires a properly configured environment. As the agent crawls directories and discovers PeopleSoft metadata, it will run utilities to acquire additional information. When run on my Oracle Enterprise Linux middle tier, the EMF Agent executes `psae` and `tnsping`.

## EMF Agents as Services

PeopleTools delivers an EMF agent service for Microsoft Windows. To install the service, open a command prompt and issue the following commands:

```
SET PS_HOME=c:\path\to\peopletools
cd %PS_HOME%\bin\client\winx86
REM -- Alternatively:
REM cd %PS_HOME%\bin\server\winx86

PSEMAgentService /install %PS_HOME%\PSEMAgent
```

The service defaults to automatic startup, which means it will auto start when booting Microsoft Windows. Unfortunately, if the EMF hub is down, the service will fail to start. Oracle recommends changing the service startup type to Manual and then starting the service only after the EMF hub is running. Alternatively, use the `StartAgent.bat` script to start the EMF agent only when needed.

For all other operating systems, create the appropriate `init` script. Unlike the Microsoft Windows service, a properly written UNIX service will continue to ping the EMF hub even if the hub is down, logging errors and retry attempts until the hub is running.

Here is a copy of the Linux Standard Base (LSB)–compliant `init` script I wrote for my Oracle Enterprise Linux 5.8 middle tier. To use this on your own server, follow these steps:

1. Update the `PS_HOME` and `DAEMON_USER` variables to values appropriate for your environment.

2. Save the script as `/etc/init.d/psemagent`.

3. Execute `chmod +x /etc/init.d/psemagent` to set the executable bit.

4. Run `chkconfig psemagent on` or `insserv psemagent` (depends on OS).

```
#!/bin/sh
### BEGIN INIT INFO
# Provides: psemagent
# Required-Start: $network
# Required-Stop: $network
# Should-Start:
# Should-Stop:
# Default-Start: 3 4 5
# Default-Stop: 0 1 2 6
# Short-Description: PeopleSoft EM Agent
# Description: PeopleSoft Environment Management Framework Agent
### END INIT INFO

# Author: Jim Marion
DAEMON_USER=psadm1
PS_HOME=/opt/oracle/psft/pt/tools
```

```
START_DAEMON_CMD=$PS_HOME/PSEMAgent/StartAgent.sh
STOP_DAEMON_CMD=$PS_HOME/PSEMAgent/StopAgent.sh
DESCR="PeopleSoft EM Agent"
NAME=psemagent
PIDFILE=/var/run/$NAME.pid

# Exit if the daemon does not exist
[ -x "$START_DAEMON_CMD" ] || exit 5

. /lib/lsb/init-functions
if [ $? != 0 ]
then
    echo "Unable to load LSB init functions" >&2
    exit 1
fi

# status code return values per http://tinyurl.com/6rfoyw9
status() {
    RETVAL=$(su - $DAEMON_USER -c "$START_DAEMON_CMD isrunning")
    if [ "$RETVAL" = "true" ]
    then
        echo "$DESCR Running"
        return 0
    else
        echo "$DESCR Not Running"

        if [ -f $PIDFILE ]
        then
            return 1
        fi

        if [ -f /var/lock/subsys/$NAME ]
        then
            return 2
        fi

        # program is not running and pid/lock files don't exist
        return 3
    fi
}
```

```
start() {
    echo -n "Starting $DESCR: "
    su - $DAEMON_USER -p -c $START_DAEMON_CMD > /dev/null 2>&1 &
    RETVAL=$?
    [ $RETVAL = 0 ] && touch /var/lock/subsys/$NAME && \
        echo $!>$PIDFILE && log_success_msg

    return $RETVAL
}

stop() {
    echo -n "Stopping $DESCR: "

    # don't stop if not running
    status > /dev/null
    RETVAL=$?
    if [ $RETVAL -ne 0 ]
    then
        # LSB defines stop when not running as success
        log_success_msg "Not running"
        return 0
    fi

    su - $DAEMON_USER -p -c $STOP_DAEMON_CMD > /dev/null 2>&1 \
        && log_success_msg || log_failure_msg
    RETVAL=$?

    [ $RETVAL = 0 ] && rm -f /var/lock/subsys/$NAME $PIDFILE
}

restart() {
    stop
    start
}

case "$1" in
    start)
        start
        ;;
    stop)
        stop
        ;;
```

```
status)
    status
    ;;
restart | try-restart | reload | force-reload)
    restart
    ;;
condrestart)
    [ -f /var/lock/subsys/$NAME ] && restart || :
    ;;
*)
    OPTS="start|stop|status|restart|try-restart"
    OPTS="$OPTS|condrestart|reload|force-reload"
    echo "Usage: $0 {$OPTS}"
    exit 2
esac

exit $?
```

## Additional EMF Agent Command Line Parameters

The EMF agent `StartAgent` program accepts an optional command as a single command line parameter. Table 6-1 contains a listing of valid `StartAgent` commands.

The following listing demonstrates how to use each `StartAgent` command:

```
[psadm1@fscm912pt PSEMAgent]$ ./StartAgent.sh isrunning
false

[psadm1@fscm912pt PSEMAgent]$ ./StartAgent.sh recrawl
INFO main EMF_CATEGORY - Proceeding with matching for AppServer
INFO main EMF_CATEGORY - Proceeding with matching for Decoupled
    AppServer
INFO main EMF_CATEGORY - Proceeding with matching for prcsserver
INFO main EMF_CATEGORY - Proceeding with matching for Host
INFO main EMF_CATEGORY - Proceeding with matching for Decoupled
    AppServer
INFO main EMF_CATEGORY - Proceeding with matching for prcsserver
INFO main EMF_CATEGORY - Proceeding with matching for WebServer
INFO main EMF_CATEGORY -  Diff: Hours 0 Minutes 0 Seconds 2

[psadm1@fscm912pt PSEMAgent]$ ./StartAgent.sh remove
Got Message :ShutDown
```

| Command | Explanation | Possible Output |
|---------|-------------|-----------------|
| `isrunning` | Displays a Boolean status of the agent: true if running, false if not running. | If running: `True`<br>If not running: `False` |
| `recrawl` | Crawls the directories listed in `configuration.properties` as if building a new inventory. Note: validate is not necessary after a recrawl. | Log output of the crawl process |
| `remove` | Unregister this host from the hub. The EMF agent must not be running. | On success:<br>`Peerid 1 has been removed.`<br>On failure:<br>`PeerID 1 could not be removed from the hub.` |
| `shutdown` | Stop the EMF agent. | If running:<br>`Shutting down Agent.... Shutdown normally`<br>If not running:<br>`Shutting down Agent....`<br>`Unable to detect a running agent...`<br>`Instance does not exist` |
| `url` | Displays the EMF hub URL. | `http:// localhost:8000/ PSEMHUB/hub` |
| `validate` | Validates components discovered by the latest crawl. | Log output of the validate process |
| `version` | Displays the EMF agent version information. | `8.52.03 Build Number:` |

**TABLE 6-1.** *EMF Agent Commands*

```
Peerid 1 has been removed.
Sending pulse from 'com.peoplesoft.emf.peer:id=1'

[psadm1@fscm912pt PSEMAgent]$ ./StartAgent.sh shutdown
Shutting down Agent....
Shutdown normally

[psadm1@fscm912pt PSEMAgent]$ ./StartAgent.sh url
http://localhost:8000/PSEMHUB/hub

[psadm1@fscm912pt PSEMAgent]$ ./StartAgent.sh validate
INFO main EMF_CATEGORY - Revalidate In progress
INFO main EMF_CATEGORY - Revalidate Completed

[psadm1@fscm912pt PSEMAgent]$ ./StartAgent.sh version
Version: 8.52.03 Build Number:
```

# Using the EMF Viewer

The EMF Viewer is an HTML container that uses Extensible Stylesheet
Language (XSL) to display information about agents registered with the EMF
hub. Before viewing agent information, connect to your EMF hub and run
the command GetEnvInfo. On Microsoft Windows run the following:

```
%PS_HOME%\PSEMViewer\GetEnvInfo.bat
```

For all other operating systems, run the following:

```
$PS_HOME/PSEMViewer/GetEnvInfo.bat
```

**NOTE**
*The GetEnvInfo command must be run from
the EMF hub. For security reasons, this command
connects to the loopback address only.*

When run, GetEnvInfo will prompt for the EMF hub listening port.
The port number should match the port you used when updating each

agent's `configuration.properties` file. Here is an example of running `GetEnvInfo.sh`:

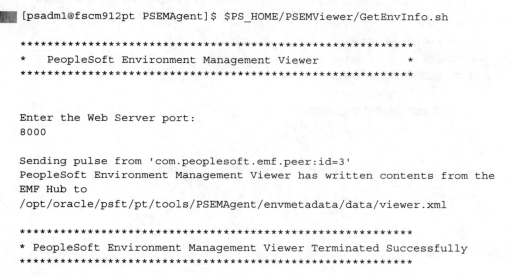

```
[psadm1@fscm912pt PSEMAgent]$ $PS_HOME/PSEMViewer/GetEnvInfo.sh


**************************************************************
*    PeopleSoft Environment Management Viewer              *
**************************************************************


Enter the Web Server port:
8000

Sending pulse from 'com.peoplesoft.emf.peer:id=3'
PeopleSoft Environment Management Viewer has written contents from the
EMF Hub to
/opt/oracle/psft/pt/tools/PSEMAgent/envmetadata/data/viewer.xml


**************************************************************
* PeopleSoft Environment Management Viewer Terminated Successfully
**************************************************************
```

The output of the `GetEnvInfo` command tells me that it generated the appropriate viewer files in `/opt/oracle/psft/pt/tools/PSEMAgent/envmetadata/data/`. To view the environment details, I will need a web browser with access to the `viewer.html` file stored in the directory `/opt/oracle/psft/pt/tools/PSEMAgent/envmetadata/data/`. Considering that this is a headless server with no web browser, I have a couple of options:

- Copy the files to my local workstation for viewing.

- Create a Samba share and open the files locally through that share.

- Expose the `/opt/oracle/psft/pt/tools/PSEMAgent/envmetadata/data/` directory to my intranet through a web server.

I chose the third option so that I could configure this once, and then ignore it. To view the file, I installed Apache 2, linked the data directory into my web server, and then secured the directory using the appropriate Apache configuration directives. With my Apache web server running,

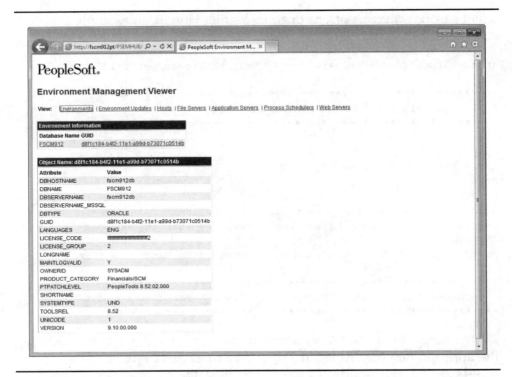

**FIGURE 6-1.** *The EMF Viewer details*

I was able to use Internet Explorer to browse to http://fscm912pt/PSEMHUB/ viewer.html to see agent details. Figure 6-1 shows my environment details.

# Securing EMF

The EMF hub uses plain HTTP connections—no encryption and no authentication. Figure 6-2 shows the information available to anyone with access to the PIA instance running the EMF hub. If you consider this information confidential, you may want to take precautions to secure this URL.

Networking, configuration, and architecture design offer a variety of ways to secure EMF. Even though the EMF does not support encryption, it is possible to encrypt agent/hub communication through the use of Secure

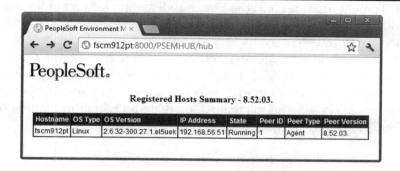

**FIGURE 6-2.** *EMF hub registered hosts*

Shell (SSH) tunnels or a combination of Secure Sockets Layer (SSL) proxies and SSL terminators. Because most Linux and UNIX servers already have an SSH daemon and client, SSH tunneling is trivial. Tunneling allows a client to communicate with a server over an encrypted channel (the tunnel). The server sees the traffic as local, allowing the client to access resources as if the client were running within the context of the server. This allows an administrator to bind services to the loopback network address, effectively hiding those services from the outside world. The first step in securing an EMF hub, therefore, is to reconfigure a standalone EMF hub to listen on the loopback address. If you're using Tomcat, edit the `conf/server.xml` file found in the Tomcat installation directory. Search for the `HTTP/1.1` Connector. The Connector's XML will resemble this:

```
<Connector port="8080" protocol="HTTP/1.1"
        connectionTimeout="20000"
        redirectPort="8443" />
```

To cause Tomcat to listen on the loopback interface only, specify the loopback address as a new attribute in the Connector element as follows, and then restart Tomcat:

```
<Connector port="8080" protocol="HTTP/1.1"
        connectionTimeout="20000"
        redirectPort="8443"
        address="127.0.0.1" />
```

With Tomcat restarted and the EMF hub listening for local EMF agents only, your remote agent pings should fail. Likewise, external requests to view the Registered Hosts Summary web page at http://your.hub.server/PSEMHUB/hub should fail. So that remote agents may continue connecting to the EMF hub, create an SSH tunnel for each computer running an agent, and then configure each agent to connect over the SSH tunnel. For example, use the following command to create a tunnel to an EMF hub running on server fscm912pt and listening on port 8080:

```
[jmarion@fscm912db ~]$ ssh -L 8080:localhost:8080 \
    jmarion@fscm912pt
jmarion@fscm912pt's password: ******
Last login: Sat Jul  7 15:06:43 2012 from fscm912db
[jmarion@fscm912pt ~]$
```

The first 8080 tells SSH to forward requests for the local port 8080 to localhost:8080 on server fscm912pt. The first port number is arbitrary. The only requirement is that nothing else is using that port number. The second port number (the one following the colon) is the port on which the target service is running.

Windows clients can create SSH tunnels by using applications such as PuTTY and Plink. The following example shows how to create an SSH tunnel to server fscm912pt using the Plink SSH client:

```
C:\Users\sarah>plink -L 8080:localhost:8080 jmarion@fscm912pt
Using username "jmarion".
jmarion@fscm912pt's password: ******
Last login: Sat Jul  7 14:03:49 2012 from 192.168.56.1
```

After establishing the tunnel, open a browser and validate the configuration by attempting to connect to the PSEMHUB web application through the URL http://localhost:8080/PSEMHUB/hub. If all is well, edit the PSEMAgent/envmetadata/config/configuration.properties and change the hubURL property to http://localhost:8080/PSEMHUB/hub. In the scenario described here, all requests for localhost:8080 are forwarded to fscm912pt:8080 over an encrypted channel.

```
# Using SSH Port Forwarding
hubURL=http://localhost:8080/PSEMHUB/hub
```

**NOTE**
*Even though my SSH tunnel has been up and active for far longer than any laptop should remain online, SSH tunnels are not known for reliability. SSH tunnels are demonstrated here because of their simplicity and ubiquity. Alternatives include stunnel, autossh, and SSL proxy/termination.*

# Database Cloning Considerations

The EMF hub identifies application instances by a Globally Unique Identifier (GUID). To generate a new GUID for a database, follow these steps:

1. Stop any active web servers, application servers, and process scheduler servers.

2. Erase the existing GUID using SQL similar to the following:

```
UPDATE PSOPTIONS
   SET GUID = ' '
```

3. Restart the application server.

4. Verify that the PSOPTIONS table contains a new GUID using a query similar to the following:

```
SELECT GUID
  FROM PSOPTIONS
```

# Conclusion

The PeopleSoft Environment Management Framework is a prerequisite for Change Assistant. With the EMF configured and secure, we can move on to installing and using Change Assistant.

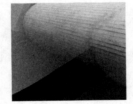

# CHAPTER
# 7

# Change Assistant

racle offers two primary methods for patching and upgrading PeopleSoft applications:

- Automated through Change Assistant
- Manual through file and project manipulation

In this chapter we will create and apply patches using Change Assistant. Appendix A explains how to apply maintenance manually.

Change Assistant is an automated upgrade project manager. It starts with a hierarchical task list complete with critical path and tasks to perform in parallel. It delegates tasks to local resources, enlisting remote resources when necessary. It reports individual task statuses as well as overall project duration. When a task fails, Change Assistant notifies someone with the authority to resolve the issue.

# Setting Up Change Assistant

Before using Change Assistant, it is important that you have properly installed and configured an instance of Change Assistant. Change Assistant is a Microsoft Windows–based program. Although it's not automatically installed with PeopleTools, the setup program is included in `%PS_HOME%\setup\PsCA`. The next few sections tell you how to install and configure Change Assistant.

## Installing Change Assistant

To install Change Assistant, launch `%PS_HOME%\setup\PsCA\setup.exe`. Work through the installation wizard, accepting the default values. Select No when Change Assistant asks if you would like to install Change Impact Analyzer. We will save a discussion of Change Impact Analyzer for the next chapter.

**NOTE**
*The Change Assistant version does not need to match the local PeopleTools install version. You can install a newer Change Assistant version if you'd like. However, the Change Assistant version* must *match the EMF hub and EMF agent versions.*

After installation and before launching Change Assistant, be sure to configure your system environment variables properly. Define `PS_HOME` as a new environment variable and then update your `PATH` environment variable to include `%PS_HOME%\bin\client\winx86` and `%PATH%\jre\bin`. To make these changes at the system level, locate your system Properties dialog (location varies by Microsoft Windows release). For most Microsoft Windows versions, you can open the system Properties dialog by right-clicking the My Computer/Computer icon and choosing Properties. Access the system's environment variables from the Advanced tab of the system Properties dialog.

## Change Assistant Environment Configuration

Change Assistant is usually installed in the `Program Files` directory, separate from other PeopleSoft applications installed in `PS_HOME`. Nevertheless, Change Assistant requires the `PATH` environment variable to contain references to files within `PS_HOME`. PeopleBooks recommends setting these environment variables at the system or user level within the Microsoft Windows operating system. These variables include setting the default Java version used by the system. I happen to have multiple Java Virtual Machines installed for a variety of different purposes. Rather than update my system default settings for Change Assistant, potentially breaking other Java-based programs, I launch Change Assistant from a batch file, shown here:

```
echo off

set PS_HOME=C:\PT8.52
set PATH=%PS_HOME%\bin\client\winx86;%PATH%\jre\bin;%PATH%

"C:\Program Files\PeopleSoft\Change Assistant\
changeassistant.exe"
```

# Configuring Change Assistant

You specify Change Assistant configuration options through Change Assistant menus. Before continuing, launch Change Assistant. Change Assistant will prompt for the appropriate *mode*. Figure 7-1 shows the Mode Selection dialog. Click Cancel to move on to configuration.

**NOTE**
*On Windows Vista or later operating system versions, Change Assistant must be launched using the Run As Administrator operating system option. Failure to launch Change Assistant as an administrator will result in the error, "Another Instance of Change Assistant Is Already Running."*

Change Assistant will immediately display the Change Assistant Options dialog. Enter appropriate values for Download, PS_HOME, Staging, and Output. Figure 7-2 shows my Change Assistant options.

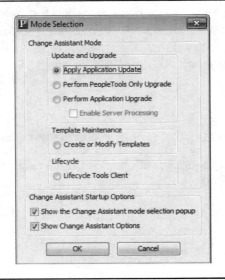

**FIGURE 7-1.** *Mode Selection dialog*

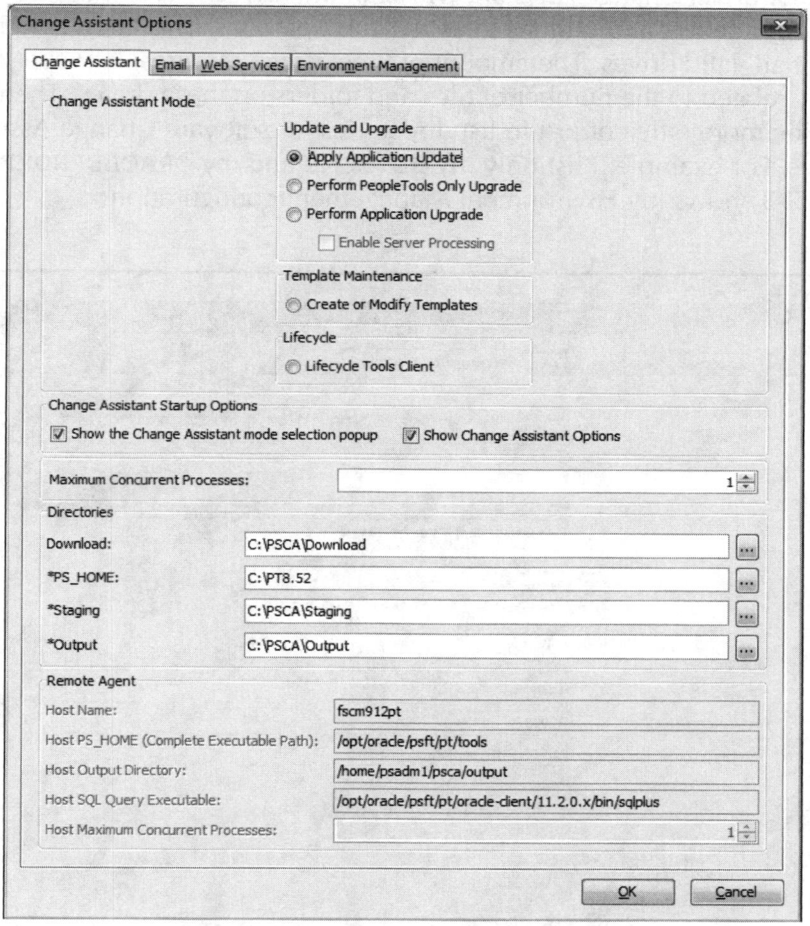

**FIGURE 7-2.** *Change Assistant Options dialog*

Switch to the Environment Management tab and set the appropriate values for Server Host and Server Port. Click the Ping button to verify your settings. Click the View button to confirm that Change Assistant, in cooperation with the EMF hub, identified each tier of your installation. Because I am communicating with my EMF hub over a Secure Shell (SSH) tunnel, I entered `localhost` as my Server Host.

The default value for Drives To Crawl is `C:|D:`. Update this value with your workstation's valid drive list. For example, delete `|D:` if you do not have a D: drive. Change Assistant will scan the drives and/or directories for installation details and utilities to assist with upgrades. The safest solution is to list all valid drives. The amount of time a scan requires, however, is directly related to the number of files and folders on these drives. Therefore, it may be more efficient just to list directories for software Change Assistant requires. For example, I list only my PS_HOME and my ORACLE_HOME. Figure 7-3 shows my Environment Management configuration.

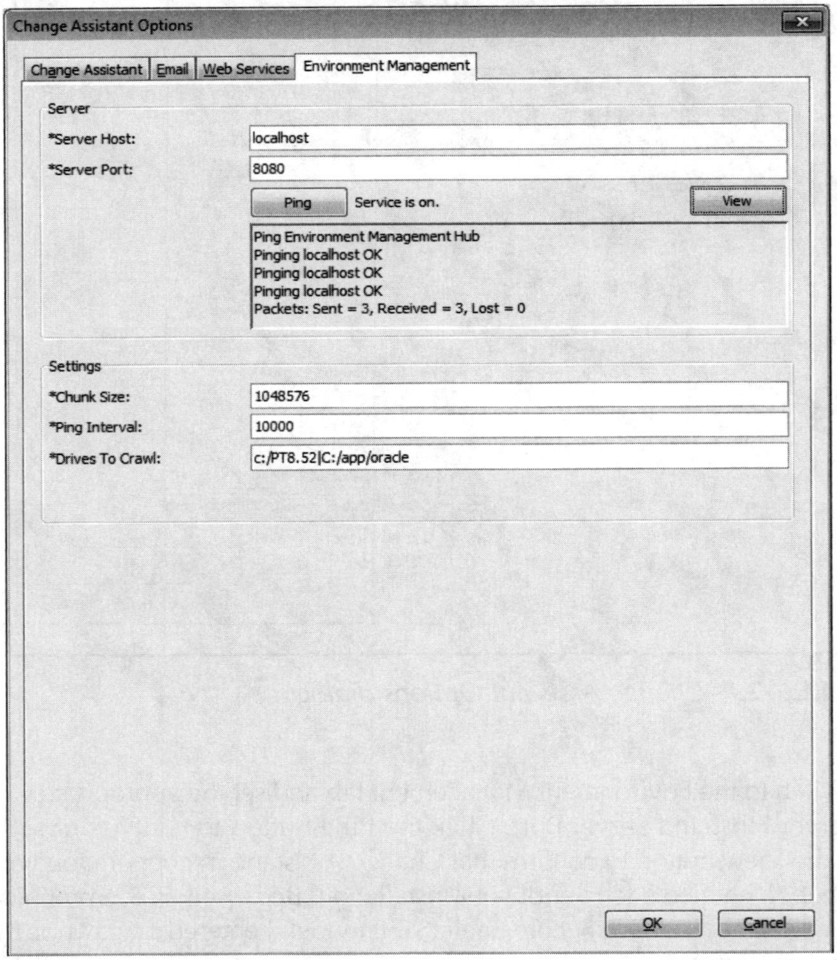

**FIGURE 7-3.** *Change Assistant Environment Management configuration*

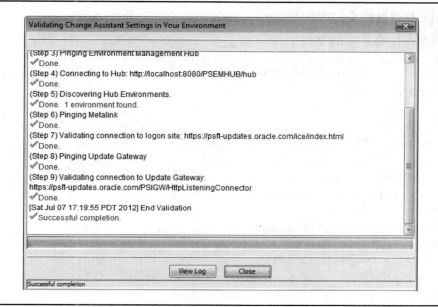

**FIGURE 7-4.** *Change Assistant validation results*

Validate the Change Assistant environment after configuration by choosing Tools | Validate from the Change Assistant menu bar. Change Assistant will respond by running a series of tests to ensure that your workstation contains the appropriate tools and can communicate with your servers as well as Oracle's update servers. Figure 7-4 shows the Change Assistant validation results.

# Applying Application Updates Through Change Assistant

Change Assistant is a convenient tool for running menial tasks and maintaining update/upgrade status, although it's not required that you use it. Prior to Change Assistant, I tracked bundle application status by printing an update's installation instructions and then placing a checkmark next to each step.

## Using the Gateway

The Update Gateway was an online service provided by Oracle. The service worked in tandem with the Environment Management Framework (EMF) to discover available updates. Oracle retired the PeopleSoft Update Gateway on July 13, 2012.

**NOTE**
*As I write, the blogosphere and forums are abuzz with customers expressing their condolences to the Update Gateway. By the time this book goes to print, Oracle will have no replacement for the Update Gateway. By the time you read this book, however, I suspect things will be a little different. Historically speaking, PeopleTools releases occur annually around the OpenWorld conference that occurs in the early autumn. Because Change Assistant is part of PeopleTools, we should not expect significant changes until the next release of PeopleTools. So keep your ears open. I do not think we have seen the last of the Update Gateway technology.*

Although the Update Gateway itself may have retired, we do not yet know the fate of the Update Gateway technology. The PeopleTools Lifecycle Management team has a lot of energy invested in the EMF and Update Gateway technology.

That said, depending on your version of Change Assistant, you may still see options for Go To Update Gateway and Download Change Packages in the Change Assistant Tools menu.

## Manual Discovery

With the Update Gateway out of commission and no replacement announced, our only option for applying maintenance is through manual discovery. Fortunately, after finding available updates, the Change Assistant manual process is nearly identical to the Update Gateway process.

## Determining Your Patch Level

Before searching for application updates, you should note your system's current patch level. Application patches and bundles often require prerequisite patches or bundles. You can discover your current patch and/or bundle level through metadata available from the EMF Viewer (described in Chapter 6) as well as from the PS_MAINTENANCE_LOG table. I typically search the PS_MAINTENANCE_LOG table's DESCRLONG field for %Bundle% and sort by UPDATE_ID in descending order:

```
SELECT *
  FROM PS_MAINTENANCE_LOG
 WHERE DESCRLONG LIKE '%Bundle%'
 ORDER BY UPDATE_ID DESC
```

## Finding Patches Online

After determining the current patch level by module, log into https:// support.oracle.com/. Locate the "Patches & Updates" section of the support site and begin searching for bundles or maintenance packs. Figure 7-5 shows an Oracle Support search for American English bundles associated with PeopleSoft SCM Strategic Sourcing version 9.1.

I usually start with the largest bundle number and review the bundle's prerequisites. If I do not have the prerequisites installed, I move down to the prior bundle number. Once I settle on a bundle for which I have the prerequisites, that bundle number should be one greater than the bundle level identified earlier by querying PS_MAINTENANCE_LOG. I can

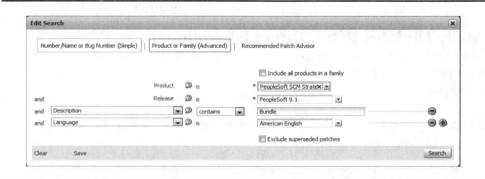

**FIGURE 7-5.** *Oracle Support bundle search*

confirm my prerequisite status by querying PS_MAINTENANCE_LOG for update IDs listed in the bundle's prerequisites. If a bundle lists several prerequisites, it might be easier to import the prerequisite IDs into a table and join to PS_MAINTENANCE_LOG to identify update IDs not found in PS_MAINTENANCE_LOG.

After identifying necessary patches and bundles, you can download the associated files. Change Assistant will prompt for the location of downloaded files, but for consistency, place downloaded Zip file(s) in your Change Assistant download directory. This is the directory you specified when configuring Change Assistant's options. I configured my workstation to use C:\PSCA\Download\. Change Assistant can pretty much take over from here.

# Patching

I happen to be running a PeopleSoft Financials and Supply Chain Management (FSCM) 9.1 Oracle VM. Based on my analysis of this system, it appears the last SCM bundle applied to this server was Bundle 16 with update ID 860100. When writing this chapter, SCM had moved on to Bundle 22. The following example demonstrates using Change Assistant to apply Bundle 17 to this FSCM instance.

To apply application updates using Change Assistant, switch to Apply Application Update mode either by selecting this mode on startup or choosing Tools | Options from the Change Assistant menu bar. Tell Change Assistant you are ready to go by selecting Tools | Apply Change Packages. Change Assistant will respond by walking you through several wizard-based dialogs. Let's walk through the wizard steps now.

## Apply Updates to the Target Environment

The first step in the wizard asks about comparisons: apply with compare or apply without a compare. A compare may generate a significant amount of output.

- If you have made no modifications, there is no reason to compare an update's changes.

- If you have made modifications but plan to roll back those modifications, it may be worth running a compare. Running a compare in this scenario may help you identify changes that the upgrade will remove.

■ If you have made modifications and intend to keep those
modifications, you definitely want to run a compare. The compare will
help you identify overwritten modifications so you can reapply them
later during the update process.

We will discuss the database compare in Part III of this book.

## Apply Updates Using the Change Impact Analyzer
Next, select the option Apply Without using Change Impact Analyzer.
(Change Impact Analyzer is the subject of Chapter 8 and I don't want to
steal its thunder by discussing it now.)

## Select a Product Line Release
During our Change Assistant configuration, we gave Change Assistant a
few details about our server. Specifically, we told Change Assistant how to
contact and query our EMF hub. Using that information, Change Assistant
discovered that I had one environment installed: Financials/SCM. Figure 7-6

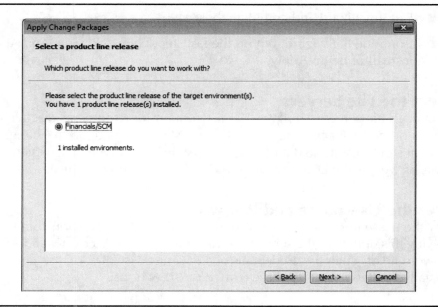

**FIGURE 7-6.** *Select a product line release*

shows this step. Ensure that your product is selected and click the Next button.

## Select a Target Environment
Select the target environment from the list of displayed environments.

## Prepare the Environment
This step of the Apply Change Packages wizard asks the administrator to confirm completion of the appropriate pre-update steps. Those steps include the following:

■ Running the SYSAUDIT and DDDAUDIT reports (see Chapter 2 for more details)

■ Resolving any issues identified by those reports

■ Creating a backup of the target environment

If you did not complete these steps, you have two options:

■ Exit the wizard and complete those steps.

■ Continue the wizard, but on the last step, choose Review And Apply instead of Begin Apply.

## Select the File Servers
Select each file server to update. The list contains environments discovered by each of the EMF agents reporting to the EMF hub identified in Change Assistant's options. If the dialog does not list any file servers, check your agents as well as the EMF Viewer (see Chapter 6 for more details).

## Enter the Username and Password
Enter the username and password of the PeopleSoft user responsible for applying this update to the selected environment. In the Access ID and Access Password fields, enter the credentials of a database system administrator. This is usually the PeopleSoft database owner: SYSADM or sa.

**NOTE**
*These credentials may be case-sensitive*
*(it depends on the database configuration).*

## Select the Apply Directory

Select the directory containing the downloaded Zip file—do not select the downloaded Zip file, just the directory containing the Zip file. If you followed my advice, then your downloaded change package is in Change Assistant's download directory. I placed mine in `C:\PSCA\Download`.

## Select Change Packages

Change Assistant searched the directory specified in the previous step. In this step, Change Assistant displays a list of all discovered updates. Select each update you want to apply. Figure 7-7 shows the update selection step.

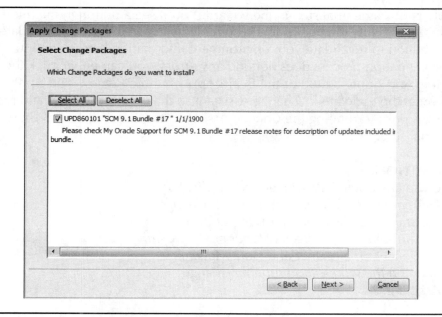

**FIGURE 7-7.** *Select Change Packages dialog*

## Select a Method for Applying Database Changes

Change Assistant allows for two database script execution methods: Automatic or Manual. If you choose Automatic, Change Assistant will build and execute database change scripts without human intervention. On the other hand, if you prefer to review and manually apply database change scripts, choose Manual. Selecting Manual will cause Change Assistant to pause, alerting the administrator that manual intervention is required. Since I am working with a vanilla Financials/Supply Chain system, I chose Automatic.

## Confirm Your Selections

In this step, Change Assistant displays the selected environment and change package. If this information is incorrect, click the Back button to select alternative values.

## Apply Now

Apply Now is the final step in the wizard. You'll see a button in the middle of the Apply Now dialog. Oracle recommends that you click this Validate Now button to revalidate your environment information before continuing. If the validation process does not find any errors, you can either click the Review And Apply button or the Begin Apply button. Review And Apply will open the template in Change Assistant so that you can review and make changes prior to running the Change Assistant template. Figure 7-8 shows this final step.

**CAUTION**
*Close any open Data Mover and Application Designer sessions before continuing. Change Assistant uses these programs to perform certain steps. These steps will not be successful if Application Designer and Data Mover are open on the workstation running Change Assistant.*

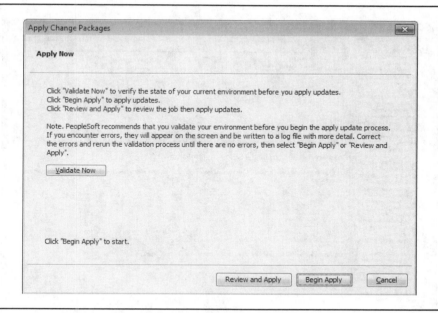

**FIGURE 7-8.** *Apply Now dialog*

Figure 7-9 shows the SCM 9.1 Bundle 17 template within Change Assistant.

If you chose Review And Apply instead of Apply, Change Assistant inserted a new chapter named Manual Stop Step for Review that includes a manual step. Mark this step as complete before running the Change Assistant template. To mark the step as complete, either right-click the step and select Complete from the context menu or select the step and press the F7 shortcut key on your keyboard.

## Run the Template

Choose Run | Run when you are ready to run the Change Assistant template. Change Assistant will display environment details and allow you to confirm your decision to run the template. The template will run unattended until it either encounters an error or a manual step. In either case, take appropriate action and run the template again. Change Assistant will start where it left off. If you plan to run Change Assistant on a Windows server within your data

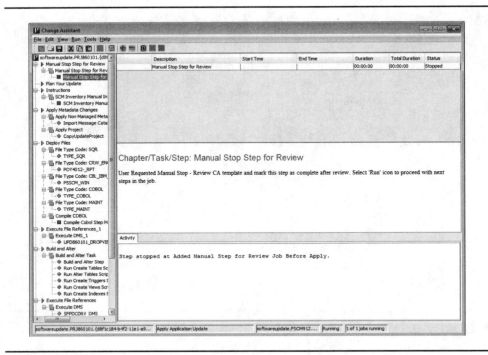

**FIGURE 7-9.** *Change Assistant template example*

center and do not want to monitor the template's status continuously, you can configure Change Assistant's e-mail settings. Change Assistant will use these settings to notify you when intervention is required.

# Dealing with Errors

Change Assistant will display a list of log files when it fails to execute a step. Review these log files for clues as to why the step failed. Common reasons for failure include the following:

- Invalid Change Assistant configuration (although unlikely since Change Assistant passed validation)

- Incorrect EMF Agent configuration

- Improper change package deployment options

- The step succeeded but a utility returned the wrong exit code

## Invalid Change Assistant Configuration

If you find yourself in this situation, review the Change Assistant–generated
log file for errors. Once you've identified them, confirm your Change
Assistant options by choosing Tools | Options. If something in your
environment has changed since you last validated Change Assistant, choose
Tools | Validate. If you are not able to identify the cause of the error, try
copying the Change Assistant command line for the command and then run
the command in a Microsoft Windows cmd.exe "black box" window.

## Incorrect EMF Agent Configuration

The following log file entry describes Change Assistant's attempt to deploy
files to an EMF agent through the EMF hub. The hub appears to identify the
correct agent, but the agent does not have write access to the decoupled
$PS_APP_HOME target directory. For identification purposes, I emphasized
the log's error notification with boldface text. The resolution in this case is
to reconfigure the EMF agent so that it is running as a user with write access
to the $PS_APP_HOME directory. Refer to Chapter 6 for more information
regarding EMF agent configuration.

```
Deploy File for TYPE_SQR
Retrieving File Reference Data.
Retrieving File:aucpdf.sqr
   File Size: 380357 bytes
   File Date: Thu Nov 03 23:27:42 PDT 2011
Contacting EM Hub.
Retrieving File:bildar.sqc
   File Size: 23097 bytes
   File Date: Sun Oct 30 22:51:32 PDT 2011
Retrieving File:pls4030.sqr
   File Size: 44809 bytes
   File Date: Mon Oct 24 17:40:56 PDT 2011
Retrieving File:pls2002.sqr
   File Size: 131820 bytes
   File Date: Wed Oct 26 17:21:34 PDT 2011
Retrieving File:cmohcost.sqc
   File Size: 69509 bytes
   File Date: Wed Oct 12 03:05:30 PDT 2011
Retrieving File:sfs6003.sqr
   File Size: 172657 bytes
   File Date: Wed Apr 06 05:42:44 PDT 2011
Deploying file to sarah-pc (PeerID: 8)
```

```
Detected the following servers installed that match the File
Reference: File Server
Deploying the following files to c:/PT8.52/sqr:
    bildar.sqc
    sfs6003.sqr
    cmohcost.sqc
    aucpdf.sqr
    pls2002.sqr
    pls4030.sqr
```
**Deploying file to fscm912pt (PeerID: 4)**
  **Detected the following servers installed that match the File**
  **Reference: Application Server, Batch Server**
  **Deploying the following files to**
  **/opt/oracle/psft/pt/apptools/sqr:**
    **bildar.sqc**
    **sfs6003.sqr**
    **aucpdf.sqr**
    **pls2002.sqr**
    **pls4030.sqr**
**FAILURE: Unable to Deploy File. No write access to the target**
  **directory.**

## Improper Change Package Deployment Options

The following log file shows a Change Assistant template that attempted to deploy COBOL source files to a web server. COBOL resides on application servers, batch servers, and file servers, but not on web servers. The error is at the end of the following log file and is highlighted in boldface text.

```
Deploy File for PSSCM_WIN
Retrieving File Reference Data.
Retrieving File:psscm.win
    File Size: 77387 bytes
    File Date: Tue Dec 07 01:14:32 PST 2010
Contacting EM Hub.
Deploying file to fscm912pt (PeerID: 6)
    Detected the following servers installed that match the
        File Reference: Application Server, Batch Server
    Deploying the following files to /opt/oracle/psft/pt/
    apptools/src/cbl/ibm:
        psscm.win
Deploying file to sarah-pc (PeerID: 8)
    Detected the following servers installed that match the
        File Reference: File Server
    Deploying the following files to c:/PT8.52/src/cbl/ibm:
        psscm.win
```

```
Deploying file to fscm912pt (PeerID: 6)
   Detected the following servers installed that match the
      File Reference: Web Server
   Deploying the following files to /home/psadm2/psft/pt/8.52/
   FSCM912/src/cbl/ibm:
      psscm.win
FAILURE: Unable to Deploy File. No write access to the target
   directory.
```

The reported error states that the EMF agent identified as Peer ID 6 does not have write access to $PS_CFG_HOME. This is true. An EMF agent configured for an application update in a decoupled install should deploy files to $PS_APP_HOME, not $PS_CFG_HOME. Interestingly, the target location listed in the error isn't actually the web server's directory. In a coupled installation, the location described as the web server's directory would actually have been my $PS_HOME. In a decoupled installation, however, the location /home/psadm2/psft/pt/8.52/FSCM912 represents my $PS_CFG_HOME. Given this information, a coupled $PS_HOME installation would have succeeded without reporting errors.

Later in this chapter you will learn how to select target server types for file references. Unfortunately, the target must be selected within Application Designer before generating the Change Assistant template. Since we cannot update the template, the appropriate action is to verify that the valid portions of the step completed successfully and then mark the step as complete. To validate the step's results, verify the file timestamps, ownership, and checksums within appropriate deployment locations and then ignore invalid deployment errors. After you've verified deployment, mark the step as complete and restart the Change Assistant template.

## Success, but Marked as Failure

A step may actually succeed, but Change Assistant might mark it as failed. Think of Change Assistant as a project management tool. It doesn't actually perform the tasks of a project, but it delegates those tasks to highly skilled, focused utilities. It expects those utilities to execute tasks properly and return the correct response code. Change Assistant places a certain amount of trust in its utilities and takes a utility's response code at face value, even if the utility reports the wrong results. Consider the following Data Mover log file produced while Data Mover was running from Change Assistant. Don't spend too much time looking for the error—there isn't one.

```
Started:  Fri Jul 13 23:20:36 2012
Data Mover Release: 8.52.03
Database: FSCM912 (ENG)
Input file: C:\PSCA\Staging\softwareupdatePRJ860101
   {d8f1c184-b4f2-11e1-a99d-b73071c0514b}\data\upd860101_msg.dat
   (ENG)
Commit done at end of record
Importing  PSMSGSETDEFN
 Import  PSMSGSETDEFN  0
 Update  PSMSGSETDEFN  2
Records remaining: 1
Importing  PSMSGCATDEFN
 Import  PSMSGCATDEFN  0
 Update  PSMSGCATDEFN  5
SQL Successful -  UPDATE PSMSGSETDEFN SET VERSION = 1 WHERE
   VERSION > (SELECT VERSION from PSVERSION WHERE
   OBJECTTYPENAME = 'PPC')
SQL Successful -  UPDATE PSSTATUS SET LASTREFRESHDTTM =
   %currentdatetimein
Ended: Fri Jul 13 23:20:36 2012
Successful completion
```

Even though the log file reported no errors, Change Assistant marked this step in error. What is an administrator to do when encountering an issue such as this? In this case the Data Mover import script was safe to run multiple times, so I ran it from the command line using the syntax generated by Change Assistant and marked the step as complete.

# Creating Custom Change Packages

In Chapter 2 we created a record definition to store some of our favorite data management URLs. Assuming we built this record definition in a development environment, let's create a change package to migrate that record definition and its contents to a test environment. This exercise will involve the following:

1. Creating data migration scripts

2. Adding fields, records, and file references to a project

3. Generating a change package

4. Updating a new Change Assistant template

5. Finalizing the Change Assistant template

6. Testing the change package

# Creating Data Migration Scripts

The OP_DM_DOCS SQL table contains a few rows of data that need to be migrated along with the project definition. Application Designer moves definitions only, not data. To migrate this data, we will have to write an export and then an import migration script. Create the export script by first logging into Data Mover in your development environment and then entering the following text:

```
-- PeopleSoft PeopleTools: Data Management and Upgrade Handbook
-- Chapter 7 Sample data export
-- Creating your own Change Assistant Templates

SET LOG OP_CH_07_OP_DM_DOCS.log;
SET OUTPUT OP_CH_07_OP_DM_DOCS.dat;

EXPORT PS_OP_DM_DOCS;
```

1. Save the file in your default %PS_HOME%\scripts directory and name it OP_CH_07_OP_DM_DOCS.dms.

2. After saving the file, run the Data Mover script. Running the script will produce a file named OP_CH_07_OP_DM_DOCS.dat in your Data Mover default output directory (configured through Configuration Manager).

3. Upon successful completion, create a new Data Mover script and name it %PS_HOME%\scripts\OP_CH_07_OP_DM_DOCS_IMPORT.dms.

4. Enter the following into the Data Mover text editor, save, and then close Data Mover:

```
-- PeopleSoft PeopleTools: Data Management and Upgrade Handbook
-- Chapter 7 Sample data import
-- Creating your own Change Assistant Templates

SET LOG OP_CH_07_OP_DM_DOCS_IMPORT.log;
SET INPUT OP_CH_07_OP_DM_DOCS.dat;

REPLACE_ALL PS_OP_DM_DOCS;
```

# Creating the App Designer Change Project

A change project is an Application Designer project definition with a few additional attributes.

## Change Project Configuration

We'll start by configuring the change project.

1. Launch Application Designer and create a new project.

2. Name the new project OP_CH_07.

3. From the Application Designer menu bar, choose File | Project Properties.

4. After Application Designer opens the Project Properties window, enter a description and check the Change Project checkbox. Figure 7-10 shows the new project's Properties window.

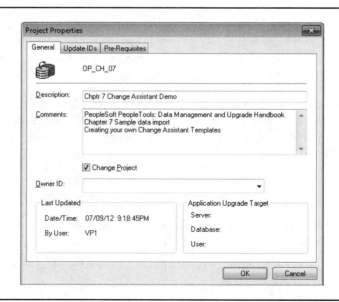

**FIGURE 7-10.**  OP_CH_07 *project properties*

5. After you've marked the project as a Change Project, Application Designer will add the Update IDs and Pre-Requisites tabs to the Project Properties dialog.

■ If your organization uses an incident tracking system (as every organization should), use the Update IDs tab to link the change project to an incident or list of incidents. Often incident requests take the form of a Development Request (DR), Change Request (CR), or Service Request (SR).

■ If your organization does not use some form of incident tracking system, then make up an ID. Application Designer requires an update ID for change packages. At a minimum, use a spreadsheet to track internal update IDs. I'm sure your Oracle sales representative would be happy to help your organization identify a more robust incident tracking system.

Update IDs may consist of alpha and numeric characters. To distinguish your updates from Oracle's updates, and to avoid update ID collisions, I recommend using your standard site-specific prefix as the prefix for update IDs created by your organization. For this book, I chose OP (Oracle Press) for our site-specific prefix. Since this is our first update, we will use the ID OP000001. Figure 7-11 shows the Update IDs tab.

Add as many update IDs as necessary. Application Designer will use the first ID added to the list as the change package's ID.

As your organization builds a library of change packages, you will find that some changes depend on other changes. Use the Project Properties Pre-Requisites tab to track these dependencies.

## Project Items

We need to tell Application Designer what to include in this change project. Insert the following into the change project:

1. Field OP_DOC_ID

2. Record OP_DM_DOCS

Adding the field and record managed definitions to our project will create a change package with structure, but no data. To migrate the data, we also need to create new file references. These file references will point

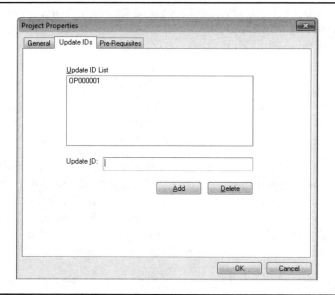

**FIGURE 7-11.** *Update IDs tab*

to the previously exported .DAT file and our untested Data Mover import script.

1. Create a new file reference definition by choosing File | New from the Application Designer menu bar.

2. In the New Definition selection dialog, choose File Reference, as shown below.

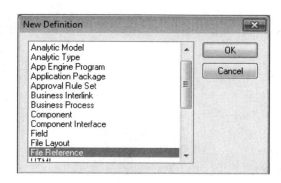

3. When the new File Reference definition window appears, select the filename and path of the .DAT file you previously exported: `C:\PT8.52\data\OP_CH_07_OP_DM_DOCS.dat`.

4. Change the PeopleSoft Server attribute to File Server. Since we will import this .DAT file through a step in Change Assistant, we won't need this file to exist on any other tier except the one running Change Assistant—the file server. As we saw earlier while applying SCM Bundle 17, selecting the correct target server is critical to Change Assistant's success. Keep the remaining attributes at their default values: Database Platform, Operating System, Unix Target Directory Security. Figure 7-12 shows my new file definition.

5. Save the new file reference and name it `OP_CH_07_OP_DM_DOCS_DAT`.

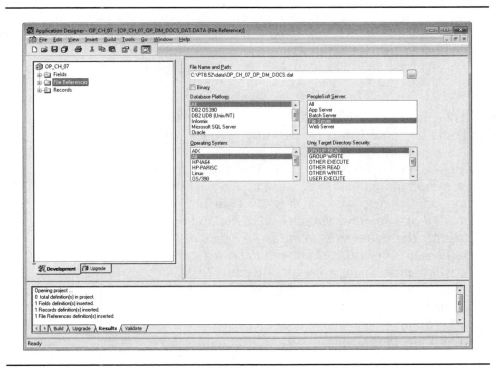

**FIGURE 7-12.** `OP_CH_07_OP_DM_DOCS_DAT` *file reference*

6. When the Save As dialog appears, choose the File Type Code of DATA. The File Type Code provides Change Assistant with the target deployment location for this file reference. For example, a file type of DATA will deploy to the `%ps_home%\data` directory, whereas a file type of COBOL will deploy to `%ps_home%\src\cbl\base`.

7. To view (or even create new) File Type codes, from Application Designer, choose Tools | Miscellaneous Definitions | File Type Codes. The Save As dialog showing the selected file type code is shown below.

8. In like manner, create a new file reference for the `OP_CH_07_OP_DM_DOCS_IMPORT.dms` Data Mover import script. For this file reference, choose the File Type Code of SCRIPTS. Figure 7-13 shows this new file reference.

**TIP**
*Rather than hard-code file paths into projects, use environment variables. File reference metadata exists in the database. The actual file does not. If multiple developers are working on the same change package, it is safe to assume that all of them have the same files, but do not assume those files exist in the same location. I rarely see two workstations with the exact same configuration. Using environment variables will allow multiple developers to generate the same change package regardless of workstation configuration. For the file references used in step 3, I could substitute `%PS_HOME%` for `C:\PT8.52`.*

When Application Designer builds a change package for this project, we want it to deploy the .DAT file and run the Data Mover script. To flag

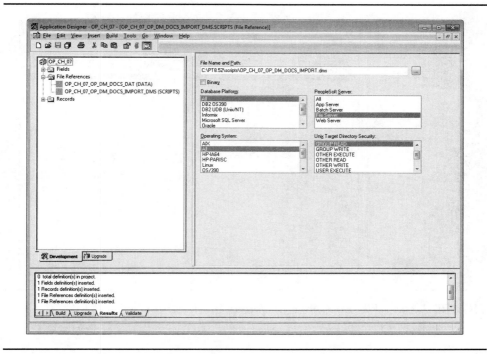

**FIGURE 7-13.** `OP_CH_07_OP_DM_DOCS_IMPORT_DMS` *file reference*

the Data Mover script for execution, in Application Designer, do the following:

1. Switch to the Upgrade tab.

2. Open the File References project item to display the list of File References.

3. Select the Execute box next to the `OP_CH_07_OP_DM_DOCS_ IMPORT_DMS` item.

Figure 7-14 shows the File Reference project upgrade attributes.

## Generate the Change Package

To create a Change Package from a Change Project, select Tools | Create Change Package. Figure 7-15 shows the Create Change Package dialog. For this Change Package, we can accept the default values. Click the OK button when you are ready to generate the package.

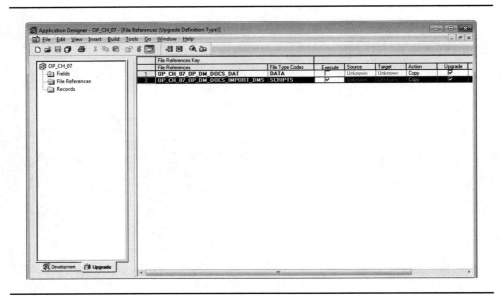

**FIGURE 7-14.** *File Reference project upgrade attributes*

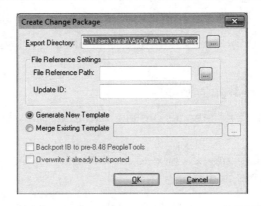

**FIGURE 7-15.** *Create Change Package dialog*

**NOTE**
*When creating a Change Package, Application Designer defaults the Export Directory to the workstation's* `%temp%` *directory. Creating the package is an intermediate step. The* `%temp%` *directory offers a convenient resting place for this file prior to finalizing the Change Project.*

**File Reference Settings**   If any of your file references included the `%FILEREFPATH%` variable, provide a value for File Reference Path and Update ID. If the variable is not included, ignore this setting.

**Generate New or Merge Existing?**   Change Packages include Change Assistant templates. If you are creating a new Change Package that does not have a template, select the Generate New Template option. On the other hand, if you have an existing template and are only regenerating the Application Designer portion of the Change Package, select the Merge Existing Template option and select an existing Change Assistant Template file.

**Backport IB Settings**   PeopleTools 8.48 significantly changed Integration Broker. If your Change Project includes Integration Broker definitions and the target for your Change Project is a pre-8.48 system, select the Backport IB To Pre-8.48 PeopleTools checkbox.

## Modify the Change Package

Based on Application Designer metadata, the Create Change Package command generated a directory named `updOP000001` (upd + our primary Update ID) containing several files. In addition to some Change Assistant metadata, the directory contains the following:

- A Change Assistant XML template

- The `OP_CH_07` project definition

- Each file reference (.DAT and Data Mover script)

- Documentation—manual application instructions for administrators who choose to manually apply this update

- A `manifest.xml` file containing the Update IDs associated with this Change Package

If you have experience applying PeopleSoft patches and bundles, you may recognize the directory contents and structure as matching that of delivered patches and bundles.

**Modify the HTML Documentation**   There is more to the install HTML document than just HTML. The generated documentation contains special XML metadata elements. If you are comfortable working with markup languages, feel free to make changes. Generally speaking, it is safe to change the text inside paragraph (`<p></p>`) HTML tags. Rather than change the markup, however, I recommend using Change Assistant's documentation editing capabilities, which are discussed in the next section.

**Modify the Change Assistant Template**   To review, and potentially change, the auto-generated Change Assistant template, launch Change Assistant in Create or Modify mode. Figure 7-16 shows the Change Assistant Mode Selection dialog after switching modes.

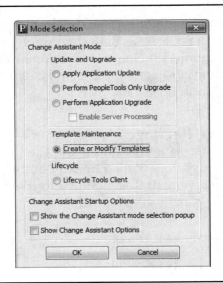

**FIGURE 7-16.**   *Change Assistant Mode Selection dialog*

**NOTE**
*You can switch modes from within Change Assistant after startup. If the Change Assistant Mode Selection dialog does not appear when you launch Change Assistant, choose Tools | Options. In the Change Assistant Options dialog, select Create Or Modify Templates.*

After you've selected the proper mode, import the template.

1. Choose File | Import template.

2. Select the Change Assistant template and click the OK button to import the template. For example, since my Change Package is at `C:\Users\sarah\AppData\Local\Temp\updOP000001` and my original project is named `OP_CH_07`, my Change Assistant template is at `C:\Users\sarah\AppData\Local\Temp\updOP000001\changeassistanttemplate\op_ch_07.xml`.

3. With the template imported, our next step is to open the template. Choose File | Open Template.

4. In the Open dialog, as shown in Figure 7-17, select the template name. In our example, the template name is `OP_CH_07`.

**FIGURE 7-17.** *Template selection dialog*

The template will appear as an outline on the left side of Change Assistant. The auto-generated documentation will appear in the center region. Figure 7-18 shows the template within Change Assistant.

5. Review the template and make any changes necessary. For example, I could change the run location of the package's data mover script by doing the following:

■ Expanding Deploy Files > File Type Code: SCRIPTS

■ Selecting OP_CH_07_OP_DM_DOCS_IMPORT_DMS

■ Choosing Edit | Step Properties

Let's add a database backup task as a Manual Stop step to our Change Assistant template. Because taking a backup could be considered part of

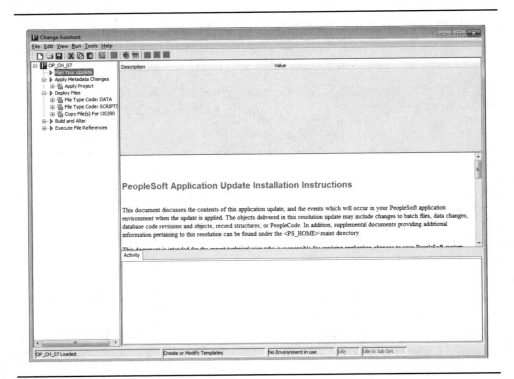

**FIGURE 7-18.** *Change Assistant template*

planning an upgrade, we will add this task and step to the "Plan Your Upgrade chapter." To add the new task and step, follow these steps:

1. On the left side of Change Assistant, choose Plan Your Upgrade.

2. Choose Edit | Insert Task. Name the new task `Backup Database`.

3. Ensure that the Backup Database task is selected. Choose Edit | Insert Step. Name the step `Create a backup`.

4. To mark this step as a Manual Stop step, choose Edit | Step Properties. Change the Type value to ManualStop.

Figure 7-19 shows the Step Properties dialog.
The following list describes the step types available in Change Assistant:

- **Application Engine**  Execute an Application Engine program.

- **Build Project**  Build a project (tables, views, and so on). The Build Project step has the same build options as the Application Designer Build Project command.

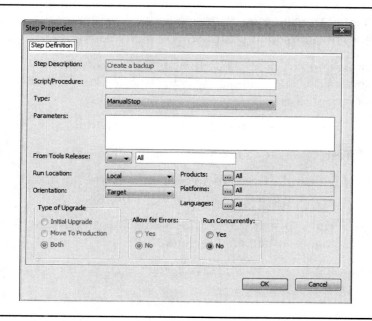

**FIGURE 7-19.**  *Create a backup step properties*

- ■ **Compare and Report**  Offers the same compare options as the Application Designer Compare and Report command.

- ■ **Copy Database**  Copy a project from one database to another—same as an Application Designer project copy.

- ■ **Copy from File**  Copy a project from a file—same as an Application Designer file copy.

- ■ **Copy to File**  Copy a project to a file—same as an Application Designer file copy.

- ■ **Create Project**  Creates a project inside Change Assistant.

- ■ **Merge Project**  Merges two projects into a single project—same as Application Designer project merge.

- ■ **Data Mover – Bootstrap**  Runs a Data Mover script in bootstrap mode.

- ■ **Data Mover – User**  Runs a Data Mover script in normal mode.

- ■ **Deploy File**  Deploys files from the Change Package.

- ■ **Execute Process**  Runs non-interactive (headless) batch files. For Change Assistant to mark the step complete, the batch file must return to completion without requiring human intervention.

- ■ **Manual Stop**  Causes Change Assistant to pause and wait for human intervention. After completing any tasks noted in the manual step, mark the step as complete.

- ■ **Process Scheduler**  Runs a process scheduler process.

- ■ **PTF Test**  Executes a PeopleSoft Test Framework test.

- ■ **SQL Command**  Executes an SQL command using the query tool specified in the Change Assistant configuration.

- ■ **SQL Script**  Executes an SQL script using the query tool specified in the Change Assistant configuration.

- ■ **SQR Report**  Executes an SQR using the PeopleTools `sqr` command line program.

Immediately following the step Type selection list is a large text box for step parameters. Use this box to enter parameters for steps that require additional information. Figure 7-20 shows our Change Package's Copy Project parameters.

Table 7-1 describes common step parameters. Consult the PeopleBook *PeopleTools: Change Assistant* appendix on "Modifying Step Properties and Parameters" to see a list of valid parameters and sample text.

Table 7-2 shows a list of common variables that may be used to reference values from Change Assistant's configuration. Others, such as PTPS_APP_HOME, are listed in PeopleBooks along with the other Change Assistant step parameters.

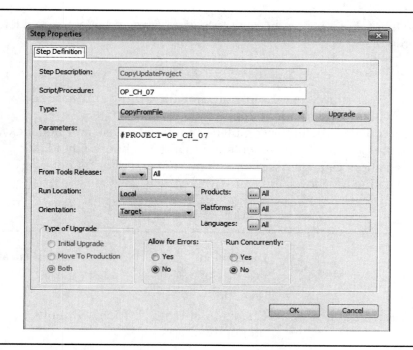

**FIGURE 7-20.** *Copy Project parameters*

| Parameter | Description | Step Type |
|---|---|---|
| #Project | Specifies a project name | Create Project, Build Project |
| #P1 through #P5 | Parameter values for SQR reports | SQR |
| #Directory | Specify a file location outside <PS_HOME>\scripts directory | Data Mover |
| #RCID | Run Control ID | Application Engine program |

**TABLE 7-1.** *Change Assistant Step Parameters*

Use these variables on the right side of a parameter expression. Here's an example:

```
#DIRECTORY=#STAGINGDIRECTORY/scripts/MAINT/
```

Figure 7-21 shows an example of using the #OutputDirectory variable within a BuildProject step.

Our template structure is complete, but our new task and step lack documentation. To add documentation to a step, choose Edit | Edit Documentation. Change Assistant will present an editor for entering documentation, as shown in Figure 7-22.

| Variable | Description | Change Assistant Location |
|---|---|---|
| #PS_HOME | PeopleSoft install location | Tools | Options |
| #OutputDirectory | Change Assistant output directory | Tools | Options |

**TABLE 7-2.** *Change Assistant Step Variables*

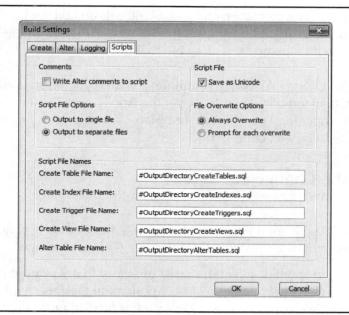

**FIGURE 7-21.** *Script filenames*

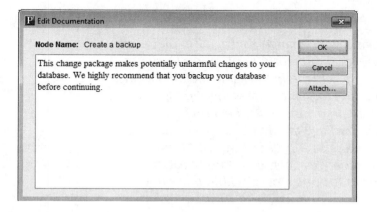

**FIGURE 7-22.** *Change Assistant documentation editor*

After making documentation changes, finalize those updates by choosing Edit | Finalize Documentation. Change Assistant will then merge new documentation into the upd*_install.htm file.

**Exporting the Change Assistant Template**     When you finish updating the Change Assistant template, export it over the Application Designer–generated template by choosing File | Export Template. When you're prompted to replace the existing file, choose Yes.

## Finalize the Change Package

Our template and documentation are ready for deployment.

1. Open Application Designer and execute the Finalize Change Package command by choosing Tools | Finalize Change Package.

2. When prompted, select the same directory that was used earlier to create the export and click OK. Application Designer will validate the change package and generate a Zip file for future deployment.

3. Since we created this change package in the highly volatile %temp% directory, now is a good time to move that change package to your corporate change package repository (most likely a shared file system location).

**TIP**
*Can't find your change package Zip file? Look in the export directory. Application Designer creates the Zip file in the same location as the export directory and names the Zip file after the directory. In my example, I exported the change package to C:\Users\sarah\ AppData\Local\Temp\updOP000001. Application Designer, therefore, created the Zip file updOP000001.zip within that same directory.*

**Test the Change Package**

You can test your Change Package by moving it to your Change Assistant download directory and then choosing Tools | Apply Change Packages. Follow the steps outlined earlier in the "Patching" section of this chapter.

# Conclusion

Change management best practices require a separation of duties. The patch creator and the patch applier should be separate people. Often times the only person with enough knowledge to apply a patch accurately, however, is the person who created the patch. As you saw in this chapter, Application Designer's change packaging and Change Assistant allow a patch creator to generate enough metadata to hand a patch over successfully to another person with minimal transition effort.

With the information contained in this chapter, you are ready to create and deploy your own change packages, improving upon your overall change management strategy.

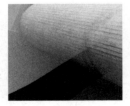

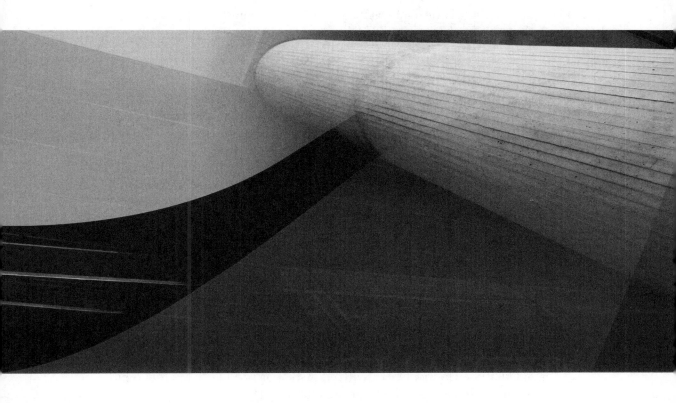

# CHAPTER
## 8

# Change Impact
# Analyzer

ou use Change Impact Analyzer to identify files, PeopleCode, and managed definitions that have been affected by changes to unrelated definitions. Change Impact Analyzer differs from compare reports tools, which reveal differences between two versions of the same definition. Basically, Change Impact Analyzer is a configurable version of Application Designer's Find Definition References command. It is capable of searching multiple definitions, infinite levels deep.

# Setup, Installation, and Configuration

Like Change Assistant, Change Impact Analyzer is a Microsoft Windows–based program. Although not automatically installed with PeopleTools, the setup program is included in `%PS_HOME%\setup\PsCIA`. To install Change Impact Analyzer, launch `%PS_HOME%\setup\PsCIA\setup.exe`. The installation wizard is rather short and asks that you indicate the JDBC driver type and install location.

Java Database Connectivity (JDBC) is a standardized Java API that defines how client applications connect to a database. The intent of JDBC is to abstract database implementation details from application code, allowing a developer to code for the common JDBC standard. The Java language includes code for these abstractions, but each database vendor is responsible for the actual implementation.

When you are prompted for a JDBC driver type, select the name that matches your PeopleSoft database platform. For PeopleTools 8.52, options include Oracle, SQL Server 2008, DB2, Sybase, and Informix.

The Change Impact Analyzer default install location is your Windows program files directory. Change Impact Analyzer allows the installer to select an alternate directory if desired.

## Installing a JDBC Driver

If your PeopleSoft database is an Oracle database and you selected the Oracle JDBC driver type when installing Change Impact Analyzer, your JDBC driver is already installed. If your site uses an alternate database platform, you will need to install the JDBC driver yourself. Here's how to install the JDBC driver:

1. Acquire (download, copy, and so on) your database vendor's type 4 JDBC driver.

2. Copy the JDBC driver into the `jdbc` subdirectory of Change Impact Analyzer's installation directory. (On my workstation, the path to the `jdbc` directory is `C:\Program Files\PeopleSoft\Change Impact Analyzer\jdbc`.)

3. The Change Impact Analyzer launcher (menu icon) created by the installation program launches a batch file. Confirm that this batch file includes your JDBC driver's jar file. To confirm, open the file `C:\Program Files\PeopleSoft\Change Impact Analyzer\pscia.cmd` and search for `jdbc`. The following listing shows the entry for my JDBC driver:

```
SET CLASSPATH=%CLASSPATH%;"C:\Program Files\PeopleSoft\
Change Impact Analyzer\jdbc\ojdbc6.jar"
```

4. If your batch file does not contain a `jdbc` line, you'll need to add one. Copy the last `SET CLASSPATH` line and replace the text after the semicolon (`;`) with the path to your JDBC driver jar file.

The Change Impact Analyzer Rules Editor also launches from a batch file. Open `psciare.cmd` and confirm/apply the same JDBC driver value. Basically, the `pscia` and `psciare` programs require the same `CLASSPATH` environment variable.

# Configuration

To configure the Change Impact Analyzer, follow these steps:

1. Launch Change Impact Analyzer and select Configure | Connectivity.

2. In the Configure Connectivity dialog, select your database type and enter connection parameters specific to your environment. Figure 8-1 shows my configuration parameters.

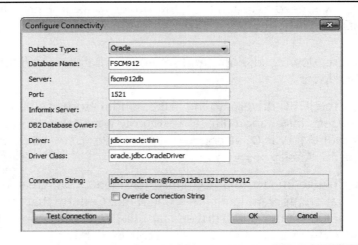

**FIGURE 8-1.** *Connectivity configuration parameters*

**NOTE**
*On Windows Vista or later versions, be sure to launch Change Impact Analyzer using the Run As Administrator option.*

3. If your JDBC driver or environment configuration requires additional or alternate JDBC parameters, select the Override Connection String checkbox and enter the appropriate values.

4. Click the Test Connection button to test the connection settings. Change Impact Analyzer will prompt for database credentials prior to connecting.

5. Configure the URL used to launch PeopleSoft pages online by selecting Configure | Reporting and Logging Options.

6. In the Options dialog, update the URL Prefix to match your PeopleSoft site's URL. Change Impact Analyzer will use this prefix when displaying relative URL definitions. Figure 8-2 shows the reporting and logging options.

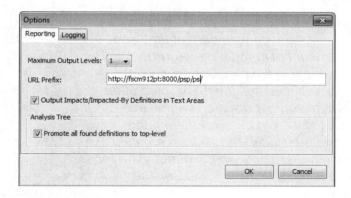

**FIGURE 8-2.** *Reporting and logging options*

# Preprocessing

Unlike other managed definitions, PeopleTools does not maintain enough metadata to perform a proper analysis of PeopleCode and file references. Change Impact Analyzer will build this metadata upon request. You need to run the preprocessing programs only if the source contents changes (PeopleCode or files) and you require a fresh version of cached metadata.

**NOTE**
*When you are running the preprocessor programs, be sure to use database credentials with write access to the Change Impact Analyzer cache tables mentioned in the sidebar "Change Impact Analyzer Authentication" later in this chapter.*

## PeopleCode and File Preprocessing

Initiate the PeopleCode preprocessor program by selecting Tools | PeopleCode Pre-Processor from the Change Impact Analyzer menu bar.

**NOTE**
*Running the PeopleCode preprocessor program may require a significant amount of time and use a fair amount of computing resources. I suggest launching the program right before heading off to a meeting, lunch, or some other activity where your workstation will be free to build metadata. On my workstation, the PeopleCode preprocessor program required approximately 20 minutes to build metadata for a Financials/Supply Chain database. The required runtime is directly related to the amount of PeopleCode within the database.*

Launch the file preprocessing program by selecting Tools | File Pre-Processor. As with the PeopleCode preprocessor, the amount of time required to run the File preprocessor is directly related to the number and size of the files to process.

# Analyzing Change

Change Impact Analyzer is capable of assessing the impact of a change to a single definition, multiple definitions, all definitions within a project, or all definitions within a change package.

## Workspaces

A Change Impact Analyzer *workspace* is a definition or a collection of definitions along with all impact reports. Initially the workspace contains no impact reports.

Create a new Change Impact Analyzer workspace by selecting File | New Workspace. Enter your database credentials. Change Impact Analyzer will prompt for the definitions to analyze in the Impact Analysis Search dialog (Figure 8-3).

The number of definitions within a workspace directly relates to the complexity of the impact analysis: more definitions equal greater complexity.

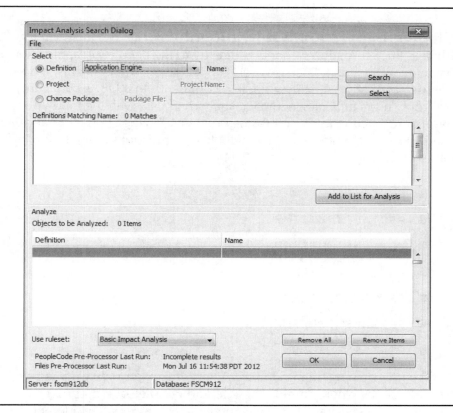

**FIGURE 8-3.** *Impact Analysis Search dialog*

Let's analyze the impact of a change to a single PeopleTools definition: record PSOPRDEFN.

1. In the Impact Analysis Search dialog, select the Definition radio button and then select Record.

2. In the Name field, enter **PSOPRDEFN**.

3. Click the Search button in the upper-right corner of the Impact Analysis Search dialog. This will populate the search results list displayed just below the search criteria.

4. Select an item from the list and click the Add To List For Analysis button located on the right side of the dialog, just under the results list.

## Change Impact Analyzer Authentication

Change Impact Analyzer connects directly to the PeopleSoft application database as a named database user. Unlike other two-tier clients, it does not use application security. Oracle recommends that DBAs configure read-only users for Change Impact Analyzer access with the following exception: To run the preprocessing programs, Change Impact Analyzer users *must* have write (insert/update/delete) permissions to the following tables:

- `PSCIAPCXREF`
- `PSCIAPCXREFTIME`
- `PSFILEPROCESSRUN`
- `PSSQLXREFDEFN`
- `PSSQLXREFITEM`
- `PSFILESQLXREFDEFN`
- `PSFILEXREFDEFN`

The user running Change Impact Analyzer requires only write access to these tables when running the File and PeopleCode preprocessor programs. If necessary, a DBA may run these processes when appropriate.

In addition to the preceding requirements, the first time a user runs the PeopleCode preprocessor program, Change Impact Analyzer will create the `PSCIAPCXREF` and `PSCIAPCXREFTIME` tables. The user who runs this initial process must also have `CREATE TABLE` access.

The lower half of the Search dialog contains a list of all selected definitions—definitions to analyze. You can add multiple definitions of a variety of types by searching for the definition and then adding it to the list of objects to be analyzed. Figure 8-4 shows the dialog containing the definition we chose to analyze: `PSOPRDEFN`.

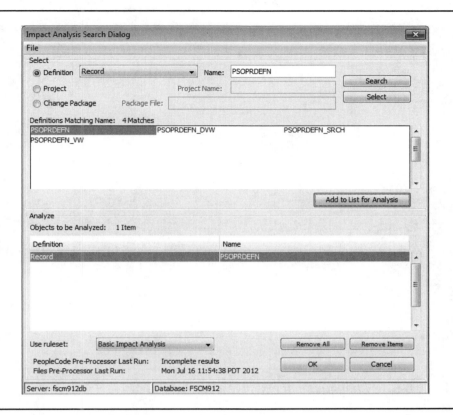

**FIGURE 8-4.**   *Impact Analysis Search dialog*

# Full Analysis

Analyze the impact of changes to definitions within the workspace by selecting Tools | Full Analysis. Change Impact Analyzer will search PeopleTools metadata for references to objects contained within the workspace. Figure 8-5 shows the Change Impact Analyzer after performing a full analysis.

PSOPRDEFN is a critical PeopleTools record definition that is referenced by hundreds of definitions. You can see the number of definitions that reference PSOPRDEFN within the Statistics pane of the Analysis Workspace. On my Financials/Supply Chain instance, Change Impact Analyzer found over 400 references.

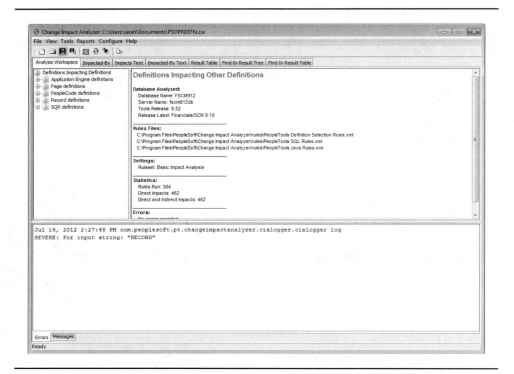

**FIGURE 8-5.** *Change Impact Analyzer full analysis*

The Change Impact Analyzer workspace is divided into seven tabs:

- Analysis Workspace
- Impacted-By
- Impacts Text
- Impacted-By Text
- Result Table
- Find-In Result Tree
- Find-In Result Table

The first tab, Analysis Workspace, will always have content. At a minimum, this tab contains the contents of the selected source definitions. The next four tabs contain relevant content only after an analysis has been performed. The remaining two Find-In tabs contain content only after running the Find In command (see the "Find In" section later in this chapter).

## Analysis Workspace

The Analysis Workspace tab displays a hierarchical list of the workspace's definitions grouped by definition type. Prior to running an analysis, this tab contains only the definitions inserted when the workspace was created. After performing an analysis, this list grows to contain all definitions searched plus all definitions impacted by the searched definitions. In the PSOPRDEFN example, the list of definitions also includes SQR reports that reference PSOPRDEFN.

## Impacted-By

Similar to the Analysis Workspace tab, the Impacted-By tab contains a list of searched and impacted definitions, but they are organized slightly differently. In this view, each impacted definition contains a node list of definitions affecting the selected definition. For example, an impact analysis of PSOPRDEFN includes the USER_GENERAL page as an impacted definition. Expanding the Page Types/USER_GENERAL node reveals a list of searched definition types that impact the USER_GENERAL page. Since I limited the scope of the search to PSOPRDEFN, this list contains only Record definitions. Figure 8-6 shows the definitions impacting the page USER_GENERAL.

## Impacts Text

The Impacts Text tab contains a text-based report that lists all definitions impacted by the analyzed definitions. The report is organized by definition headers with a list of impacted definitions below each heading.

## Impacted-By Text

The Impacted-By Text tab is exactly the opposite of the Impacts Text tab. Each heading is an impacted definition and contains a list of definitions causing that impact.

**FIGURE 8-6.** *Impacted-By tab*

## Result Table

When analyzing the impact of a definition, I find the Result Table tab to be
the most valuable. The Result table contains one row for each definition.
Rows with a blank Impacted Definition column are impacted definitions
that have not been analyzed. These rows represent definitions impacted by
the analyzed definitions. Analyzed definitions, by contrast, have values in
the Impacted Definition and Impacted Name fields. Figure 8-7 shows the
Result table. The upper rows represent unanalyzed impacted definitions,
whereas the lower rows represent analyzed definitions. In this example, I
analyzed only the PSOPRDEFN table, which is why the Name field contains
the value PSOPRDEFN.

You may open a definition in Application Designer by right-clicking a
row and then selecting Open Impacted in PSIDE.

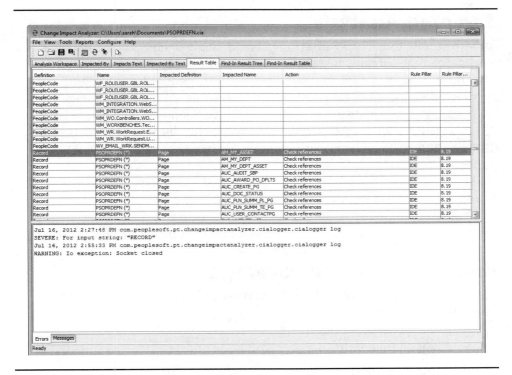

**FIGURE 8-7.** *Result Table tab*

## Traversing the Impact Tree

When I ran the impact analysis of PSOPRDEFN, Change Impact Analyzer found over 400 definitions and added each to the workspace. If I run the Full Analysis again, Change Impact Analyzer will expand the impact analysis to more than 400 definitions. On my PeopleSoft instance, this resulted in 1864 additional references. Running it a third time produced 9394 additional references. On the fourth run, Change Impact Analyzer identified nearly 40,000 references! I started with a little over 400 definitions that actually referenced PSOPRDEFN. The downstream impact, however, reached tens of thousands of definitions!

# Targeted Analysis

Earlier you saw that it is possible to analyze a single definition by creating a workspace that contains just that one definition. After analyzing that one definition, you may be interested in seeing the impact of changing an impacted definition. For example, USER_GENERAL is a definition impacted by PSOPRDEFN. I can analyze the USER_GENERAL definition by right-clicking USER_GENERAL within the Analysis Workspace results. Figure 8-8 shows the USER_GENERAL analysis results within the previously analyzed PSOPRDEFN results.

The analysis of USER_GENERAL shows that a change to USER_GENERAL would impact the component USERMAINT. By analyzing USERMAINT, I can see that changing USERMAINT would impact the component interfaces SYNC_USER_PROFILE, USER_PROFILE, and USER_PROFILE_SYNC.

# Analyzing Change Packages

To analyze the impact of an Oracle-delivered change package, follow these steps:

1. Create a new workspace.

2. In the Impact Analysis Search dialog, select the downloaded change package by choosing the Change Package radio button on the left side of the dialog and then clicking the Search button.

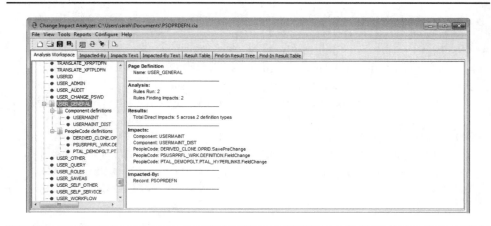

**FIGURE 8-8.** USER_GENERAL *analysis results*

3. Click the Select button to view a list of definitions included within the change package. Mark each item you want to analyze, or mark the top item to select all items.

4. In the Package Items dialog shown in Figure 8-9, click Add To Search to add each selected item to the list of definitions to analyze.

5. Click OK to create the workspace.

Figure 8-10 shows the Impact Analysis Search dialog containing each of the change package's definitions.

**FIGURE 8-9.**   *Package Items dialog*

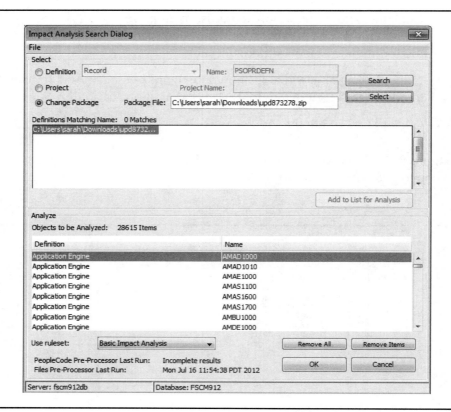

**FIGURE 8-10.** *Change package Impact Analysis Search dialog*

# Find In

You can search for references to workspace definitions by selecting Tools | Find In from the Change Impact Analyzer menu bar. The selection mechanism is similar to Application Designer's Find In feature, but with additional scope options as well as the ability to search for multiple strings. Figure 8-11 shows the Find In dialog configured to search HTML definitions for the text `isCrossDomain`.

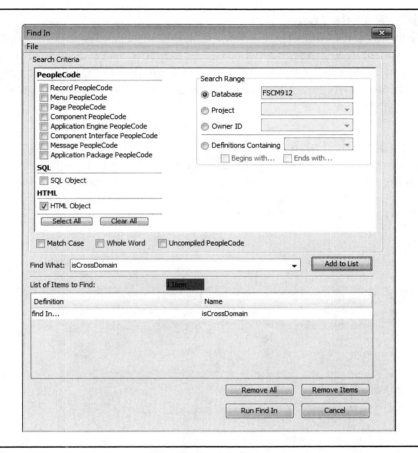

**FIGURE 8-11.**   *Find In dialog*

**CAUTION**
*The Find In command performs searches by
loading large quantities of text into memory.
Oracle recommends limiting the Find In scope
by selecting specific PeopleCode program
types, not all program types. You can fine-tune
the amount of memory available to Change
Impact Analyzer by modifying the* -Xms
*and* -Xmx *values specified in the pscia.cmd
Windows batch file.*

## Find-In Result Tree

After running the Find In command, Change Impact Analyzer populates the
Find-In Result Tree tab with a list of results categorized by definition type and
item name. Figure 8-12 shows the Find-In Result Tree tab displaying each line
in which the HTML definition PT_SAVEWARNINGSCRIPT contains the text
isCrossDomain.

## Find-In Result Table

The Find-In Result Table tab contains a tabular listing of each definition
containing the text isCrossDomain. To view a definition within Application
Designer, right-click the row containing the definition you want to view and
then choose Open in PSIDE from the context menu.

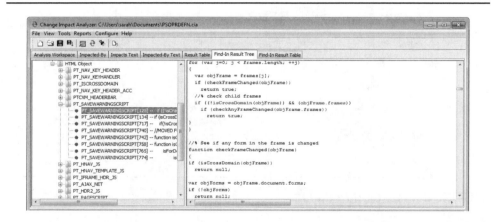

**FIGURE 8-12.**  *Find-In Result Tree tab*

# Rules

Change Impact Analyzer uses configurable rule sets to identify affected definitions. To view the list of installed rules, choose Configure I Rules. Figure 8-13 shows the default rules files installed with Change Impact Analyzer.

You can use the Change Impact Analyzer Rules Editor to do the following:

- Create new rules files

- Add new rules to existing rules files

- Change existing rules

- Override existing rules

Let's launch the Change Impact Analyzer to view rule sets.

1. When the main rules editor program appears, select File I Load Rules File. Delivered rules are installed in the rules subdirectory of the Change Impact Analyzer installation directory.

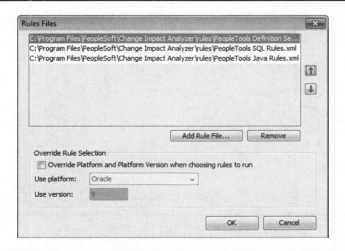

**FIGURE 8-13.** *Installed rules files*

2. Select the PeopleTools `Definition Selection Rules.xml` file. In a standard Change Impact Analyzer installation, the full path to this rules file is `C:\Program Files\PeopleSoft\Change Impact Analyzer\rules\PeopleTools\Definition Selection Rules.xml`. Figure 8-14 shows the Rules Editor main window.

3. Using the outline on the left side of the Rules Editor window, expand the nodes Rules/CHANGED: DefinitionSelection/Impacted: SQC/Rule Set: DefinitionSelection/Pillar: PT/Version: 8.00/DB Platform: default to view the rule(s) associated with SQC files. Figure 8-15 shows the rule criteria editor.

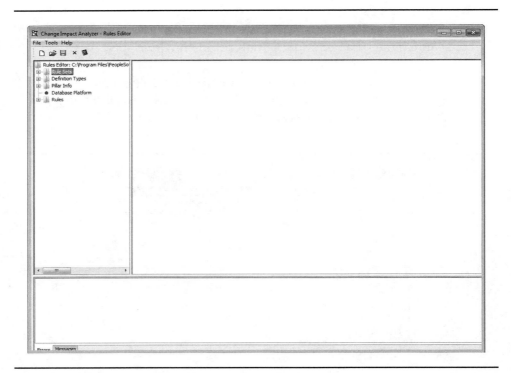

**FIGURE 8-14.** *Rules Editor main window*

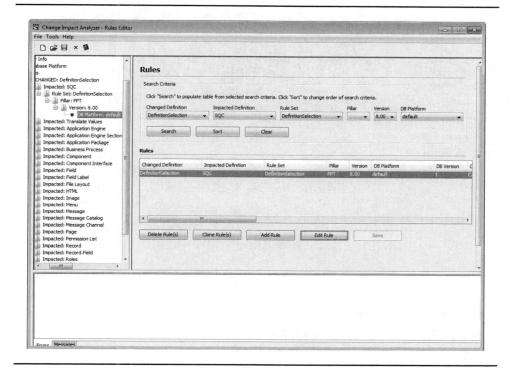

**FIGURE 8-15.** *Rule criteria editor*

**4.** To view the SQL associated with a rule, select the rule from the list of rules and then click the Edit Rule button. Figure 8-16 shows the SQC rule definition in the Edit Rule dialog.

**NOTE**
*The WHERE clause in Figure 8-16 uses like criteria with a bind variable. Typically a bind variable used with like criteria must be concatenated to wildcard characters. In Change Impact Analyzer rules, wildcards can be part of the bind variable string.*

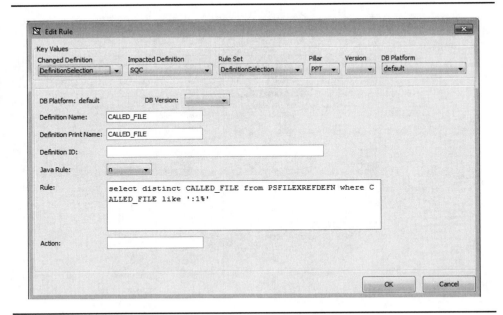

**FIGURE 8-16.** *SQC rule definition*

Rule definitions contain the following fields:

- Definition Name
- Definition Print Name
- Definition ID
- Java Rule
- Rule
- Action

# Definition Name

Enter the name of the SQL Result column containing the definition's ID. For example, if the rule is supposed to identify records impacted by a change to a field, the value for Definition Name would be RECNAME.

# Definition Print Name

The Definition Print Name field identifies the SQL result column containing the human-readable description of the impacted definition. When choosing a human-readable column, you should carefully consider the intent of displaying the column. Generally speaking, developers use the DESCR or NAME field when displaying information to users. PeopleSoft's delivered rules, however, usually share the same column for Definition Name and Definition Print Name. Displaying the internal ID makes it easier for users to find displayed definitions within Application Designer. Oracle recommends using the same value for Definition Name and Definition Print Name.

# Java Rule

Change Impact Analyzer allows administrators to define rules as Java classes. For the most part, these Java rules combine SQL and Java business logic to identify and display results. Oracle uses Java rules to create complex selection logic that cannot be written using standard, database-independent SQL.

**NOTE**
*Considering the differences between database platforms that run PeopleSoft applications, this makes sense for Oracle. For a customer, however, considering the power of a modern database procedural language, I don't think Java rules are necessary. I believe a creative programmer can achieve the same results using the target database's procedural language.*

# Rule

For Java Rules, the Rule field contains the Java class name. Otherwise, the rule is an SQL rule and should contain valid SQL. Here is an example of a rule that selects record definitions impacted by a change to a field definition:

```
SELECT DISTINCT RECNAME
     , FIELDNAME
  FROM PSRECFIELD
 WHERE FIELDNAME = ':1'
 ORDER BY RECNAME
```

# Conclusion

Change Impact Analyzer is a powerful tool for analyzing relationships between definitions. Consider the following Manager/Analyst conversation:

**Manager:** What would be the impact of adding a *Remote Worker* flag to the User Profile?

**Analyst:** Let me open the User Profile page within Change Impact Analyzer to identify the downstream effect of that change. One moment.... It appears that adding the *Remote Worker* flag to the User Profile would require updating only three component interfaces. If the field is optional, then we should be OK. If it is marked as a required field, then we may have to review an additional 13 PeopleCode programs that use those component interfaces.

In this chapter you learned how to use Change Impact Analyzer to navigate through a definition impact path to answer questions just like this one intelligently. This text covered most of Change Impact Analyzer's features and configuration options. For a complete list, refer to the PeopleBook *PeopleTools: PeopleSoft Change Impact Analyzer.*

# CHAPTER
## 9

# Change and
# Version Control

*hange control* is simply a mechanism used for controlling change. In its simplest form, change control consists of locking items within the change control system to prevent users from changing those items. *Version control*, on the other hand, involves managing versions of items, with no provisions for preventing change.

Change and version control systems are commonplace in the typical development lifecycle. Developers write code using a fancy text editor, run some automated tests, and then check that code into a version control system. We rarely differentiate the two terms because most version control *systems* include change control as a core feature.

The typical version control system offers the following services:

■ **Locking**   A checkout process ensures that only one developer can modify a file at a given time.

■ **Versioning**   Historical copies, or deltas, are retained for the purpose of reverting to or comparing revisions.

■ **Tagging**   This mechanism identifies changes.

Mercurial, Git, Concurrent Versions System (CVS), and Apache Subversion (SVN) are all popular version control systems. These systems work well for text and binary file management—the bulk of the average code base. Java, web, and .NET programmers use these tools daily through their integrated development environments (IDEs). But what about an application comprising database metadata with sprinklings of code to implement business logic? This is the situation for most PeopleSoft developers. A PeopleSoft development team may benefit from using Git or SVN to track changes to SQR, COBOL, shell scripts, and even SQL scripts, but how do you version a PeopleTools stylesheet spread across multiple relational tables and rows within a database?

# PeopleTools Change Control

Application Designer's Change Control feature supports *locking*, *history*, and *stamping*. A developer can lock a definition prior to modification to prevent other developers from changing the same object.

**NOTE**
*"History" refers to PeopleTools' ability to maintain a history of change control locking, not versioned history.*

# Locking

Before an electrician begins work on a circuit, that electrician uses a lockout tag to lock a circuit to prevent others from energizing the system. In this scenario, the lockout tag performs the following functions:

■ Specifies that a circuit should remain offline

■ Identifies the single person allowed to energize the circuit

For an electrician, failure to follow proper lockout procedures may result in death. Application Designer has a similar lockout mechanism, though without such dire consequences.

When a developer locks a definition, Application Designer makes note of the developer and allows only that developer (or an administrator) to unlock the definition. Locking applies only to definitions maintained within Application Designer. It does not apply to other upgradeable definitions. When locking is enabled, a developer can edit a definition only if

■ the definition is unlocked (not locked by someone else)

■ the developer first locks the definition

# History

When change control history is enabled, Application Designer records the timestamp, action, and user who initiated a change. Events that automatically trigger history include creating, deleting, locking, unlocking, renaming, and copying a definition. A developer may record a new history event at any time. In addition to the automatically recorded information, a developer can also specify a project name, incident ID, and comment describing the reason for the change.

# Stamping

*Stamping* refers to marking definitions with the *timestamp* of the last change as well as the ID of the user who performed the change. Stamping is a native feature of PeopleTools and is always enabled. This stamping mechanism allows Application Designer to classify changes during project and database compares: custom, changed, and unchanged.

# Configuring Change Control

Configuring Change Control involves establishing security online and enabling Change Control within Application Designer.

## Types of Security

Application Designer Change Control security includes three responsibilities:

- Restricted access
- Developer access
- Supervisor access

These responsibilities define access only when Change Control is enabled. At all times, these responsibilities determine the contents of Application Designer's Tools | Change Control menu item.

**Restricted Access**    When Change Control is enabled, users with restricted access may open definitions in read-only mode. The definition's lock state is irrelevant. This is an appropriate responsibility for functional analysts who assist with problem definition, but aren't responsible for changing definitions. Users with restricted access do not have a Tools | Change Control menu item in Application Designer. When Change Control is enabled, this user can view history through the Change Control toolbar buttons. When Change Control is disabled, restricted users cannot view history.

**Developer Access**    Grant developer access to users who need to edit definitions. A user with developer access will be able to lock unlocked definitions as well as definitions he or she previously locked. A developer cannot unlock someone else's definitions. Users with developer access may view Change Control history regardless of the state of Change Control.

**Supervisor Access**     A user with supervisor access can do the following:

- Unlock someone else's definitions
- Access the Change Control Administration dialog
- Lock all definitions at once

Users with supervisor access could be considered Change Control super users with full access to the Change Control system.

## Configuring Security
Change Control responsibilities are an attribute of standard PeopleTools Permission Lists. Both PeopleTools and applications deliver Permission Lists preconfigured for Change Control responsibilities. Unfortunately, however, it seems those Permission Lists grant most Application Designer users the supervisor access responsibility. For example, the following PeopleTools Permission Lists grant supervisor access:

- PTPT1100—Security Administrator
- PTPT1200—PeopleTools
- PTPT1300—Portal Administrator

The PTPT1200 Permission List is very common among developers. Granting every developer supervisor access is not an effective Change Control strategy, however. Securing developer access requires either modifying the delivered PTPT1200 Permission List or cloning PTPT1200 and its associated PeopleTools role. Both require rework at upgrade time. If you choose to clone the Permission List and Role, you will have to apply updates to the cloned versions. If you choose to modify the delivered Permission List, you will have to reset the Change Control responsibility after upgrade.

Likewise, some application-specific Permission Lists include Change Control responsibilities. For example, the EPPV1000 (ePro Requisitions) Permission List gives its users developer access.

You can configure Permission Lists by logging into your PeopleSoft application online.

1. Use the Main Menu to navigate to PeopleTools | Security | Permissions & Roles | Permission Lists.

2. Select the Permission List you want to edit, and then switch to the PeopleTools tab.

3. Under the PeopleTools Permissions section, you will see a Tools Permissions link. Click that link to set the Change Control responsibility. Figure 9-1 shows the Tools Permission editor window.

By querying the PeopleTools security tables, you can determine Change Control responsibility membership. The following query displays the Change Control responsibilities granted by each Permission List.

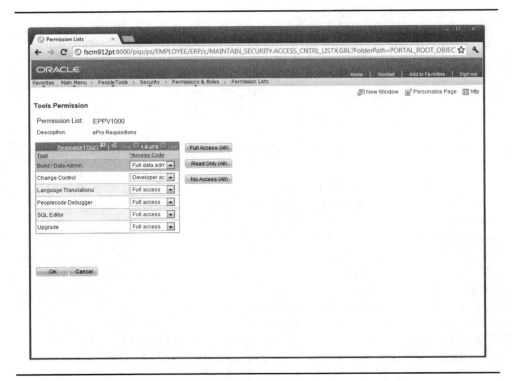

**FIGURE 9-1.** *Tools Permission editor window*

On my Financials/Supply Chain 9.1 demo system, this query identifies 17 Permission Lists that specify some form of Change Control responsibility; 14 of those Permission Lists give supervisor access!

```
SELECT CLASSID
     , CASE AUTHORIZEDACTIONS
            WHEN 2 THEN 'Restricted Access'
            WHEN 3 THEN 'Developer Access'
            WHEN 4 THEN 'Supervisor Access'
       END AS RESPONSIBILITY
  FROM PSAUTHITEM AUTH
 WHERE MENUNAME LIKE 'APPLICATION_DESIGNER%'
   AND BARNAME = 'CHANGE_CONTROL'
```

## Shared Identities

A locked object can be changed only by the lock owner. This approach does not work well for collaborative projects, however. For example, consider a corporation with developers working in several different time zones: India, Romania, United Kingdom, and the United States. During the span of 24 hours, a U.K. worker may lock and change a definition, intending to pass that definition off to his U.S. counterpart at the end of the day. If that U.K. developer leaves for home without unlocking the definition, the U.S. employee will require someone with supervisor access to unlock the definition. Some organizations choose to work around this issue by sharing Application Designer developer IDs between members in the same group, but this is a double-edged sword: On one hand, it cleanly cuts

### Definition Security

Collaborative teams often require a *two-phase locking solution*—an outer lock to keep the rest of the organization from touching a group of definitions and an inner lock to signal individual team members. For the outer lock, I recommend Definition Security. Definition Security allows a security administrator to create groups of definitions and secure them by Permission List. Used in this manner, Definition Security allows a team to lay claim to a set of definitions. The team members can then use Change Control locking on those secured objects to avoid internal team conflicts. For more information, see the *PeopleTools PeopleBook: Security Administration* chapter entitled "Implementing Definition Security."

through the sharing issue; unfortunately, however, the other side of the blade cuts through many of the audit and history benefits obtained through Change Control.

# Enabling Change Control

To enable change control, do the following:

1. Log into Application Designer as a user with Change Control supervisor access.

2. Select Tools | Change Control | Administration from the Application Designer menu bar.

3. Enable the Change Control features you require. I recommend enabling both Change Control Locking and Change Control History in the Change Control Administrator dialog, shown next:

# Using Change Control

Once Change Control is enabled, users can manage locks, view history logs, and add new history comments.

## Locking and Unlocking Definitions

The easiest way to lock or unlock a definition is to insert the definition into a project and then right-click the definition within the project workspace. When Change Control locking is enabled, the context menu contains the commands Lock Definition and Unlock Definition. Because projects are change controlled definitions, be sure to lock the project before attempting to insert definitions.

## Identifying Lock Owners

Restricted users can identify the owner of a lock in one of two ways:

■ Compare View History comments for Lock/Unlock pairs

■ Look for the lock owner's ID in parentheses next to the definition ID within the project workspace. If a locked definition doesn't have an ID beside the definition, then the logged-in user owns the lock.

Figure 9-2 shows Application Designer with the OP_DOC_ID field locked by developer JKIM.

In addition to the methods available to restricted users, supervisor and developer users have one more option: use the Locked Objects dialog. Open this dialog by selecting Tools | Change Control | View Locked Definitions from the Application Designer menu bar.

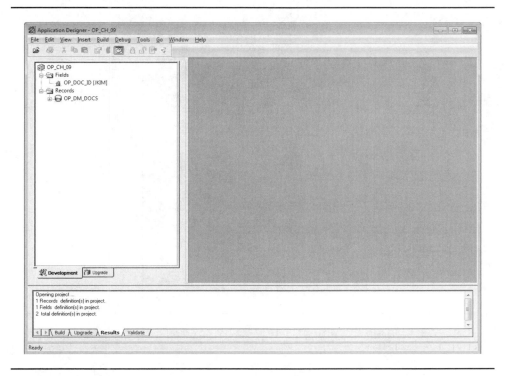

**FIGURE 9-2.**  *Application Designer locked definition*

## Adding and Viewing History Comments

Restricted, developer, and supervisor users can manually add history comments by using the Insert Comment toolbar command, which opens the Insert Comment dialog shown in Figure 9-3.

Additionally, developer and supervisor users can add history comments by doing one of the following:

■ Right-clicking a definition within the PROJECT WORKSPACE and selecting Insert Comment.

■ Opening a definition and then selecting Tools | Change Control | Insert Comment from the Application Designer menu bar.

Application Designer will automatically insert a history comment when creating a new definition or when locking a definition. When locking a definition, Application Designer will prompt you for comment details. Canceling the Insert Comment dialog will cancel the lock request, leaving the definition in an unlocked state.

**FIGURE 9-3.** *Insert Comment dialog*

## Change Control Preferences

Application Designer does not automatically prompt for history comments when saving a definition. Developers can configure automatic prompting on a per-workstation basis by enabling the Prompt For Comments When Definition Is Saved Application Designer Change Control option. To enable this option, select Tools | Options from the Application Designer menu bar and switch to the Change Control tab. Figure 9-4 shows the Change Control workstation Options dialog.

**NOTE**
*Enabling comment prompting will cause Application Designer to prompt on every save. Some may find this behavior annoying. However, a developer does not need to enter a comment every time Application Designer prompts for comments.*

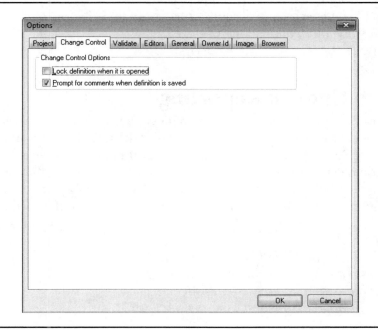

**FIGURE 9-4.** *Application Designer Change Control Options*

With Change Control locking enabled, Application Designer displays a warning message for each definition a developer opens. A developer can bypass this warning by configuring Application Designer to lock definitions automatically when opened. The Lock Definition When It Is Opened checkbox is shown with the Prompt For Comments When Definition Is Saved option in Figure 9-4.

**TIP**

*Even though choosing the first option eliminates the annoying warning message, I strongly discourage the use of this setting. Developers and analysts often open definitions just to review their contents. Automatic locking requires manually unlocking these unchanged definitions upon closure. Forgetting to unlock a definition will block another user from changing that object. Furthermore, each lock request adds another row to the history table. Locking objects you don't intend to change can add a significant amount of unnecessary information to the Change Control history tables.*

# Change Control Reporting

Within Application Designer, a user can view change history as well as identify the user holding a lock on a particular definition. That is about the extent of PeopleSoft's Change Control reporting. Nevertheless, since Application Designer writes Change Control information to database tables, you can write your own queries and reports. The following Oracle-specific query identifies locks that have been outstanding for more than a month.

**NOTE**

*The following SQL statements are meant to serve as a guide for creating your own reports. You can create much more sophisticated reports through PeopleSoft Query, Oracle BI Publisher, and SQR.*

```
SELECT OPRID
     , CASE WHEN OBJECTID1 =  18 THEN 'Activity'
            WHEN OBJECTID1 =  66
             AND OBJECTID2 =   0 THEN 'AE Program'
            WHEN OBJECTID1 = 104 THEN 'App Package'
            WHEN OBJECTID1 =  85 THEN 'Approval Ruleset'
            WHEN OBJECTID1 =  64 THEN 'Business Interlink'
            WHEN OBJECTID1 =   7 THEN 'Business Process'
            WHEN OBJECTID1 =  10
             AND OBJECTID2 =  39 THEN 'Component'
            WHEN OBJECTID1 =  74 THEN 'CI'
            WHEN OBJECTID1 =   6 THEN 'Field'
            WHEN OBJECTID1 =  71 THEN 'File Layout'
            WHEN OBJECTID1 =  90 THEN 'HTML'
            WHEN OBJECTID1 =  91 THEN 'Image'
            WHEN OBJECTID1 =   3 THEN 'Menu'
            WHEN OBJECTID1 =   9 THEN 'Page'
            WHEN OBJECTID1 =  11 THEN 'Project'
            WHEN OBJECTID1 =   1 THEN 'Record'
            WHEN OBJECTID1 =  65 THEN 'SQL'
            WHEN OBJECTID1 =  94 THEN 'Stylesheet'
       END AS DEFN_TYPE
     , OBJECTVALUE1 AS NAME
     , TRUNC(SYSDATE - CAST(DTTM_STAMP AS DATE)) DAYS_OUT
     , PROJECTNAME
     , DESCRLONG
  FROM PSCHGCTLLOCK
 WHERE DTTM_STAMP < ADD_MONTHS(TRUNC(SYSDATE), -1)
```

To see a list of all definitions created since the last change package was applied, run the following SQL:

```
SELECT OPRID
     , CASE WHEN OBJECTID1 =  18 THEN 'Activity'
            WHEN OBJECTID1 =  66
             AND OBJECTID2 =   0 THEN 'AE Program'
            WHEN OBJECTID1 = 104 THEN 'App Package'
            WHEN OBJECTID1 =  85 THEN 'Approval Ruleset'
            WHEN OBJECTID1 =  64 THEN 'Business Interlink'
            WHEN OBJECTID1 =   7 THEN 'Business Process'
            WHEN OBJECTID1 =  10
             AND OBJECTID2 =  39 THEN 'Component'
            WHEN OBJECTID1 =  74 THEN 'CI'
```

```
            WHEN OBJECTID1 =    6 THEN 'Field'
            WHEN OBJECTID1 =   71 THEN 'File Layout'
            WHEN OBJECTID1 =   90 THEN 'HTML'
            WHEN OBJECTID1 =   91 THEN 'Image'
            WHEN OBJECTID1 =    3 THEN 'Menu'
            WHEN OBJECTID1 =    9 THEN 'Page'
            WHEN OBJECTID1 =   11 THEN 'Project'
            WHEN OBJECTID1 =    1 THEN 'Record'
            WHEN OBJECTID1 =   65 THEN 'SQL'
            WHEN OBJECTID1 =   94 THEN 'Stylesheet'
      END AS DEFN_TYPE
    , OBJECTVALUE1 AS NAME
    , DTTM_STAMP
  FROM PSCHGCTLHIST HIST
 WHERE CHGCTRL_ACTION = 'A'
   AND DTTM_STAMP > (
SELECT MAX(DTTM_IMPORTED)
  FROM PS_MAINTENANCE_LOG )
 ORDER BY DTTM_STAMP DESC
```

The *PeopleTools: PeopleSoft Application Designer Developer's Guide* chapter, "Using Change Control," contains additional information regarding Change Control field values.

# Managing Multiple Databases

PeopleSoft customers generally configure several environments: Demo, Development, Test, QA, and Production. Each environment maintains its own set of Change Control attributes. Change Control attributes do not follow a definition as it migrates from database to database. The lock status of a definition in Development, for example, is unrelated to the lock status in other environments. Likewise, the Change Control history of a definition in Development is not likely to match the Change Control history of that same definition in another environment. This has significant implications for the practice of cloning environments. It is common for an organization to replace the QA, Test, and even Development environments with a copy of the Production environment. Doing so, however, will eliminate existing locks as well as change history.

# Change Control with Upgrades

Applying maintenance and upgrades requires a static database—developers must freeze active development. This allows administrators and subject matter experts to identify and resolve upgrade conflicts. Administrators may use a variety of mechanisms to secure a database during this critical upgrade juncture:

- ■ **Communication**  Communicate downtime and expect all developers to honor that request. Unfortunately, this strategy is challenging in today's distributed workplace.

- ■ **Network isolation**  Change Domain Name System (DNS) entries, use routers/firewalls, and so on, to close standard network access routes, effectively isolating the database.

- ■ **Change Control**  Use Application Designer's system-wide lock feature to lock all definitions.

Application Designer's system-wide lock is effective at preventing developers from changing definitions. Apply or remove a system-wide lock by selecting Tools | Change Control | Administrator from the Application Designer menu bar. Select the Lock All Definitions checkbox to enable a system-wide lock. Deselect the Lock All Definitions checkbox to remove a system-wide lock.

**TIP**
*Change Control locks are an effective method for securing definitions. A developer cannot change a locked definition. Though effective, locks are not a substitute for PeopleTools Definition Security.*

The unfortunate side effect of a system-wide lock, however, is that it deletes all developer-specific locks. When an administrator unlocks the system, all definitions will be unlocked. Developers who previously held locks will need to reapply those locks. Below is the warning message a Change Control supervisor will see when applying a system-wide lock.

# Version Control

Everyone implements some form of version control. While writing this book, for example, I made backup copies of files prior to implementing changes. If I didn't like the result of the changes, I could revert to the backup version. With PeopleSoft, we often implement versioning by cloning Application Designer definitions into *backup* definitions. On a much larger scale, we may even clone environments. In fact, the backup step listed in nearly every Change Assistant template is an attempt at version control. If something within the Change Assistant template fails or if we don't like the results, we can revert to the last saved version.

## File-based Version Control

Odds are pretty good that your organization already uses a version control system (or maybe even several). With modern distributed version control systems (DVCS), such as Git and Mercurial, your cubical partner may even be committing changes to a local DVCS without anyone else's knowledge.

The following sections describe the four levels of version control for PeopleSoft.

### Level 1: Version Control for Files
A lightweight approach to version control for PeopleSoft is to check file system code and configuration files into a version control system. Files such as COBOL, Data Mover scripts, SQL, SQR, PS/nVision layouts, BI Publisher templates, and configuration files make excellent candidates for version control.

## Level 2: Version Control for Project Definitions

After standard files, the next step on the journey to version control is to export PeopleSoft Application Designer projects regularly and check them into a version control system.

## Level 3: Version Control for PeopleCode

Version control for Application Designer project definitions is great for retaining history but is not very valuable in regards to compare and merge. It may be too much to ask a file-based version control system to offer side-by-side page and component comparisons. At a minimum, however, we should expect a PeopleCode "diff" and compare. Level 3 involves exporting PeopleCode and storing it as plain text files within a version control system. Application Designer contains two mechanisms for exporting PeopleCode as plain text:

- Using the Find In menu command to search for semicolons (;)

- Exporting PeopleCode projects to file, and then extracting PeopleCode from the resultant XML file

## Level 4: Version Control for Data

The pinnacle of file-based version control is storing relational data within the version control system. This level requires an intimate knowledge of the database's relational model. To reach this level, a developer with knowledge of an object's relational model would write Data Mover scripts to copy information into .DAT files, and then check those .DAT files into a version control system.

Unfortunately, the view from level 4 is not that great. Much like level 2, level 4 offers versioning, tagging, and branching, but not much with regard to compare. At a minimum, an organization should implement level 1 version control.

# Specialized Version Control Products

Although better than nothing, the file-based version control system leaves a lot to be desired:

- Workflow

- Native PeopleSoft definition support

- Rollback
- Configuration management
- Segregation of duties
- Compliance

Even though system management and developer productivity are important, the greatest motivator for a specialized version control system is legislative compliance. Local and international regulations often require strict control over enterprise application code and configurations. The following Oracle partners sell specialized version control systems to fill this void:

- Phire, Inc.: www.phire-soft.com/
- Quest Software: www.quest.com/stat-peoplesoft/
- GreyHeller: www.greyheller.com/Products/version-control.html
- mcAMDIOS: www.mcamdois.com/

# Conclusion

In this chapter, you learned how to configure and use PeopleSoft's Change Control features to ensure codebase integrity throughout the development cycle. We discussed version control, even laying out a blueprint for a custom-built solution. At the beginning of this chapter, we asked how a person can version an object spread across multiple tables while participating in several peer and parent/child relationships. Oracle has not answered this question, allowing partners to create their own solutions.

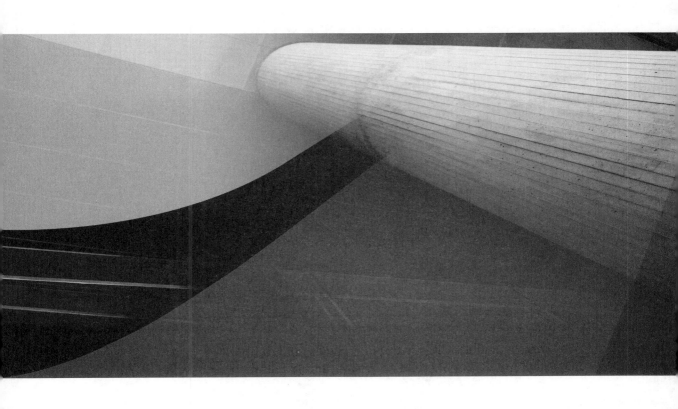

# PART
# III

## Upgrades

# CHAPTER
## 10

# Upgrade Overview

"Ever-newer waters flow on those who step into the same rivers."
—Heraclitus, c. 475 B.C.

"Our new Constitution is now established, and has an appearance that promises permanency; but in this world nothing can be said to be certain, except death and taxes."
—Benjamin Franklin in a letter to Jean-Baptiste Leroy, November 13, 1789

oth the Greek philosopher and the Early American statesman would probably agree that the primary constant in life is *change*. For organizations, change is also a constant. Two primary factors motivate change in organizations: pain and gain.

With regard to software, change equals upgrades, which often include new features, new interfaces, streamlined process flows, and fixes to old software problems—the gain. Software change also requires software reconfiguration, user manual updates, and current business process realignment with system process—the pain. Upgrades bring new opportunities and great potential for efficiencies. But these changes involve work and the allocation of scarce resources: labor, time, and, ultimately, money.

When perceived gains outweigh costs (when the gain seems greater than the pain), organizations implement change. Several common pain factors motivate upgrades:

- Regulatory requirements

- Costly support contracts

- Discontinued support

- Competitive pressure

When motivated by regulatory requirements, cost is irrelevant. For other pain-motivated decisions, the benefits derived from an upgrade must exceed implementation costs. The following common costs are often associated with a software upgrade:

- Potential consulting fees

- Hardware upgrades

- Labor for IT and subject matter experts
- System integration work
- Training
- Potential downtime and lost productivity

# Does Change Require an Upgrade?

Traditionally software companies have bundled new features into periodic software releases. This was motivated by both economics and psychology. From an economic perspective, if a company is going to implement change, it often wants to implement more changes at one time rather than living in a constant state of change. That way, the company has to pay for the change only once. From a psychological perspective, users often avoid change, even positive change, for several reasons: fear and anxiety, as well as the effort required to change habits and behaviors. Longer durations between upgrades allowed software users to "settle in" to a day-to-day routine rather than live in a constant state of change.

More recently, software companies are promoting the benefits of shorter release cycles with incremental but continuous change. The "big bang" approach to software upgrades has proven to be too disruptive and costly, prohibiting many organizations from upgrading. PeopleSoft continues to release major upgrades for those who are not current. For those who are current, however, Oracle now provides periodic feature pack updates that a customer can apply to an existing system using the same techniques described in Part II of this book.

# PeopleSoft Upgrades

In this part of the book, we offer tips and instruction to help your organization lower its costs when upgrading PeopleSoft software.

## Compare Reports

The term "upgrade" often brings up great emotion: excitement and the antithesis—sheer terror! A demonstration of the new features, modern user interface, and simplified user experience provided by a software upgrade often generates enthusiasm and anticipation. On the darker side, upgrades bring to mind chaos, budget overruns, lost productivity, and user resistance to change.

It doesn't have to be this dramatic, however. We'll offer tips and instructions to help your organization lower its upgrade costs and carefully consider the appropriate options.

Compare reports identify and categorize change. Some changes require special attention, and other changes can be ignored. In Chapter 11, you will learn how to generate and interpret compare reports so that you can differentiate between changes that require attention and changes you can ignore.

## PeopleSoft Test Framework

Proper testing is critical to upgrade success. Testing, however, requires people—not just warm bodies, but functional experts. Few companies have enough excess labor capacity to dedicate their brightest human resources to upgrade testing. In Chapter 12 you will learn how to use PeopleSoft's Test Framework to build and maintain an automated test suite that can repeat the mundane tasks that normally require functional experts.

## Upgrade Tips and Techniques

Upgrading PeopleSoft requires knowledge of each of the subject areas covered in this book. A complete, operating system–independent upgrade guide could easily cover 600 pages. In fact, Oracle creates version-specific upgrade guides that describe how to perform an upgrade. In Chapter 13 you will learn a few tips and techniques to streamline the upgrade process, including virtualization shortcuts.

## Pain Avoidance

The Wong-Baker Faces Foundation publishes a universal pain scale used by physicians and patients to gauge pain. You can see the pain scale at http://www.wongbakerfaces.org/. On the Wong-Baker pain scale, routine maintenance ranges from 0 (doesn't hurt) to 4 (hurts a little more). Upgrades, on the other hand, start at 4 (hurts a little more) and end somewhere around 9 (hurts a whole lot). Part II of this book covered change management regarding patches and routine maintenance. In Part III, we offer tips and instructions to help your organization stay below the "hurts a little more" range of the pain scale.

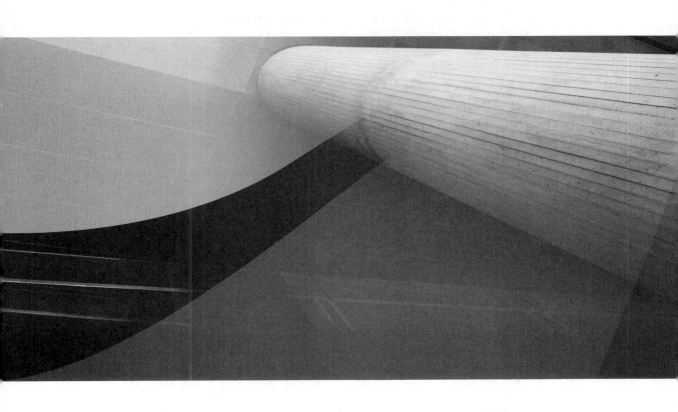

# CHAPTER
## 11

## Compare Reports

pgrades, patches, bundles, and maintenance packs contain Application Designer change projects. A *change project* is a collection of PeopleTools definitions that Oracle changed since the last release. Most of the definitions within a change project differ from a customer's version because Oracle changed its own code (new version). Other differences exist because the customer made changes (a customized version). When applying these change projects, an upgrade team must decide which version of a definition to keep:

- The original version

- A customized version

- The new version

In this chapter you will learn how to use the compare process to identify, report, and appropriately tag definitions. A successful compare has a significant impact on the upgrade process.

# Our First Compare

A comparison involves two code repositories: these can be either two PeopleSoft applications or a combination of a project file and a PeopleSoft application. When you perform a compare between two PeopleSoft systems, both systems must be on the same PeopleTools release. As you will see later, application release is negotiable. For file compares, release is irrelevant.

## Creating a Sample

Before we perform a compare, we need two code repositories. I've been working in a PeopleSoft Financials/Supply Chain 9.1 instance, so this represents one repository. To keep it simple, let's export a project from this system and use that project file as the second code repository.

### The Source Project

We've already created several custom definitions. We can add some of those to the project. For completeness, we should also add some delivered definitions to the project.

Log into Application Designer using two-tier mode. (Application Designer does not support compare operations in three-tier mode.) Create a new project definition named OP_CH_11 and insert the following definitions into the project:

- Field OP_DOC_ID

- Page USER_GENERAL

- Record OP_DM_DOCS

- Record PSOPRDEFN

- Record PSROLEDEFN_VW

- Message Catalog Entry 3, 1

Figure 11-1 shows the Message Catalog Entries in the Insert Into Project dialog.

Open the record PSOPRDEFN and choose View | View PeopleCode from the Application Designer menu bar. The PeopleCode editor will open to the OPRID FieldChange event. Choose Insert | Current Definition into Project

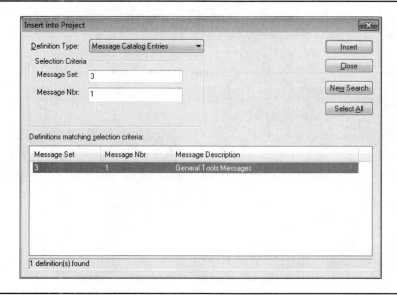

**FIGURE 11-1.**   *Message Catalog Entries in the Insert Into Project dialog*

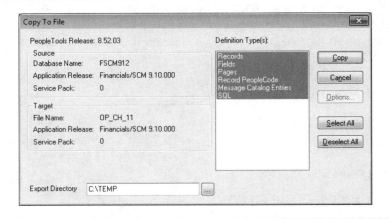

**FIGURE 11-2.** OP_CH_11 *project definition*

(or press F7) to insert this PeopleCode definition into the project. Figure 11-2 shows the Application Designer project definition. Unfortunately, PeopleCode definitions and Message Catalog entries do not appear in the development tab of the project workspace, so make sure you manually add them to the project.

Export this project to a file by choosing Tools I Copy Project I To File from the Application Designer menu bar. It does not matter where you place this file. Nevertheless, be sure to note the location. I recommend something short and easy to remember, such as C:\TEMP. Figure 11-3 shows the

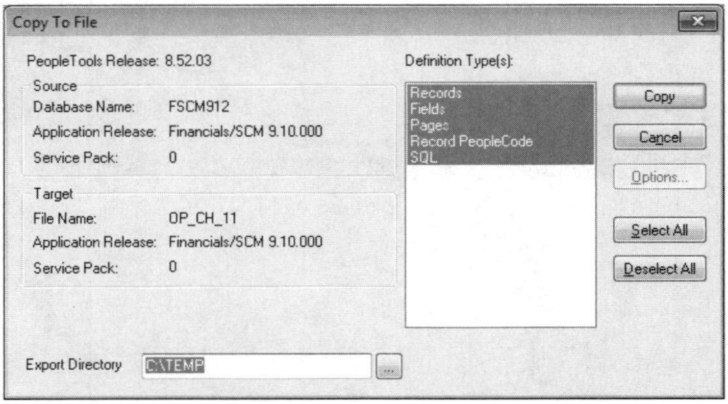

**FIGURE 11-3.** *Copy To File dialog*

project Copy To File dialog. We will use this project as the source for compare operations.

At this point, running a compare report against the project file will yield very little. Each definition in the file is identical to the definition within the database. But since this is our first opportunity to run a compare report, let's go ahead and run one anyway.

Choose Tools | Compare and Report | From File. When the Compare and Report From File: Select Project dialog appears, ensure that you are viewing the directory containing the initial project export. For this example, I chose C:\temp. Just below the file and folder selection area is a list containing each project definition within my temp directory. Select the OP_CH_11 project and click Select. Figure 11-4 shows the project Compare And Report From File: Select Project dialog.

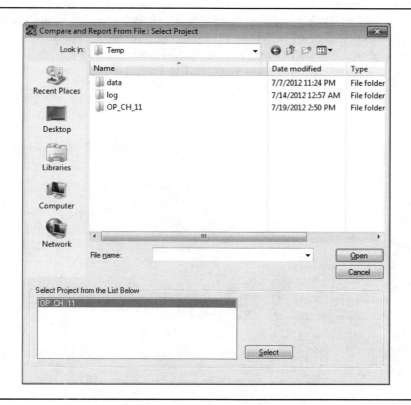

**FIGURE 11-4.** *Compare And Report From File: Select Project dialog*

To perform a compare, Application Designer copies a project definition's structure into the current database. It does *not* copy the project items—just the structure. My database already has a project named OP_CH_11. When I click the Select button, Application Designer will recognize the project name and ask if I want to overwrite the database version of the project definition with the file version. Again, this is just the project structure, not the project's items. Choosing Yes, Replace, will have no impact on PSOPRDEFN or any other item within the project. Nevertheless, it is important to note that the Compare From File operation overwrites the database's version of a project definition. Figure 11-5 shows the Compare And Report From File dialog. Notice that Message Catalog Entries are not in the list of definitions to compare. Click the Compare button to begin the compare process.

When the compare is finished, use the project workspace and switch to the Upgrade tab. Double-click each of the folders listed in the Upgrade tab to view the compare status of each item. Notice that all of the definitions except Message Catalog Entries show Same/Same for the source and target columns. We expect Same/Same, because we haven't changed any definitions. Message Catalog Entries contain the value Unknown/Unknown. Application Designer does not manage Message Catalog Entries. This is why change packages include Message Catalog Data Mover scripts.

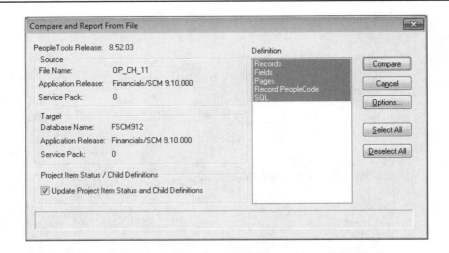

**FIGURE 11-5.** *Compare And Report From File dialog*

The compare process generated several reports, all of which are currently open in Application Designer. If you prefer, feel free to review them now. At this point, however, they are all empty—no changes, no rows. We'll review them later when a compare has some differences to report.

## Customizing

To gain value from this compare, something has to be different. We will tread lightly since most items in our project are delivered definitions, and making the wrong change could render the system unusable. Fortunately, we have a backup project file, but nevertheless, we must proceed with caution.

1. Within the Upgrade tab, double-click the Fields folder to open the list of fields.

2. Double-click the OP_DOC_ID field to open the definition.

3. Add a new label to the list of field labels. Set the Label ID to OP_UNIQUE, the Long Name to Unique Identifier, and the Short Name to Unique ID. Figure 11-6 shows the field with its new label.

4. Save and close the field definition.

5. While still viewing the Upgrade tab, expand the PeopleCode node and then double-click the Record PeopleCode folder.

6. Double-click the PSOPRDEFN.OPRID.SavePreChange PeopleCode row to open the item in Application Designer's PeopleCode editor. We don't need to change the behavior of the PeopleCode program. We just need to change the contents.

7. We can evoke change by adding a comment to the very end of the event's code listing. Add the following to the bottom of the code editor, and then save and close the PeopleCode definition.

   ```
   REM ** A as in aisle... G as in gnome... T as in tsunami;
   ```

**CAUTION**
*Don't forget the line terminating semicolon!*

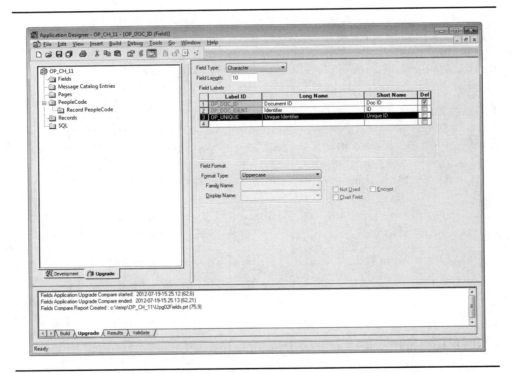

**FIGURE 11-6.** OP_UNIQUE *field label*

We can make a similar change to the SQL for the view PSROLEDEFN_VW. Open the view in Application Designer, switch to the Record Type tab, and then click the Click To Open SQL Editor button. Add a multiline comment somewhere within the body of the SQL statement similar to the following (the comment is in bold). Then save and close the definition.

```
SELECT rolename
 , descr
 , %TextIn(descrlong)
 , rolestatus /* I am a comment. I have no impact. */
  FROM psroledefn
WHERE rolename <> 'PeopleSoft Administrator'
```

# Running the Compare

With some changes in place, let's run a compare.

1. Launch the compare by selecting Tools | Compare And Report | From File from the Application Designer menu bar.

2. When prompted, select the project file you previously exported. In the preceding example, I exported to `C:\temp`.

3. When the Compare And Report From File dialog appears, click the Options button.

4. The Upgrade Options dialog appears. Each tab within this dialog specifies a comparison or a reporting option. When running a compare, Application Designer will use compare options to set project definition upgrade options. Reporting options define what to report, how to report it, and where to place generated reports.

## Compare Options Tab

Figure 11-7 shows the Compare Options tab of the Upgrade Options dialog. The tab is divided into several areas.

**Compare Type**     Compare Type asks if you want to perform a project or a database compare. When comparing to a file, you have only one option: project compare. When comparing to another PeopleSoft instance, however, you may choose project or database compares. For minor change projects with a small number of changes, a project compare is best. Use a database compare when performing an application upgrade. Chapter 12 offers more information about the database compare.

**Target Orientation**     You may choose from one of two target orientations: PeopleSoft Vanilla or Keep Customizations. Vanilla is a flavor enhancer added to many desserts; it also represents a base flavor. A *vanilla system* is a base system—one that contains no customizations. The orientation tells Application Designer how to set upgrade flags while performing a compare. If the target system has customizations and you want to remove those customizations, choose PeopleSoft Vanilla. If you want to keep your customizations, choose Keep Customizations. You can change upgrade settings

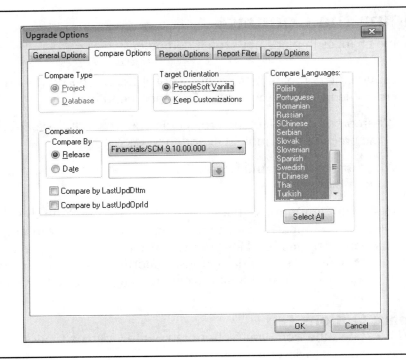

**FIGURE 11-7.** *Compare Options tab of the Upgrade Options dialog*

on a definition-by-definition basis after the compare completes. Generally speaking, a customer chooses PeopleSoft Vanilla and then later reintroduces customizations on an as-needed basis.

**Compare Languages**     Several definition types support multi-language design. For example, a base language page definition may appear different from an Arabic language page. Select the language you want to compare. You will most likely select all languages (the default) for compare operations.

**Comparison**     The Compare By options allow you to choose a particular release label for comparisons. To use Compare By Release, both the source and target systems must have a release label in common. A PeopleSoft database will likely have several release labels. The source and target do not have to have the same number of release labels, but they must have at least one release label in common. If two systems have no release in common, choose Compare By Date. I use this option when comparing custom cross-product utilities—for example, when I'm comparing definitions between Human Capital Management (HCM) and Financials applications.

## Report Options Tab

Figure 11-8 shows the Report Options tab. This tab is also divided into several areas.

**Report Output**    The Report Output area is where you specify display and report type options. Click the Font button to select a different font. Select the Generate Browser Reports checkbox to create an HTML viewer for sharing reports or viewing them offline. Application Designer will generate the HTML

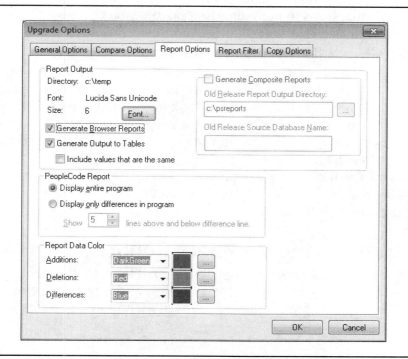

**FIGURE 11-8.**    *Report Options tab*

report in a subdirectory of the folder identified at the top of the Report Output section. Figure 11-8 shows the report output directory as c:\temp.

**PeopleCode Report**    Use the PeopleCode Report section to specify how much of a PeopleCode listing to display. Printing an entire PeopleCode program is generally safer, because the full program listing offers enough context to identify a change's location. Printing each changed program, however, can generate some very large reports. Alternatively, you can select Display Only Differences In Program and select the number of lines to show above and below the change. Be sure to select enough lines to identify the change properly.

**Report Data Color**    If you prefer, you may select alternative colors for additions, deletions, and differences. Compare reports will set the font color according to the selected colors. For example, when using the default color scheme, a PeopleCode compare report will use a dark green color to display PeopleCode that exists in the source, but not the target.

### Report Filter Tab
The Report Filter tab contains a grid that allows you to choose what types of change to display within compare reports. The grid represents an intersection of the source and target systems. The default filter identifies customizations and ignores vanilla changes. Generally speaking, a customer is concerned with reviewing only changes that impact customizations. Figure 11-9 shows the Report Filter tab.

Click the OK button at the bottom of the Upgrade Options dialog to dismiss the dialog. Click the Compare button on the Compare And Report dialog to perform the compare.

## Interpreting the Compare Report
Running the compare process generated a report for each definition type within the project. The records, fields, pages, and reports are empty because we did not make changes to those definitions. The SQL and

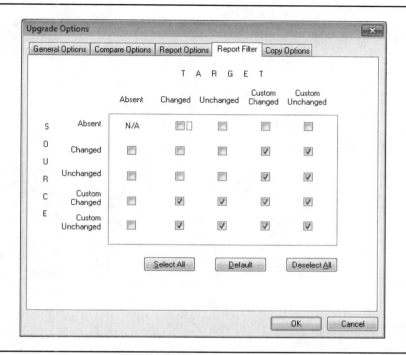

**FIGURE 11-9.**  *Report Filter tab*

record PeopleCode reports, however, contain side-by-side comparisons.
Figure 11-10 shows the PeopleCode compare report.

**TIP**
*Compare reports can be rather wide. Closing
the project workspace panel provides more
display area for viewing reports.*

Each compare report uses a similar layout: definition identification,
child item identification, upgrade options, and differences.

**Definition Identification Columns**  The first column identifies the definition.
Some definition types, such as pages and SQL, require multiple fields to identify
the definition uniquely.

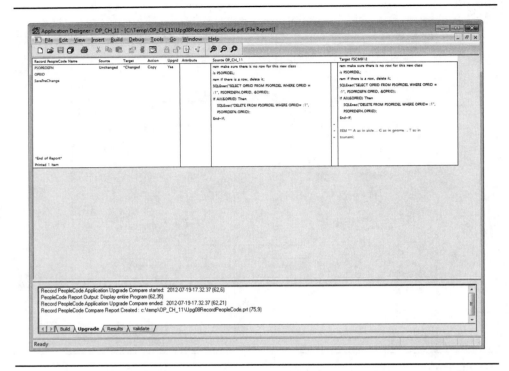

**FIGURE 11-10.** *PeopleCode compare report*

**Definition Child Item Identification Columns**    The second set of columns identifies the portion of the definition that differs between the source and target. The page report, for example, lists page fields that differ between releases.

**Upgrade Options Columns**    The next set of columns—Source, Target, Action, and Upgrade—specify how Application Designer would apply the change project if it were imported immediately following a compare operation.

**Difference Columns**    The final set of columns display differences. In Figure 11-10, for example, the last two columns contain side-by-side code listings, highlighting the differences between the source and target systems. The final two lines are displayed with a red font to signify that these lines would be removed if I chose to apply this project (or change package, upgrade, and so on).

# Interpreting Upgrade Flags

Running the compare process performs two critical operations: generating differential reports and setting project upgrade options. While Application Designer is identifying changes, it marks a flag within the project specifying whether a changed definition should be copied, deleted, or ignored. The value chosen by the compare process depends on whether the user running the compare chose Vanilla or Keep Customizations. Figure 11-11 illustrates the impact these flags have on the compare process.

To view upgrade flags, use the Project Workspace to switch to the Upgrade tab. Double-click each folder to open the category's list of definitions. In our example, we added the USER_GENERAL page to the project but made no changes. Since the compare process did not find any changes, it marked the source and target as being the same, set the Action to None, and left the Upgrade flag empty. As far as Application Designer is concerned, there is no reason to act upon this unchanged definition. Figure 11-12 shows the Page definition upgrade flags window.

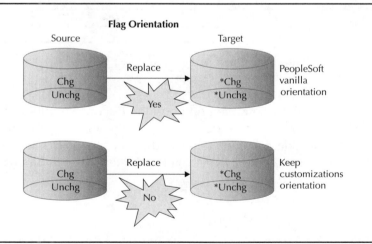

**FIGURE 11-11.** *Flag orientation*

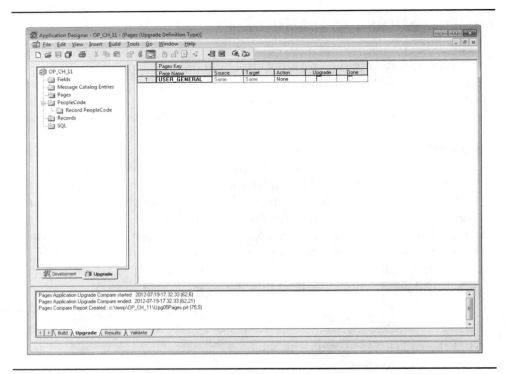

**FIGURE 11-12.**   *Page definition upgrade flags*

Expand the PeopleCode node and open the Record PeopleCode folder. Figure 11-13 shows the PeopleCode upgrade flags. We copied a delivered, unmodified PeopleCode definition to file and then changed that definition. After making changes, the compare process marks the file Source as Unchanged and the database Target as *Changed.

## Source and Target Columns
The compare process classifies change with one of four categories:

- **Unchanged**   The definition has not changed since the last release.

- **Changed**   The definition has changed since the last release.

- **\*Unchanged**   The definition is a custom definition and it has not changed.

- **\*Changed**   The definition is a custom definition and it has changed.

## When Does Same + Same = Copy?

When the compare process identifies identical definitions between source and target definitions, it sets the upgrade action to None and leaves the Upgrade flag unchecked. If two definitions are identical, Same/Same, why waste time copying one over the other? Answer: To update the target system's Application Server cache. Copying items from a source system to a target system happens at the database level. The Application Server is not aware of the transaction. When the Application Server receives a request for a definition, it compares its cached version to the database's version. If they have the same version number, then the Application Server uses its cached version.

A *content reference* is a definition that someone could migrate from a source system to a target system. Have you ever copied a content reference from one system to another, but the target never seems to show the new content reference? I have—I've even gone into the portal registry of the target and tried to create the copied content reference. What's interesting is that trying to create a content reference that doesn't show in the portal registry, but was migrated through a project, results in the application displaying a message saying the definition already exists. If it exists, then why isn't the application displaying it? The Application Server maintains its own cache and is not aware of the new content reference.

Content references present an interesting dilemma. A user's primary interaction with a content reference is through system menus and navigation collections. If the Application Server is not aware of the content reference, it has no reason to check the database for a new version. If a user can't see a content reference in the menu, that user can't initiate the request.

The Application Server caches content references based on the portal registry hierarchy. When requesting a content reference, the Application Server also makes note of the content reference's child items. The solution to the content reference cache issue, therefore, is to copy the content reference's parent folder even though it has not changed. Copying the parent will increment the target system's version information. When someone accesses the parent content reference, the Application Server will reload the parent and make note of the new child content references.

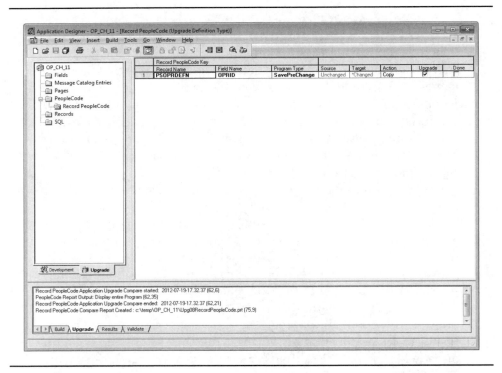

**FIGURE 11-13.** *PeopleCode upgrade options*

The asterisk (*) signifies customization. The lack of an asterisk identifies a Vanilla definition.

How the compare process determines change depends on compare options: Compare by release, by date, by LastUpdDttm, and by LastUpdOprId. This is why either a source or a target can show Changed or Unchanged, meaning either the source or the target may have a newer version.

## Action Column
The Action column specifies the upgrade action Application Designer intends to take if asked to copy the definition into the target. The compare process derives the action from a combination of the Vanilla/Customization

compare option as well as the Source/Target column values. For example, if you choose the Vanilla compare option and the target is marked as Custom Changed (*Changed), then the compare process will set the Action column to Copy. Likewise, if the Source column contains the value Absent, then the Action column will be set to Delete.

### Upgrade Column

The Upgrade column is a confirmation flag stating whether or not to perform the action specified. The Upgrade column is automatically marked if the Action is set to Copy.

## Selecting the Source

As you saw earlier when performing a project file compare, we can use Application Designer to log into the target database. When performing a database to database comparison, you log into the source database. At compare time, Application Designer will prompt for the target database's two-tier credentials. Figure 11-14 illustrates this process.

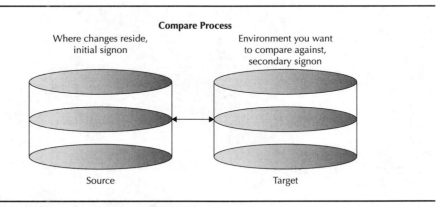

**FIGURE 11-14.**  *Signon database compare process*

# Running a Compare and Report Against a Maintenance Pack

In Chapter 7 we used Change Assistant to apply SCM 9.1 bundle 17 to a vanilla PeopleSoft instance. In Appendix A, we will manually apply bundle 18. Let's prepare now by running the compare report. I've already downloaded the bundle and extracted the change project.

To run the compare, I select Tools | Compare and Report | From File. After running the compare, I have several compare reports. In this case I'm running a vanilla system, so the compare reports are empty—no customizations to report. Figure 11-15 shows the Record upgrade settings for bundle 18.

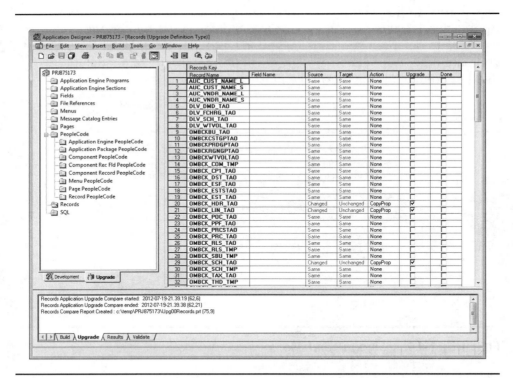

**FIGURE 11-15.** *Record upgrade settings*

# Filtering Results

The compare process marked several records as Same/Same. When you're trying to determine the impact of a change project, definitions that haven't changed represent "noise"; they make it hard for you to understand the big picture. We can filter these results by selecting View | Filtering | Custom Filtering from the Application Designer menu bar. When the Custom Filtering dialog appears, uncheck the Show Definitions Which Are Identical In Source And Target checkbox. Figure 11-16 shows the Custom Filtering dialog.

Filters offer a very effective mechanism for changing upgrade flags based on compare results. For example, when copying a large number of pagelet and navigation collection content references from one database to another, I also copy the parent content reference. Because the source and target versions of these parent definitions are the same, the compare process won't copy the definitions. After the compare process, I manually change the upgrade flags by using a filter to select all *unchanged* definitions.

The filter in this case is exactly the opposite of the prior filter. To select all definitions that are the same in the source and target, select View | Filtering | Custom Filtering. Click the Deselect All button to remove all checkboxes and then check only the Show Definitions Which Are Identical In Source And Target checkbox. This will hide all definitions that differ

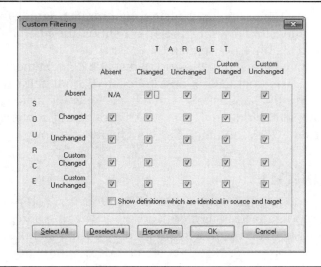

**FIGURE 11-16.**    *Custom Filtering dialog*

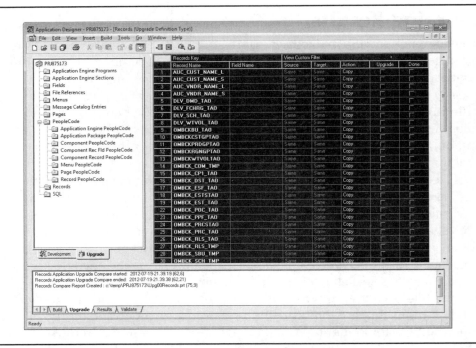

**FIGURE 11-17.** *Upgrade options grid with visible rows selected*

between the source and target. With only Same/Same definitions showing, click the little gray box in the upper-left corner of the upgrade options grid. This will select all visible rows. Figure 11-17 shows the filtered upgrade options grid with visible rows selected.

Right-click anywhere within the grid to reveal a context menu containing several segments. The upgrade options are located about halfway down the menu and allow us to change the selected items' upgrade action, tag them for upgrade, or reset their done flag. In the case of parent content references, I select Set Action | Copy, and then Tag For Upgrade.

# Conclusion

In this chapter you learned how to generate and review compare reports. Running the compare process is a critical step in the upgrade process. Compare reports help an upgrade team identify customizations. A side-by-side PeopleCode compare assists that team in determining how to merge customizations back into an upgraded system. In the next chapter we will run through a full upgrade.

# CHAPTER
## 12

# PeopleSoft Test
# Framework

he PeopleSoft Test Framework (PTF) is a client-side, metadata-aware automated testing facility. It uses Internet Explorer to record and run functional test scripts. In this chapter you will learn how to install, configure, and use the PeopleSoft Test Framework.

# Installing PeopleSoft Test Framework

PTF is a multitier testing tool. As we saw in Chapter 2, Application Designer may connect in two-tier, direct-to-database, or three-tier Application Server mode. PTF connects to the web server. Although I'm tempted to call this "four-tier mode" (client, web server, application server, database), most sites will configure proxies, load balancers, Secure Sockets Layer (SSL) accelerators, and other network devices between the client and the web server.

The first step in the installation process is to verify system connectivity and prerequisites. Once satisfied, we can run the installation process.

## Environment Prerequisites

PTF accesses test metadata through an HTTPS connection to Integration Broker. This means a properly configured environment includes Integration Broker and has SSL enabled.

### Enable SSL

PTF requires SSL communication between the PTF client and the PeopleSoft Integration Gateway. It is not enough to terminate SSL early using an SSL load balancer or SSL accelerator. PTF's service operations are marked as requiring SSL, causing Integration Broker to verify that data is transmitted over a secure protocol. Integration Broker will fail if the incoming request is sent over HTTP.

**NOTE**
*Carrying SSL through to the PeopleSoft web server is required only for web services. Standard PeopleSoft Internet Architecture (PIA) access still supports early SSL termination.*

## Configure Integration Broker

Integration Broker's architecture is very similar to PeopleSoft's Pure Internet Architecture, but with a lot more flexibility and a lot fewer conventions. It consists of Application Server processes and a gateway service. Online applications have portals, integration tools have gateways, but portals and gateways are the same: they both have the definition gate, door, or entrance. The following steps offer a basic outline to assist you in configuring Integration Broker.

**Enable Pub/Sub**    Configure the Application Server to start the Integration Broker Publication and Subscription services. Figure 12-1 shows the `psadmin` configuration menu.

**Gateway Configuration**    Next, log into your PeopleSoft online application as an administrator and do the following:

1. Navigate to PeopleTools | Integration Broker | Configuration | Gateways.

2. Open the LOCAL gateway and verify the URL setting.

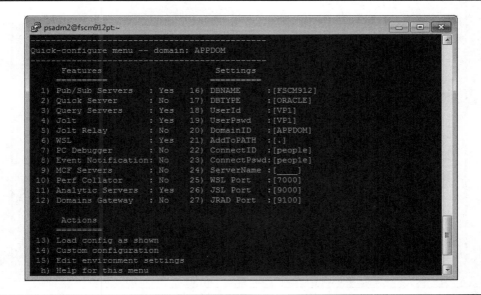

**FIGURE 12-1.**  *Configuration menu for* `psadmin`

3. If the Connectors grid is empty, click the Load Gateway Connectors button to populate the grid. Figure 12-2 shows the LOCAL gateway's settings.

4. The gateway URL points to Integration Broker's servlet. You can click the Ping Gateway button to confirm the URL, but a properly secured gateway may contain a URL that is not accessible outside the application's network. My gateway URL, for example, is http://fscm912pt:8000/PSIGW/PeopleSoftListeningConnector. Notice the protocol is HTTP, not HTTPS, and the server name lacks a domain. Services inside my secure PeopleSoft network communicate through plain HTTP. Any service trying to connect from outside that network, however, must use SSL and specify a fully qualified server/domain name. The URL, therefore, to ping my gateway from outside the PeopleSoft network is https://fscm912pt.example.com/PSIGW/PeopleSoftListeningConnector. Verify that your gateway is running

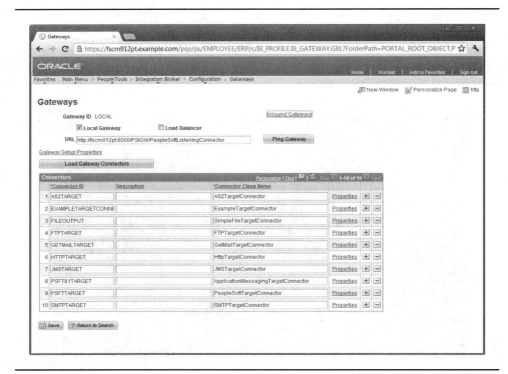

**FIGURE 12-2.** *LOCAL Gateway settings*

by attempting to access the fully qualified HTTPS (secure) URL for your gateway. A properly configured gateway will appear similar to the one shown next.

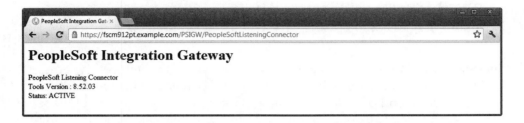

**5.** Select the Gateway Setup Properties link to configure PeopleSoft nodes with which this gateway will communicate. At a minimum, configure the gateway's default Application Server and the default local node's Application Server. Figure 12-3 shows the LOCAL gateway's node settings.

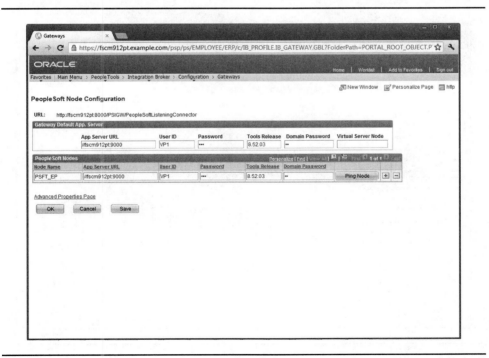

**FIGURE 12-3.**   *Gateway node settings*

**NOTE**
*PeopleSoft stores these settings in the* `integrationGateway.properties` *file within the* `PSIGW/WEB-INF` *servlet directory. Regenerating PIA will overwrite this file, requiring reconfiguration.*

**Service Configuration**     To facilitate moving definitions between systems, PeopleSoft does not hard-code web service end points in schemas. Configure the web service end point for Integration Broker by navigating to PeopleTools | Integration Broker | Configuration | Service Configuration. If you are using PeopleTools 8.51, enter the Target Location and Secure Target Location. For PeopleTools 8.52 and later, click the Setup Target Location link and enter the appropriate URLs. Figure 12-4 shows a PeopleTools 8.52 service target configuration.

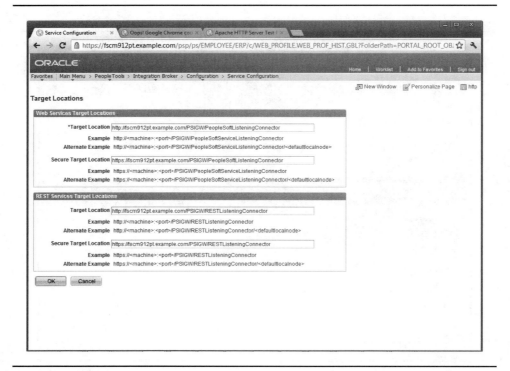

**FIGURE 12-4.**   *Service target configuration*

**Node Configuration**  Integration Broker is a form of Enterprise Service Bus (ESB), routing information between nodes. To function properly, Integration Broker needs to know a message's sender and the intended recipient. PTF uses two nodes: ANONYMOUS and the default local node. Both the ANONYMOUS and the default local node are delivered by PeopleSoft. Configure nodes by navigating to PeopleTools | Integration Broker | Integration Setup | Nodes. Select the ANONYMOUS node and update the Default User ID. Figure 12-5 shows the ANONYMOUS node configuration.

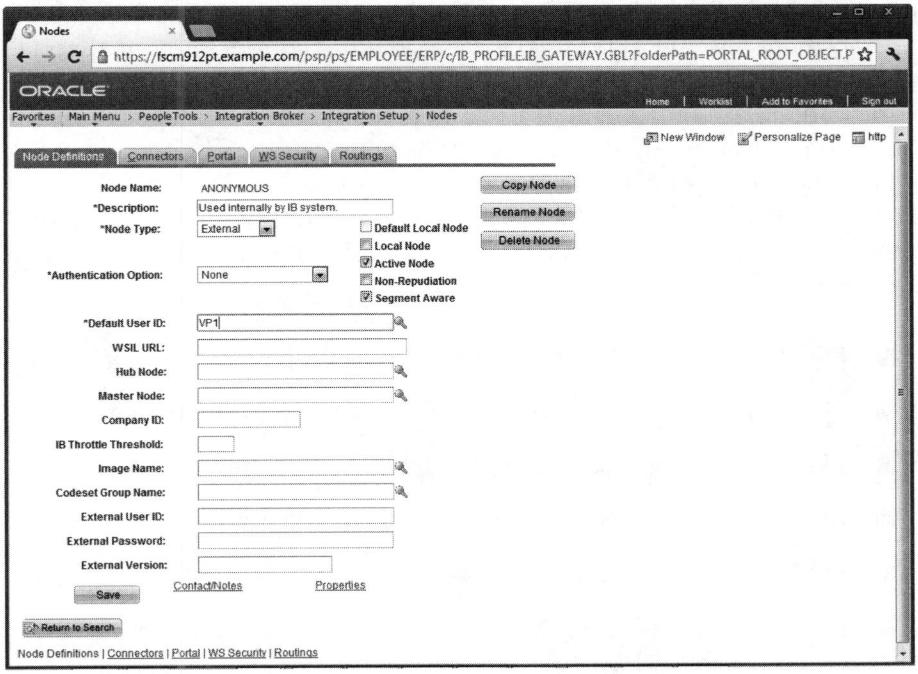

**FIGURE 12-5.**  *ANONYMOUS node configuration*

**NOTE**
*PTF's use of the ANONYMOUS node is not necessarily intentional. ANONYMOUS is the name of the node Integration Broker uses for anonymous service requests.*

A node's default user must have access to any service operations requested by that node. PTF uses the PTTS_TEST service. Following the principle of least privilege, I recommend creating an unprivileged user and adding only permission lists required to execute anonymous services. Whichever user you choose for the ANONYMOUS node, ensure that the user has permission to execute PTTS_TEST service operations (PTF User role is discussed later in the section, "User Configuration").

After saving the ANONYMOUS node, identify your default local node. From the node search page, find the node that has a *1* in the Local Node column, and a *Y* in the default local node column. The default local node of a fresh PeopleSoft installation always starts with `PSFT_`. The following list contains the names of each delivered application's default local node. Your default local node will have this name only if this is a new, preconfigured installation. A production system should *not* use these node names (see the upcoming Caution).

- **PSFT_CR**   PeopleSoft Customer Relationship Management

- **PSFT_EP**   PeopleSoft Financials/Supply Chain Management

- **PSFT_HR**   PeopleSoft Human Capital Management

- **PSFT_HR**   PeopleSoft Campus Solutions 9.0 (same as HCM 9.0)

- **PSFT_LM**   PeopleSoft Enterprise Learning

- **PSFT_PA**   PeopleSoft User Interaction Hub (formerly PeopleSoft Enterprise Portal)

- **PSFT_PF**   PeopleSoft Enterprise Performance Management

**CAUTION**
*Node names play a significant role in PeopleSoft security. No two nodes should have the same name. A PS_TOKEN generated by one server will be accepted by another server if that other server is configured to trust the node identified by the PS_TOKEN. For example, a developer may have access to authenticate as a manager in a development Human Capital Management (HCM) system but not in a production system. If your development and production nodes have the same names and your Financials system is configured to trust the HCM system, then that developer can craft a PS_TOKEN cookie to authenticate against the Financials production system as the manager identified by the PS_TOKEN cookie.*

Open the node and switch to the Connectors tab. Click the Ping Node button to verify the default local node's configuration. A ping attempts to connect to the application server identified within the Gateway node configuration. Since this is the default local node, we are really asking the application to ping itself. If you see "Success" in the Message Text column, then the node is configured properly. Figures 12-6 and 12-7 show the node Connectors tab and ping results, respectively.

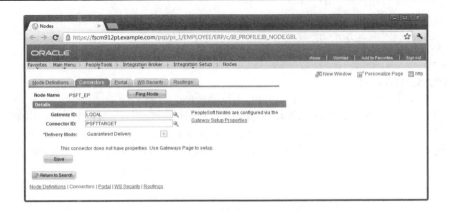

**FIGURE 12-6.** *Default local node Connectors tab*

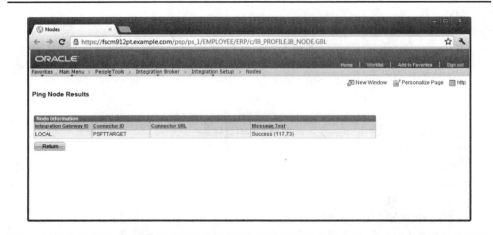

**FIGURE 12-7.** *Connector ping results*

**Domain Status**   Navigate to PeopleTools I Integration Broker I Service
Operations Monitor I Administration I Domain Status and confirm that your
domains are active. Depending on your configuration, you may have
multiple domains. Not every domain has to be active. PTF will have to
connect to the Application Server Pub/Sub services, so at least one domain
will have to be active. Figure 12-8 shows the Domain Status page.

**NOTE**
*If your site has multiple domains and you aren't
familiar with the domain configuration, find out
who configured your domains and ask that
person which one to activate.*

## User Configuration
PTF includes three roles: PTF User, PTF Editor, and PTF Administrator. The
*PeopleTools PeopleBook: PeopleSoft Test Framework* chapter "Installing
and Configuring PTF," section "Setting Up Security," shows an excellent
table describing the access provided by each role. In summary, to run tests

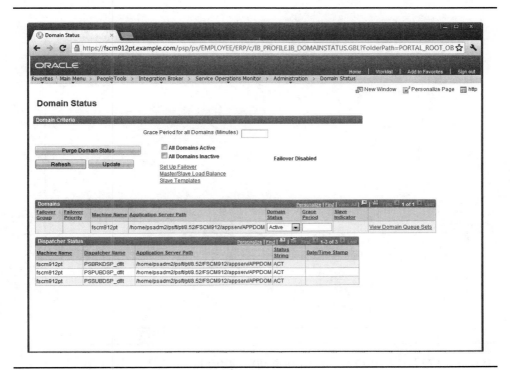

**FIGURE 12-8.** *Domain Status page*

only, you'll grant a user the PTF User role. If a user will change, create, or run tests, then you'll give that user the PTF Editor role. Users who run PTF reports as well as modify and run tests require the PTF Administrator role.

## Web Profile Configuration

Identify the web profile in use by the system you plan to test. The only sure way to determine which web profile your server uses is to check the value of the `WebProfile` key within the portal servlet's `configuration.properties` file. If your architecture uses only one web profile (as opposed to two separate web servers running KIOSK and PRO), then you can determine the currently loaded web profile from PeopleTools | Web Profile | Web Profile History. The profile that has the most recent Profile Was Loaded value is the one that is currently in use.

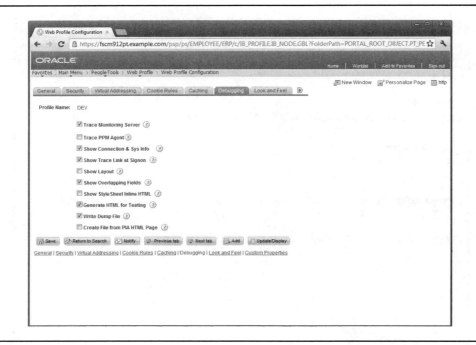

**FIGURE 12-9.** *Web Profile Debugging options*

Edit the web profile by navigating to PeopleTools | Web Profile | Web Profile Configuration. Switch to the Debugging tab and verify that the following checkboxes are selected:

- Show Connection & Sys Info
- Generate HTML for Testing

Figure 12-9 shows the Web Profile Debugging tab.

## PTF Online Configuration Options

As previously mentioned, PTF requires SSL. You may configure PTF to allow untrusted SSL connections by navigating to PeopleTools | Lifecycle Tools | Test Framework | Define Configuration Options and selecting the Allow Untrusted SSL checkbox. This is important if your site uses an untrusted, self-signed digital certificate.

Trust in this regard is a matter of implicit versus explicit trust. PTF will implicitly trust a certificate signed by a known certificate authority. You must explicitly choose to trust a certificate that is not signed by a reputable certificate authority.

**CAUTION**
*Be aware that accepting untrusted SSL certificates may compromise security.*

While viewing the PTF online configuration options, you can add a row for each Process Scheduler you intend to use with PTF.

### Browser Settings
PTF is a .NET application that records and plays tests through Microsoft's Internet Explorer. Add the site you will be testing to your browser's trusted sites security zone. For more information about Internet Explorer's security zones, see Microsoft's documentation online. Microsoft maintains configuration steps for each browser and operating system version.

## Install PTF
The PTF installation program is delivered with the PeopleTools file server installation. Launch the installation program, `%PS_HOME%\setup\PsTestFramework\setup.exe`. The installation wizard is rather short, allowing you to select a target install location, and that is it. Accept the defaults, clicking Next and Finish when prompted.

# My First Test
When a user performs a functional test, that user logs into PeopleSoft and visually verifies something—a value on a page, results of a calculation or process, and so on. An automated test, therefore, must be able to navigate to a particular location within the PeopleSoft application and then verify "something." Automated tests often include some type of action, such as

adding a new row or changing a value on a page, but this is not required. Later in this chapter, we will create a PTF test that performs the following:

1. Logs into PeopleSoft as user CROTH

2. Navigates to PeopleTools | Security | User Profiles | User Profiles

3. Adds the role PTF User to operator ID AERICKSON

4. Verifies that AERICKSON has the role PTF User

Before creating this test, however, PTF requires some configuration. Specifically, we have to create a connection profile to tell PTF where to find and store tests, and we need to create an execution profile to identify the system to test.

## Creating a Profile

Launch PeopleSoft Test Framework. When the Signon dialog appears, create a profile for the system you plan to test. Figure 12-10 shows the PTF Signon dialog with a fully configured profile.

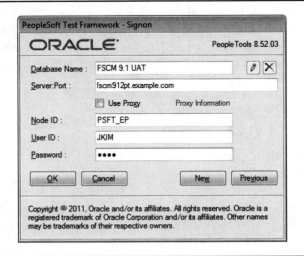

**FIGURE 12-10.** *PTF Signon dialog with a configured profile*

**NOTE**
*On Windows 7, launch PTF by right-clicking
the icon and selecting Run As Administrator.
Administrator access is required to attach to
and record browser sessions.*

A profile consists of a name, a connection string, proxy information,
the target node ID, and credentials.

## Database Name
The Database Name field uniquely identifies a profile. The field is not used
within a connection string, so it does not have to contain the target database's
name. Enter a unique, meaningful description.

## Server:Port
PTF uses the value entered into Server:Port to generate a web service end point.
If the target system uses the default SSL port (443), the port is not required.
Alternatively, you may enter the full HttpListeningConnector URL. A full URL
may be necessary if a particular implementation uses URL fragments to
reverse-proxy SSL requests as in https://peoplesoft.example.com/**fscm**/PSIGW/
HttpListeningConnector. If you choose to use a full URL, be sure to use the
HTTPS protocol. PTF attempts a secure tunnel connection regardless of the
URL's protocol.

## Use Proxy Checkbox
If your network architecture requires you to connect to PeopleSoft
through a proxy server, select the Use Proxy checkbox and fill in the
Proxy Information section. Later you will see how to use an HTTP
debugging proxy to troubleshoot PTF connection issues.

## Node ID
Node ID is required only if the target Integration Broker gateway is shared
among multiple PeopleSoft applications. The node ID is not required if the
target node is configured as the gateway's default application server.

## User ID

Enter a PeopleSoft user ID that has one of the three roles: PTF User, PTF Editor, or PTF Administrator. If your environment has no PTF test cases or Execution profiles, log in as a PTF Administrator. You will need this role to create an Execution profile. The PTF user ID does not require access to the PeopleSoft features you plan to test. Later you will create an Execution Profile that specifies the PeopleSoft Operator ID.

**NOTE**
*Tests run as valid PeopleSoft application users. The PTF access ID is not necessarily the same operator ID used to perform tests. Test case operator IDs are stored with preconfigured execution options that can be shared by multiple tests.*

## Password

Enter the PTF user's password.

# Troubleshooting Connections

The following is a list of common connection issues and potential solutions.

## Connection Errors

When PTF is improperly configured, you may experience one of the following errors while trying to log into PTF.

**There was an error when PeopleSoft Test Framework was trying to login**    This is a very generic error. In a few paragraphs you will learn how to use Fiddler to determine the root cause of this error message.

**InnerException: The remote name could not be resolved**    DNS resolution failed. Try pinging or using `nslookup`, `dig`, or another command-line tool to determine whether the host is accessible through your network.

**InnerException: Unable to connect to the remote server**    PTF was able to determine the IP address for the target host but was not able to connect. Verify the port number as well as your local and server firewall rules.

**InnerException: The remote name could not be resolved: 'http'**     This
error means the URL entered into the Server:Port field was prefixed with
*http* instead of *https*. Since the URL did not begin with *https*, PTF assumed
the part before the colon (:) was the server name and the part after the colon
was the port number. In this case, the part before the colon is *http*, causing
PTF to attempt to connect to a server named *http*.

## Authentication Errors

Have you ever seen the error in Figure 12-11? PTF displays this error
message if its authentication service operation failed. This does not
necessarily mean that you entered the wrong password.

The service operation might fail for several reasons:

- Invalid password

- Invalid user ID

- User does not have a PTF role

- Network configuration

You need to see the XML response to know exactly why the
service operation failed. Since Integration Broker writes failures to the
`errorLog.html` file, it is possible to review errors from a web browser
by navigating to your site's integration gateway—for example, https://
fscm912pt.example.com/PSIGW/errorLog.html. I find this approach works

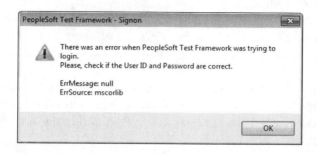

**FIGURE 12-11.** *Generic error dialog*

well the first time, but browsers, proxies, and even WebLogic prefer to cache this HTML document, making it nearly impossible to reload. Furthermore, a secure PeopleSoft installation would not allow web access to the `errorLog.html` (or `msgLog.html`) file. These files may contain highly confidential information and should be tightly guarded.

An alternative method is to place a "man in the middle" (see the OWASP web site at www.owasp.org/index.php/Man-in-the-middle_attack) to capture and decipher PTF's SSL communication. The Fiddler debugging proxy works very well for this. Fiddler is a web-debugging proxy tool that appears as a standard proxy server with this difference: Fiddler logs and organizes communication for analysis purposes.

**Debugging with Fiddler**    Fiddler is an extremely valuable debugging tool. I use it to troubleshoot all kinds of connection issues—from report node configuration to Integration Broker. You can download Fiddler from www.fiddler2.com/.

To view SSL-encrypted communication, you will need to configure Fiddler to pretend to be the server receiving the SSL request. Open Fiddler and choose Tools | Fiddler Options from the Fiddler menu bar.

Switch to the HTTPS tab and select the Decrypt HTTPS Traffic checkbox. When prompted to Trust the Fiddler Root certificate, select No. Selecting Yes will add this bogus certificate to your trusted certificate store and could pose a significant security risk. Figure 12-12 shows the Fiddler Options dialog for HTTPS.

When configured to decrypt HTTPS traffic, Fiddler will receive SSL CONNECT requests and present its own certificate. Any application receiving this certificate will know it is untrusted and will automatically generate an error. PTF, in fact, will accept Fiddler's certificate only if you enable Allow Untrusted SSL within PTF's online options. After Fiddler negotiates a secure connection with the client, it logs the request and then plays the client role, connecting to the destination server using SSL as if Fiddler were the real client.

Next, while still viewing Fiddler's options, switch to the Connections tab. The Connections tab specifies the port Fiddler uses to listen for proxy requests. Look for the box labeled Fiddler Listens On Port and make note of the port number. The default is port 8888.

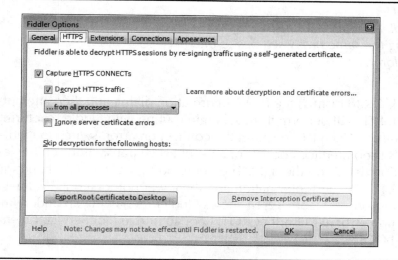

**FIGURE 12-12.** *Fiddler Options dialog*

After configuring Fiddler, launch PTF and configure it to use Fiddler as the proxy server by enabling the Use Proxy option, and then selecting the Proxy Information link. If Fiddler is running on your local workstation, enter the server name **localhost** and the port on which Fiddler listens (usually 8888). Figure 12-13 shows the Proxy Information dialog.

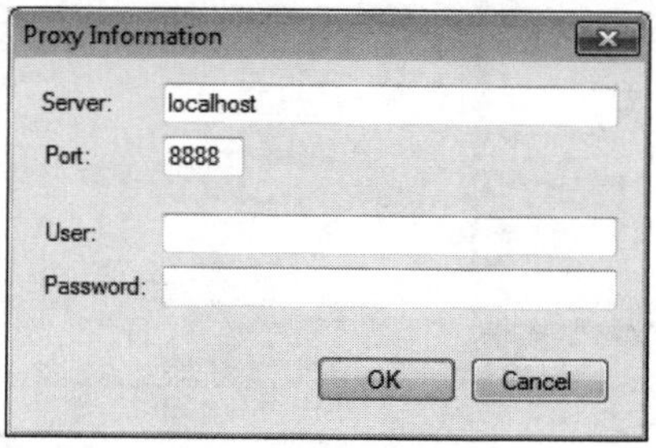

**FIGURE 12-13.** *PTF Proxy Information dialog*

**NOTE**
*Fiddler connects to upstream proxy servers using the same proxy settings as Internet Explorer.*

Click OK to dismiss the Proxy Information dialog and then attempt to connect. PTF will perform its usual login routine with Fiddler capturing all of the traffic. When PTF displays the connection error, switch to Fiddler. Fiddler's user interface consists of a list of HTTP transactions on the left and transaction details on the right. The upper portion of the right-hand frame contains PTF request information and the lower portion contains Integration Broker responses. Figure 12-14 shows Fiddler identifying an underlying connection error as "UserID CROTH not authorized for Service Operation PTTST_LOGIN."

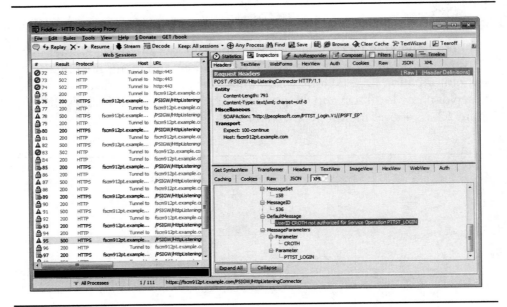

**FIGURE 12-14.** *Fiddler analysis window*

**TIP**
*Fiddler automatically updates your web
browsers to run all traffic through Fiddler. You
can pause browser logging by removing the
checkmark next to the File | Capture Traffic
menu item. Fiddler will continue to log all
traffic for applications specifically configured
to use Fiddler, such as PTF.*

The following is a list of connection errors and potential solutions:

- **User password failed. (158,45)**   Either the user ID or the password
  is incorrect.

- **UserID XYZ not authorized for Service Operation PTTST_LOGIN**   User
  XYZ is not a member of one of the three PTF roles.

- **Https required for Service Operation PTTST_CONFIG**   Network
  configuration issue. SSL termination occurs before Integration Broker.

# Execution Profiles

Execution profiles (also known as execution options) tell PTF how to connect
to the system under test. PTF stores execution profiles within the database to
which the session is connected. Each database may have several execution
profiles. All PTF users connecting to that server may share these profiles.
Because the information contained within an execution profile is potentially
sensitive in nature, only PTF Administrators may update the profiles.

   To create an execution profile, look for the very first menu item in the
PeopleSoft Test Framework menu bar. The menu item is named after the
Connection profile name used to connect to PTF. Since I named my
profile FSCM 9.1 UAT, my menu item is named FSCM 9.1 UAT. From
this menu item, select Execution Options. Click the Insert button in the
upper-right corner of the dialog to create a new execution profile.

## General Options

As shown in Figure 12-15, each execution profile identifies the target system, the application user credentials, a process scheduler server, as well as miscellaneous runtime options.

**NOTE**
*As with any PeopleSoft password, execution profile passwords are stored and transported as encrypted strings.*

When you're naming an execution profile, create a name that identifies the target system as well as the application user. This will assist PTF users in selecting the correct profile. Additionally, profile names may not contain the following characters: &, ?, /, \, *, ', ", or spaces.

Unlike the PTF connection URL, the Execution Option Application URL may be HTTP or HTTPS. Although its use is strongly encouraged, SSL is not

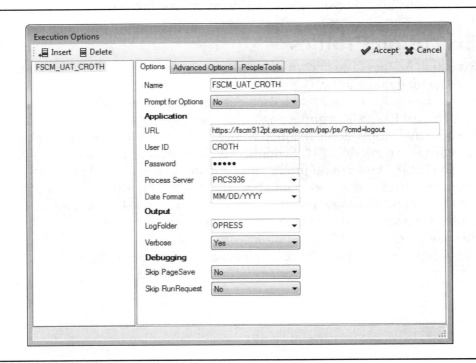

**FIGURE 12-15.** *Execution Options dialog*

required. Potentially sensitive information may pass between the client and server while a test is being performed.

The Execution Options dialog also allows an administrator to specify whether or not to save a component or submit a process run request. When these options are set to Yes, a user can test transaction and run control pages without actually saving data. This allows a PTF user to repeat tests without database changes.

## Advanced Options

The Advanced Options tab allows an administrator to configure multiple portals (EMPLOYEE, CUSTOMER, SUPPLIER, and so on) for a test. A supply chain test, for example, may use both the EMPLOYEE and the SUPPLIER portals.

The Advanced Options tab also allows an administrator to specify whether or not the execution profile supports persistent variables. Figure 12-16 shows an execution profile's Advanced Options dialog.

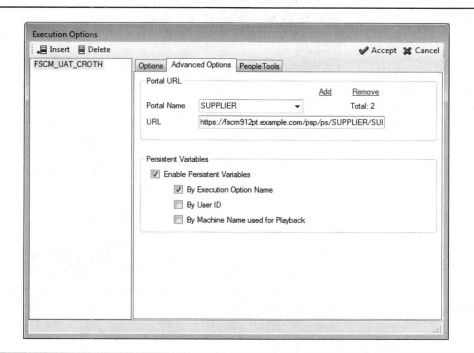

**FIGURE 12-16.** *Advanced Options dialog*

## PeopleTools Options

Switch to the PeopleTools tab and enter information about your local workstation. PeopleTools options are used by a small number of tests. Changing these options requires the PTF Administrator role to prevent PTF users from selecting databases and PS_HOME configurations that administrators have not approved. Figure 12-17 shows the PeopleTools tab.

## Maintaining Execution Profiles Online

A PTF Administrator can maintain most Execution Profile options online by navigating to PeopleTools | Lifecycle Tools | Test Framework | Define Execution Options. From this component, an administrator can maintain all options except passwords.

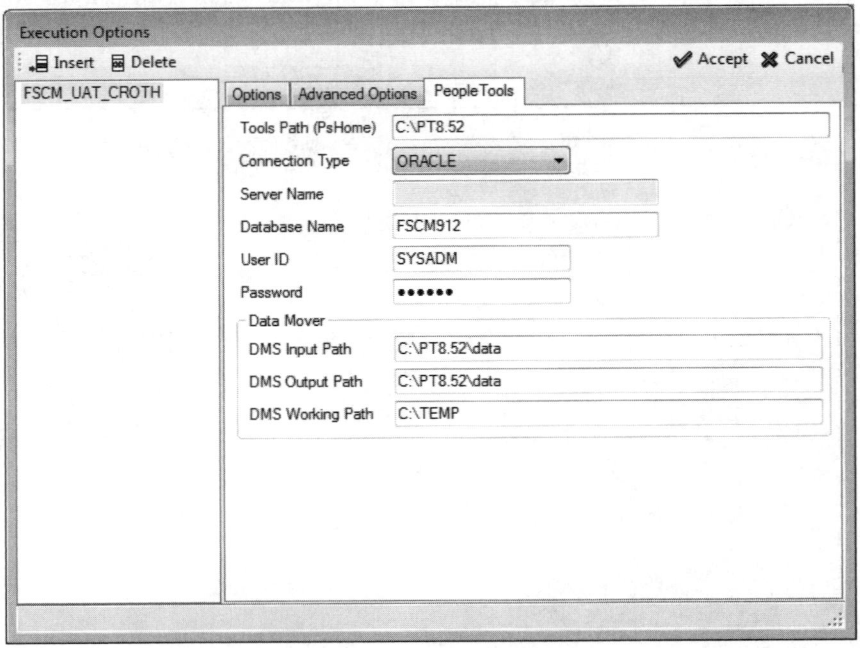

**FIGURE 12-17.** *PeopleTools tab*

# Creating a Test

With PTF configured, we can create a test. The test we will create inserts the PTF User role into a user profile and then confirms this change. This test will use the FSCM_UAT_CROTH execution profile we created earlier.

Figure 12-18 shows the PTF Application window showing the PTF Explorer. The server I'm using has no test cases, so the PTF Explorer is empty. Nevertheless, the Explorer does contain a single folder named myFolder, which is a special folder that contains tests created by and visible only to the logged-in user. Even members of the PTF User role can create and maintain tests in myFolder. Since this is just a sample, we will create our new test within myFolder.

## Create a Folder

PTF stores tests, test cases, and logs within a folder. Select myFolder from the PTF Explorer and then choose Create | Folder from the PTF menu bar. Name the new folder ADD_ROLE_TO_USER. As with execution profile names, folder names may not contain spaces, &, ?, /, \, *, ', or ". Figure 12-19 shows the new folder within PTF Explorer.

## Create a Test

To create the test, select the ADD_ROLE_TO_USER node within myFolder. Choose Create | Test from the PTF menu bar. PTF will display a new, empty test editor window (Figure 12-20).

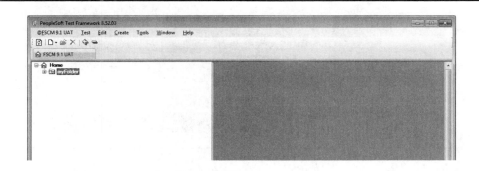

**FIGURE 12-18.** *PTF Application window showing the PTF Explorer*

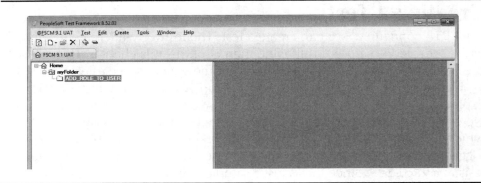

**FIGURE 12-19.** *PTF Explorer with a new folder*

## Record Test

Open the test recorder by selecting Test I Open Test Recorder from the PTF menu bar. The PTF Recorder toolbar will appear (Figure 12-21).

From the Recorder toolbar, click the Home button. When you move your mouse over the button, the Recorder toolbar's status bar will display the text, "Start web client and go to the default URL." The default URL is the URL identified in the execution options as the application URL.

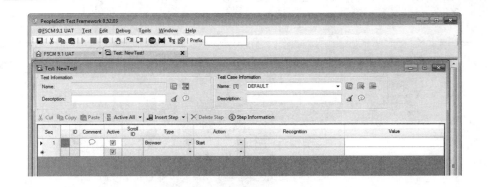

**FIGURE 12-20.** *New PTF test*

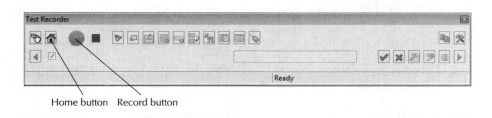

Home button   Record button

**FIGURE 12-21.**   *Recorder toolbar in Test Recorder*

When PTF is ready to record, the right side of the status bar will contain the text, "Ready." If it displays the text "Browser not hooked," it means PTF is not able to record actions within Internet Explorer. If the status bar says, "Ready," you can click the Record button. The recorder listens for changes within the state of PeopleSoft pages and records those changes. Figure 12-22 shows the Recorder toolbar while a test is being recorded.

**NOTE**
*PTF will display the message "Browser not hooked" if you are using Windows 7, have User Account Controls enabled, and did not launch PTF as an administrator. To fix this issue, run PTF as an administrator.*

With the recorder running, switch to Internet Explorer and log in. The Recorder toolbar will display each action and each changed value. Notice that the Recorder toolbar displays an encrypted password rather than the plaintext password.

Verify button

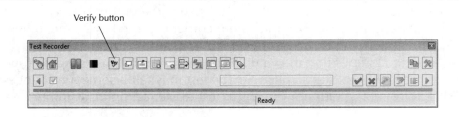

**FIGURE 12-22.**   *Recorder toolbar while recording a test*

Complete the following actions:

1. Navigate to PeopleTools | Security | User Profiles | User Profiles.

2. Open a user profile. Since I am using the FSCM demo database, I chose AERICKSON.

3. Switch to the Roles tab.

4. Add a new row to the User Roles scroll area.

5. Enter the role name **PTF User**.

6. Save the component.

7. Return to the User Profile search page and reopen the User Profile you were just editing.

8. Find the PTF User role within the User Roles scroll area.

9. Drag the Verify button from the Recorder toolbar over the PTF User value. This will add a Verify step to the test case to confirm that the PTF User role exists within the user's list of available roles.

10. Log out.

11. Click the Stop button in the Recorder toolbar.

Your test case should look something like Figure 12-23. Save the test case as ADD_ROLE_TO_USER.

## Clean the Recorded Test

We have now satisfied our initial requirements: Create a test that adds the PTF User role to AERICKSON and verify the results. At this very moment, this snapshot in time, the test works exactly as recorded. As recorded, the test makes some assumptions that may change and aren't necessary for successful execution. For example, the recorder captured every menu item click. The underlying assumption is that the menu will never change. The test also assumes that the value PTF User will exist in a specific row number of the User Roles scroll area. The test may fail if someone changes AERICKSON's roles. Our objective is to test existence, not row number.

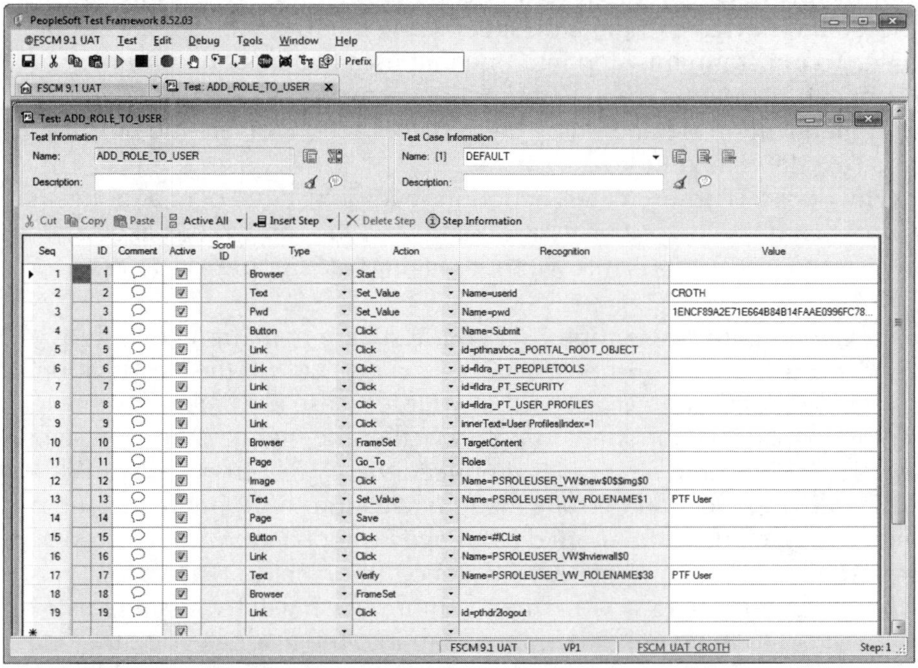

**FIGURE 12-23.** *Test case*

The test contains one more significant flaw: It recorded the username and password entered when logging into PeopleSoft. My concern is not the presence of the password, because it is encrypted. The problem is that the test case is supposed to run using the Execution Profile credentials, not credentials hard-coded into the test case. Let's fix these issues: credentials, navigation, and scroll handling, as well as other issues we identify while cleansing the test case.

**Dynamic Authentication**    Our test case should run using the credentials specified within the selected Execution Profile, not as the user specified while recording the test case. The first step in the test case editor has a Type of Browser and an Action of Start. Valid Type values include Browser, Link, Button, Text, as well as several others. The Browser value tells PTF to perform a Browser action. The Start action tells PTF to launch Internet Explorer and navigate to the URL specified within the selected Execution Profile. To transform this step into one that uses the Execution Profile's authentication options, change the Action from Start to Start_Login. Now that authentication is handled by the browser action, delete the next three steps: Text, Pwd, and Button.

Why does PTF insert a Start action instead of a Start_Login action? The answer: flexibility. If your system is configured for anonymous access, you may want to test components without logging into PeopleSoft.

**Direct Component Navigation**    If your test case contains active steps that have `id=pthnavbca_PORTAL_ROOT_OBJECT` in the Recognition column, then odds are very good that your test case uses menus to navigate to components. It is important to note whether the menu navigation steps are active. With some recordings, I noticed that PTF correctly identifies the target component and inserts menu navigation steps, but marks them as inactive, preferring the more direct Page/Prompt action. If PTF properly inserted a Page/Prompt action with Recognition set to `MAINTAIN_SECURITY.USERMAINT.GBL`, then your test case will bypass menus and go direct to the component. If you fall into the first category, the one without a Page/Prompt action, then identify the first row containing `id=pthnavbca_PORTAL_ROOT_OBJECT`. If you deleted the extraneous credential information, this step should be the second step. Change the Type column value to Page and the Action to Prompt. In the Recognition column, enter **`MAINTAIN_SECURITY.USERMAINT.GBL`**. This represents the menu, component, and market of the target component. Enter **`update`** in the value column. We want PTF to navigate to the component's search page in update mode as opposed to add or correct history mode. Delete the remaining Link rows that identify the component's menu navigation path.

**Correct Search Page Handling**    A search page allows a user to find and select a specific transaction. Identifying a transaction usually involves entering information into search keys, clicking the search button, and then selecting a particular row from the search results. Unless you are testing a search page, configure your test case to use Level 0 search keys and to use the Page/PromptOk action instead of the `#ICSearch` Button/Click action. In this test case, the `#ICSearch` button immediately follows the AERICKSON row (the fourth row). For that #ICSearch row, change the Type to Page and the Action to PromptOk. Delete the value in the Recognition column.

**Returning to a Search Page**    When recording the test, we clicked the Return To Search button to reload the AERICKSON user profile. PTF recorded that Return to Search action as a #ICList button click. This is acceptable, but we can do better. We don't actually want to return to the search results. Rather, we want to relaunch the component as if performing a brand new search. Change the #ICList row to a Page/Prompt action that navigates to MAINTAIN_SECURITY.USERMAINT.GBL in update mode (just like the initial navigation).

Depending on how PTF recorded your test, the row following the #ICList row contains either a Page/PromptOk action or a Link/Click action. Regardless of the current action, change it to a Text/Set_Value action. Set the Recognition field to Name=PSOPRDEFN_SRCH_OPRID and enter **AERICKSON** into the value field. We want to perform the same sequence as our initial search.

Add a new row just below the Text/Set_Value row you just edited. Set the Type to Page and select PromptOk for the Action.

Insert a Page/Go_To action immediately following the Page/PromptOK action. Set the Recognition field to Roles. This action tells PTF to switch to the Roles tab within the component.

**Scroll Handling**    The Text/Verify action within our test case expects to find the value PTF User in row 38. As previously mentioned, that may or may not be the correct location. The test's only stated requirement is that PTF User exist within the User Roles scroll area. Whether it is in row 38 is irrelevant.

We just finished configuring the Return to Search behavior. The step immediately following the Return to Search and Page/Go_To Roles steps is an Image/Click step that commands PTF to click the View All link within the User Roles scroll area. We clicked this link while recording the test case to view row 38. Effective scroll handling does not require this step. Replace the existing Image/Click action with a Scroll/Key_Set action. Make the following changes to the Scroll/Key_Set row:

- Set the Scroll ID column to 1.

- Change the Recognition field to Type=Text;Name=PSROLEUSER_ VW_ROLENAME.

- Set the Value field to PTF User.

The Scroll/Key_Set action configures PTF to perform a scroll-based key search. When creating your own scroll searches, be sure to create a row for each key within the Scroll area.

Insert a row immediately following the Scroll/Key_Set row and configure it as follows:

- Set the Scroll ID to 1.

- Set Type to Scroll.

- Set Action to Action.

- Enter `ret=&Scroll1` into the Recognition field.

- Enter `sel` into the Value field.

This new row commands PTF to execute the key-based search that we configured through the Scroll/Key_Set steps. The phrase `ret=&Scroll1` tells PTF to place the return value of the selection action (the row's index) in a variable named `&Scroll1`.

The final step is to configure the Text/Verify step to use the row identified by the Scroll/Action row. The row immediately following the Scroll/Action row should have a Recognition value of `Name=PSROLEUSER_ VW_ROLENAME$`*xx*, where *xx* represents a row number. Change the Recognition field to this: `Name=PSROLEUSER_VW_ROLENAME&Scroll1`.

The recorded test case initially contained 22 steps. After cleanup, we are down to 18 steps. Figure 12-24 shows the updated PTF test case.

## Run a Test

Run the test by choosing Test | Run from the PTF menu bar. PTF will launch Internet Explorer and run through each of the recorded steps. Upon completion, PTF will open the test execution log for review. Confirm that the result field contains the text "Pass." If it doesn't, review the log for errors, resolve any issues, and then rerun the test. Figure 12-25 shows part of the execution log.

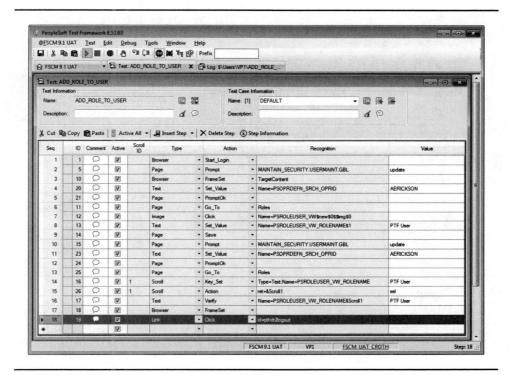

**FIGURE 12-24.** *Updated PTF test case*

**TIP**

*Does your site have a lot of test cases and nested test hierarchies? When communicating with colleagues, rather than sending the navigation path, right-click the test case and chose Copy Link To Clipboard. Send the clipboard contents to your coworker, instructing him or her to paste the contents into the Quick Open dialog available by choosing the Window | Quick Open PTF menu item.*

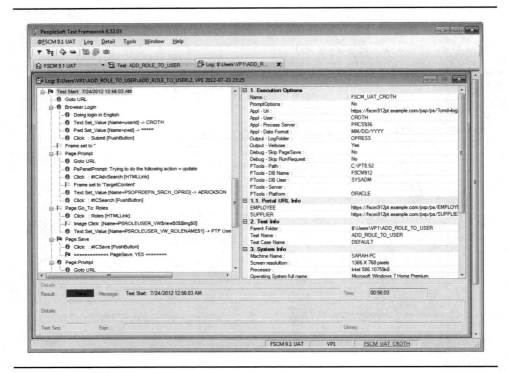

**FIGURE 12-25.** *Test case execution log*

## Stop on Error

If we attempt to rerun the ADD_ROLE_TO_USER test case, PTF will insert the role PTF User a second time. This insertion will generate a unique constraint error when PTF attempts to save the component. We can avoid this problem by raising an error if the PTF User role exists and configuring PTF to stop when it encounters an error. To determine whether the role already exists, locate the first Page/Go_To action and insert two rows below that action. In the first row, do the following:

- Set the Scroll ID to 1.
- Change the Type to Scroll.

- Select the Action of Key_Set.
- Enter a Recognition of **Type=Text;Name=PSROLEUSER_VW_ ROLENAME**.
- Set the Value field to **PTF User**.

In the second row, do the following:

- Set the Scroll ID to 1.
- Change the Type to Scroll.
- Select the Action of Action.
- Enter a Recognition of **&ret=&Scroll1**.
- Set the Value field to **not**.

Before running the test, choose Debug | Stop on Error from the PTF menu bar. Now when the test runs, it will exit if AERICKSON already has the PTF User role. Figure 12-26 shows the modified test case.

**NOTE**
*Rather than expecting each user to configure Stop on Error, run the test from a shell test and add an Execution/StopOnError step.*

# Reviewing Logs

PTF creates and retains logs of important test case information. PTF's log viewer presents this information in a graphical hierarchy showing the status of each step within a test case. The first step in our ADD_ROLE_TO_USER test case, for example, contains the action Browser/Start_Login. PTF's log viewer expands this step into two hierarchical branches in a tree, the login having multiple child branches. Each node within the tree contains an icon

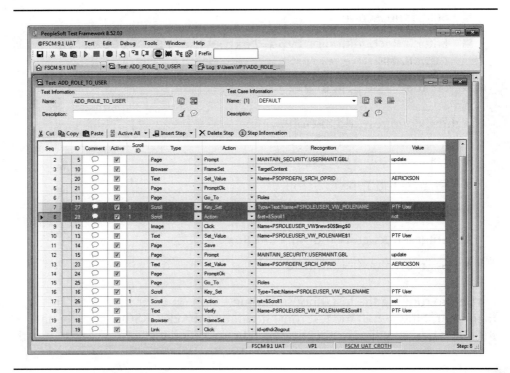

**FIGURE 12-26.** *Test case that uses the not action*

depicting the step's execution status. This icon makes it visually easy to identify errors within a PTF log.

When a script fails, PTF records a screenshot of the active page and saves it with the offending action in the test execution log. You may view the screenshot at any time by double-clicking the LogScreenShot node within PTF's log viewer. Figure 12-27 shows a log with three separate executions, each with a different result: a script failure, a success, and a step failure.

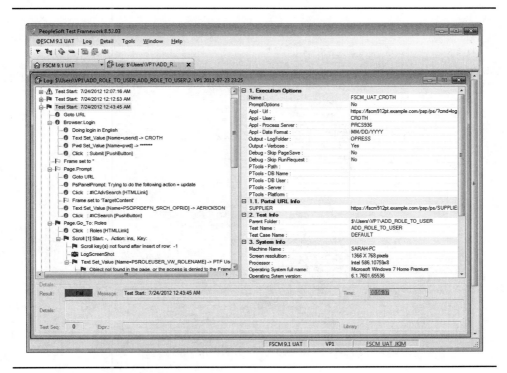

**FIGURE 12-27.**   *PTF log viewer*

# Using PTF to Verify and Reset Configurations after Upgrade

After upgrading, you may find that a patch contains information that overwrites site-specific configurations. For example, a patch that includes node configuration changes may overwrite the Default User ID of the WSDL_NODE. We can record a simple PTF test case to verify this type of configuration reset and run that test after applying maintenance. Figure 12-28 shows a simple eight-step test that verifies the Default User ID of the WSDL_NODE.

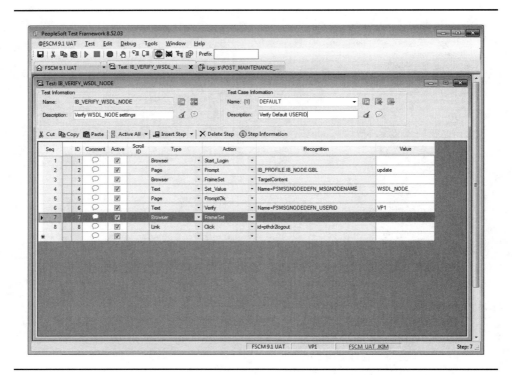

**FIGURE 12-28.** *WSDL_NODE validation test*

Using conditionals, we can configure this test and actually change the value of the WSDL_NODE if PTF discovers the value is incorrect. Figure 12-29 shows the altered test case. Notice that the test case performs a save using Integration Broker's custom save button and then performs a Verify step to confirm the results.

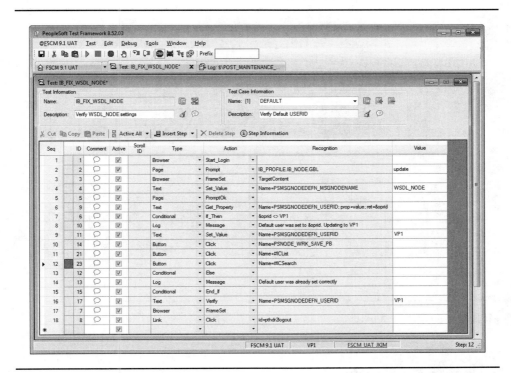

**FIGURE 12-29.** *Test case that resets the WSDL_NODE*

Saving an Integration Broker definition displays a Save confirmation dialog. Configuring Message Recognition allows PTF to respond to such dialogs. To access Message Recognition, click the second button to the right of the test name—the icon with a green checkmark. Figure 12-30 shows the Message Recognition dialog for the WSDL_NODE reset test case.

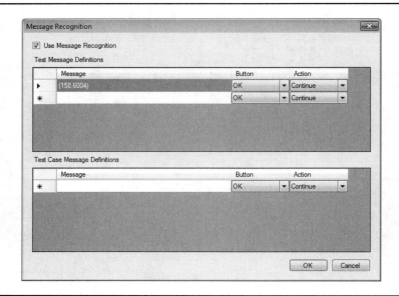

**FIGURE 12-30.** *Message Recognition dialog*

# Library Tests

A *library* is a reusable test case fragment. As you develop tests and recognize common patterns, you can extract those patterns into test libraries. Test libraries allow test editors to adhere to the Don't Repeat Yourself (DRY) software development best practice. The DRY principle simplifies tests by minimizing the amount of steps per test and reduces test maintenance by centralizing common actions.

Create a test library as you would any other test. To designate the test as a library, open the test's properties and check the box labeled Library Test. Optionally, enter any parameters other tests should pass to this test. Figure 12-31 shows a library test that copies the default Workflow Operator ID into a variable for use by other tests.

Call a PTF library by inserting a Test/Exec action step into your PTF test case. When inserting a test library, PTF will add an ellipsis (...) button to the Recognition field. Click the button to select a library and test case, or type the library name into the Recognition field and enter the test case name into the Value field. For tests that contain parameters, enter them in the Recognition field along with the library name using this format:

```
OP_DEF_WORKFLOW_OPRID_LIB;FirstName=Jim;Spouse=Sarah;Children=3
```

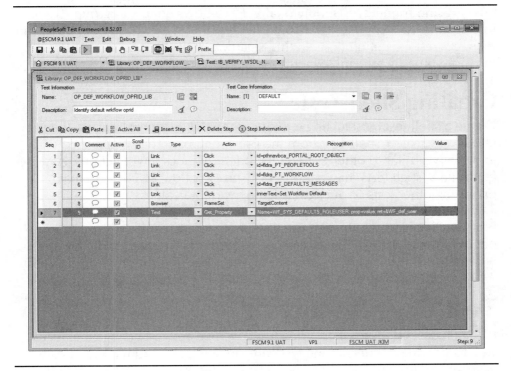

**FIGURE 12-31.**   *Example PTF library test*

Do not include spaces after the semicolons. A library designed to use parameters references them in Recognition and Value fields using the syntax `%param.FirstName%`.

When calling a library, make sure you understand its runtime context and place the library within your test case accordingly. For example, if you create a test case that verifies a page value against a library's variable and the library requires navigation, call the library first. Likewise, when writing libraries, consider and document the runtime context. If a library includes navigation, note this in the comments.

# Automated Test Suites

PTF attempts to emulate the online user experience: entering data, clicking buttons, pausing for results, and so on. A test pretty much consumes the workstation (or remote desktop session) of the logged-in user. Rather than opening and running tests individually, PTF allows editors to group PTF tests into *shell tests*. A shell test is a controller test that sets execution options and manages test execution flow. In this regard, a shell test is synonymous with the more broadly recognized term *test suite*.

## Creating Shell Tests

Create a shell test by selecting a folder in the PTF Explorer tree and then choosing Create | Shell Test from the PTF menu bar. The shell test editor looks very similar to other test editors, but it includes fewer actions. As controllers, shell tests may perform only process flow actions, such as executing other tests or queries or setting variable values.

When you are creating shell tests to serve as traditional test suites, the best practice is to create each test as an autonomous unit, logging in and out of the browser within each test. Alternatively, shell tests may comprise multiple test case libraries, acting as a test case composition or orchestrator.

# Test Case Reporting

PTF includes reports for identifying test coverage and test change impact as well as viewing test details and test comparisons. A PTF administrator can access these reports from the PeopleTools | Lifecycle Tools | Test Framework navigation. Of particular note are the coverage and change impact reports. Both of these reports search for tests related to project definitions. The coverage report identifies items within a project that are not "covered" by tests—which means those items are not tested. The change impact report identifies tests that may be affected by a change project. For example, if a change project removes a component from a menu, Page/Prompt actions using that menu/component combination will fail.

# Conclusion

In this chapter you learned how to record, modify, and run PTF tests. Follow all the normal best practices when writing tests. Most important, *Primum non nocere*: First, do no harm. Next time someone in your organization performs functional testing, instead of running that test from a printed script in a notebook, record the test. Recording the test will help your organization build a test library and reduce your standard functional testing effort.

# CHAPTER
## 13

# Upgrade Tips
# and Techniques

ince you are reading this book, you or someone you know has probably been through an enterprise software implementation. It is no secret that software implementations are difficult. You don't have to look far to find tombstones in the software implementation graveyard!

Upgrades are difficult as well. In a sense, an upgrade is a micro-reimplementation. Upgrades provide an organization the opportunity to change the way they do business or make another pass at aligning software with internal business processes. The way your organization does business should be part of its strategic advantage. You want your software to move your organization toward that strategic advantage.

When you know the location of a dangerous section of road, you can act accordingly. This chapter is full of warning signs. We mark the hazardous sections of the upgrade road map, and, whenever possible, point out an alternative, shorter route.

From the Oracle Support web site, a customer can download a 300-page upgrade guide containing step-by-step instructions for performing an application- and version-specific upgrade. Although the high-level steps involved in an upgrade remain the same across PeopleSoft applications, upgrade details and complexity differ widely. For example, the "Human Capital Management (HCM) 9.0 to 9.1" upgrade guide contains nearly 400 pages, whereas the Enterprise Portal upgrade guide is about 300 pages. Not only do upgrade steps differ by application, but also by version. The steps required to upgrade an HCM 8.9 system to 9.1 differ from those required to upgrade HCM 9.0 to 9.1. Because PeopleSoft installations vary widely among customers, it is impossible to write a standard, "one size fits all" upgrade guide. Given the number of hardware and software configurations available to a customer, it would be difficult to identify a "standard" installation.

Using this chapter to detail all of the steps required for an upgrade would be akin to software malpractice. A complete upgrade reference manual could easily fill 800 pages. Rather than attempt to document every possible step based on an ever-changing and unknown environment, this chapter highlights some tips to help you perform a successful upgrade.

# Planning the Upgrade

Your upgrade will be about as unique as your fingerprint. Each customer implements PeopleSoft a little differently. One customer may use Microsoft's SQL Server on 32-bit Windows, whereas another may implement the same PeopleSoft application on DB2 UDB for z/OS. In this section, you will learn about important considerations for planning an upgrade.

# Upgrade Types

PeopleSoft customers perform two types of upgrades: PeopleTools upgrades and application upgrades.

### PeopleTools Upgrade

A PeopleTools upgrade is usually easier than an application upgrade. PeopleTools upgrades rarely change the application's appearance or behavior. This is because PeopleTools upgrades include new features, but no physical implementations of those features. It is entirely possible to upgrade PeopleTools without functional users even noticing the change. Likewise, PeopleTools upgrades are simpler because they rarely touch customer-modified definitions, so there is little customization rework. Because PeopleTools upgrades do not change application behavior, testing requirements are minimal in comparison to an application upgrade.

A PeopleTools upgrade can become complex if the upgrade requires architecture changes, such as 32-bit to 64-bit migration, operating system upgrades, and so on. For example, migrating a database from 32-bit to 64-bit hardware may require a full database export and import.

I prefer small, incremental adjustments over dramatic changes. It is easier to identify the cause of a new error when you're making small changes. Furthermore, small changes usually require shorter system outages. The more you attempt to accomplish within an outage window, the less margin available for error.

Stay current with PeopleTools and system infrastructure. With all prerequisites met, an administrator can easily apply a PeopleTools upgrade over a weekend.

## Application Upgrade

An application upgrade is a lot more complicated than a PeopleTools upgrade. Application upgrades often include changes to existing business processes as well as the addition of new business processes. These changes require a significant amount of functional testing and end user change management.

Application upgrades are further complicated by the fact that they usually require PeopleTools upgrades. PeopleSoft applications always require a minimum PeopleTools version—usually the version released closest to the application's release date. This is because new application features require PeopleTools enhancements. For example, Human Capital Management (HCM) 9.1 Feature Pack 2 included new operational dashboards. HCM 9.1 Feature Pack 2 required a minimum PeopleTools version of 8.52 because prior versions of PeopleTools did not include the features necessary to build those dashboards, specifically header pagelets and pagelet icons. When planning an application upgrade, ensure that your PeopleTools release is certified for the target application release. If it isn't certified, you will need to include a PeopleTools upgrade in your application upgrade plan.

# Upgrade Timeframe

The amount of time required for an upgrade varies widely by customer. I upgraded an HCM 9.0 application that was running PeopleTools 8.49 to HCM 9.1 FP2 running PeopleTools 8.52.06 over a weekend. I performed this upgrade against a small, vanilla HCM system requiring no hardware changes. The average HCM upgrade, however, requires six to nine months. The Financial/Supply Change Management upgrade averages nine to twelve months. The following factors influence the time required for an upgrade:

- Amount of data to convert
- Number of customizations to merge into the upgrade
- Number and complexity of integrations
- Availability of resources (testing, development, and so on)
- Training and documentation (organization change management)
- Patching and maintenance cycles during the upgrade
- Multipass migration requirements

- Software prerequisites

- Hardware changes

Let's review each of these factors in detail.

## Amount of Data to Convert

Application upgrades often include data conversion routines. The larger your data set, the longer these routines run. Through hardware and SQL tuning, you may be able to shorten conversion runtime, but the amount of time spent optimizing the conversion will likely be greater than the amount of time gained from the optimization. Nevertheless, optimization is often required to make conversion programs complete within the allotted production upgrade downtime.

Another very important optimization technique is to reduce the amount of data prior to performing an upgrade. As demonstrated in Chapter 4, Data Archive Manager is a valuable tool that can reduce the volume of transactions within your PeopleSoft system. Keep in mind that pre-upgrade data structures may not match post-upgrade table definitions. It may not be possible to restore from an archive without also performing a conversion against history tables. Considering that archived data is not accessible from PeopleSoft transaction pages, a history table data conversion can be run after the upgrade go-live date.

## Number of Customizations to Merge into the Upgrade

It is very common for an initial PeopleSoft implementation to contain a significant number of customizations designed to align PeopleSoft with an organization's business model. Oftentimes these customizations are based on the customer's perception of PeopleSoft and an implementation consultant's understanding of the customer's business. With use, a customer will often discover a configuration that satisfies a business requirement.

An upgrade is an excellent time to evaluate customizations. The upgrade process will overwrite customizations, requiring you to reapply any customizations you intend to keep. An upfront customization evaluation will save valuable time in customization rework. Here is a list of a few customizations that you may no longer require:

- Business process changes you can implement through configuration

- Customizations requested at implementation, but never used

- Features you implemented through customization that are now part of the delivered product

## Number and Complexity of Integrations

PeopleSoft applications participate in a much larger enterprise software ecosystem. You may have to change integration code to align existing integrations with changes to transactions and data structures.

## Availability of Resources

Upgrades require labor: performing upgrades, applying customizations, testing transactions, and so on. Generally speaking, increasing the number of people dedicated to an upgrade project will shorten the overall upgrade project duration. Trying to manage a normal workload while performing functional testing can jeopardize a project.

## Training and Documentation

By definition, an upgrade involves change: new features, streamlined business processes, and so on. It is very likely that your organization created step-by-step user guides that an upgrade will invalidate. Likewise, these changes may require additional functional user training.

## Patching and Maintenance Cycles During Upgrade

When planning your upgrade, you will pick a target release version. For example, if you currently have HCM 8.9 installed, you may target HCM 9.1. If HCM 9.2 releases two months into your upgrade, will you switch to the newer target release? What about bundles, maintenance packs, and feature packs? Generally speaking, it is best to avoid all but necessary maintenance until after going live on an upgraded system.

## Multipass Migration Requirements

A customer applying an upgrade usually chooses the latest version available. Depending on your current version, however, you may not be able to perform a direct upgrade. For example, if your HCM release version is 8.3 and you would like to be using 9.1, you will first have to upgrade to 8.9 and then perform a second upgrade to 9.1.

## Software Prerequisites

Application upgrades often require PeopleTools upgrades, and a PeopleTools upgrade may require a newer version of your operating system, database, WebLogic, Tuxedo, or any number of software components.

When planning an application upgrade, be sure to allow time for a PeopleTools and infrastructure upgrade. To ensure maximum system stability, I recommend incremental changes. In regard to PeopleTools upgrades, an incremental change approach would involve breaking the entire upgrade process into smaller architecture changes, such as applying a Tuxedo upgrade to your current PeopleTools version. After each of the software and architecture prerequisites is working in your current PeopleTools version, perform a PeopleTools upgrade. Depending on the gap between your current PeopleTools version and your target release, you may have to upgrade everything as a single unit. Newer versions of prerequisite software may not be compatible with older versions of PeopleTools.

The alternative to small, incremental changes is to upgrade every piece of a PeopleSoft application and its corresponding infrastructure at once; this is known as the *Big Bang* approach (http://en.wikipedia.org/wiki/Big_bang_ adoption). This type of upgrade is risky, but if successful, it can reduce overall upgrade costs. If not successful, the Big Bang approach can exponentially increase costs. The approach is risky because an organization cannot gauge the project's success rate until go-live. Furthermore, the Big Bang contains no natural early termination points. The incremental approach allows a team to reevaluate future direction at each milestone. If a team chooses to forgo the remainder of an upgrade project, that team can claim each prior milestone as a success. The Big Bang team, on the other hand, has nothing unless the project completes on time and on budget.

## Hardware Changes

Oracle certifies and decertifies hardware for PeopleTools based on hardware manufacturer support policies and software requirements. For example, PeopleTools releases 8.50 to 8.52 included more 64-bit software prerequisites. Prior to 8.50, a customer could run PeopleSoft on either 32-bit or 64-bit hardware. As of 8.50, PeopleTools is certified for 64-bit hardware only. If your application upgrade requires a PeopleTools upgrade, be sure to check the target PeopleTools hardware requirements.

Also, be sure to include enough computing resources for at least one "copy of production" system when planning hardware changes. Likewise, include enough space to accommodate backups at various stages of the upgrade.

# Upgrade Team

An upgrade often requires a significant investment in talented technical and functional labor. Technical team members apply upgrades, customize the system, and create integrations. Functional team members identify requirements, apply configurations, and make implementation decisions. All members should be flexible and willing to adapt to change during this exciting process. This is a challenging but worthwhile endeavor with great rewards ahead.

An upgrade team often consists of the following roles.

## Upgrade Project Manager

The upgrade project manager is responsible for timelines, budgets, status reports, and the overall upgrade big picture. He or she should have a functional and technical understanding of the PeopleSoft product. Patience and a great sense of humor are also helpful. This person often sets the tone for the entire project.

## Technical Resources

Upgrade technical staff must be familiar with PeopleSoft upgrades, database systems, SQL, PeopleTools, Change Assistant, Data Management Tools, and Application Engine.

## Database Administrator

The DBA position may require either a part-time or full-time employee. A DBA assists technical staff in reviewing scripts, performing backups, and troubleshooting and tuning the database.

### Network/System Administrator

The network and system administrator role is often a part-time position. This member manages network security and connectivity, often providing valuable network architecture recommendations.

### Developers

A project's PeopleSoft developers must be familiar with your organization's customizations and how those customizations will affect an upgrade. Developers should have experience in SQR, COBOL, PeopleTools, Application Engine, and PeopleCode. These members are responsible for reapplying customizations during the upgrade process.

### Functional Resources

Functional members represent the broader user community. Functional members should be experts within their modules, with a full understanding of module configuration options. These experts establish the testing strategy used to test the upgraded system. They must acquire knowledge regarding changes introduced with the upgrade, which allows them to create appropriate test cases and documentation for coworkers.

### Executive Sponsor

Although not required, an executive sponsor from your organization's senior management team adds a significant amount of value. A senior manager assists with the procurement of adequate project resources and helps communicate a common vision.

# Performing the Upgrade

Here are a few tips to simplify your upgrade.

# Creating a New Demo Database

During an upgrade, you perform a comparison between the target version's demo database and your own copy of production. This allows you to identify changes between the two releases, specifically identifying any customizations affected by an upgrade.

When performing a new PeopleSoft installation, Oracle allows for two options: create an empty database or create a database with seeded, demo transaction data. A demo database allows a customer to interact with new PeopleSoft features without performing configuration steps. A demo database contains a fully implemented, fully functional instance of a PeopleSoft application.

A few years ago, the only way to create a demo database was to perform a complete PeopleSoft installation. Then Oracle released a couple of PeopleSoft Oracle VM (OVM) templates. This allowed OVM customers to import a fully configured demo instance into Oracle's Xen-based hypervisor. These OVM templates significantly reduce the time required to create a demo instance from two days to 15 minutes. In 2012, Oracle stepped up support for OVM by releasing an OVM template for every PeopleSoft 9.1 application and updating many of them to the latest maintenance and feature packs midyear. Customer adoption of these PeopleSoft templates has been hampered by the OVM requirement. Not every customer has experience with Xen-based hypervisors or hardware available for Xen virtualization.

Don't worry, though; for those who don't use OVM, the PeopleSoft community maintains documentation that describes how to convert PeopleSoft OVM templates into Oracle VirtualBox instances that can run on any laptop, desktop, or server. You can find a list of documents on my blog at http://jjmpsj.blogspot.com/2012/08/peoplesoft-ovm-virtualbox-conversion.html.

Today you have several options for creating a demo instance:

■ Install a PeopleSoft demo instance from the Oracle provided installation media.

■ Import a PeopleSoft OVM template.

■ Convert a PeopleSoft OVM template to another virtualization platform—VirtualBox, for example.

■ Apply any combination of the above, such as install a PeopleSoft demo database from Oracle's installation media but deploy the PeopleSoft middle tier as an OVM template.

A demo instance has minimal hardware requirements. Oracle recommends a minimum of two CPUs and 4 gigabytes of RAM for a full database, application server, and web server installation. For generating an upgrade compare report, we will use the database portion of a demo configuration only.

# PeopleTools Upgrade

Unless you've kept current with PeopleTools upgrades, your application upgrade will likely require a PeopleTools upgrade. As mentioned, select a PeopleTools version certified for your target application release and ensure that your hardware is certified for the PeopleTools release. You can usually upgrade to a higher version of PeopleTools than the version required for the target application, but this can increase project risk. Some application features extend PeopleTools features. Installing a higher version of PeopleTools may require additional application patches. To reduce risk, upgrade PeopleTools to the application version's recommended PeopleTools version. After the application upgrade, apply the additional PeopleTools upgrade desired for go-live.

With a decoupled `PS_HOME`, `PS_CFG_HOME`, and `PS_APP_HOME`, a modern PeopleTools upgrade really isn't much of an upgrade. It is more like a fresh PeopleTools installation with database upgrade scripts. Oracle provides documentation detailing each step required for a PeopleTools upgrade. Rather than repeat Oracle's documentation, this section focuses on a *virtual upgrade*.

## Virtual Upgrade

The easiest way to perform a PeopleTools upgrade is to skip the installation phase. If you plan to run PeopleSoft on a 64-bit Linux operating system, then you can leverage the work of the PeopleTools OVM team. Oracle's PeopleSoft OVM templates contain the latest PeopleTools Linux 64-bit binary distribution. Rather than install PeopleTools and all of its required components, mount the OVM `TOOLS.img` disk image. The `TOOLS.img` file contains a complete Tuxedo (`TUXDIR`), WebLogic, Oracle Client (`ORACLE_HOME`), and PeopleTools (`PS_HOME`) installation.

The OVM template mounts the `TOOLS.img` disk into `/opt/oracle/psft/pt`. Depending on your architecture, you may either mount the disk directly using losetup, mount it virtually through your virtual OS media manager, convert the disk to a new format, or temporarily mount the disk so you can copy its files into a different partition.

The files within the `TOOLS.img` disk are owned by three users: root, psadm1, and psadm2. The following command listing describes the users and groups required by the `TOOLS.img` disk image. You are not required to use the same users, but you will need an understanding of file ownership so you can make the appropriate changes. It is easiest to use Oracle's recommendations. Otherwise, you will have to make the same changes for subsequent upgrades.

```
# groups
groupadd -g 505 oracle
groupadd -g 506 appinst
groupadd -g 54321 oinstall
groupadd -g 54322 dba

# users
useradd -u 54321 -g oracle oracle
useradd -u 505 -g oracle psadm1
useradd -u 506 -g oracle psadm2
useradd -u 507 -g appinst psadm3
```

Part of the reason for separating files into PS_HOME, PS_CFG_HOME, and PS_APP_HOME is to make it easy to swap application and PeopleTools files without actually performing an upgrade—sort of a virtual upgrade.

## Virtualizing the Application Upgrade

Through the use of OVM templates and PS_APP_HOME, you can virtualize a portion of the application upgrade. Just like the PeopleTools OVM template, the application OVM template includes a complete PS_APP_HOME file system that you can mount into your server's file system, giving you all of the application's updated scripts, reports, and other application-specific files.

## Adjusting Upgrade Flags

During the course of an upgrade, you will perform a compare for the purpose of copying upgraded definitions into your copy of the production system. Generally speaking, you want to apply all changes included with an upgrade. Failure to apply an Oracle-delivered change may render a portion of your system unusable. Rather than blindly apply each change, however, it is wise to review and adjust definition upgrade action and upgrade flags. You may find that the compare process set a flag to delete a definition that you intended to keep.

Considering the number of definitions included in an upgrade project, customers often apply the "divide and conquer" approach, with multiple people adjusting flags within the same project. If multiple people are working on the same change project, be very careful to avoid changing the same definition types. Application Designer's optimistic locking design will allow multiple people to view the same project, but only one user can actually save changes. Successive user save attempts will fail.

# Reconfiguring the Application

PeopleTools and application upgrades include their own configuration data. At times, upgrade configuration data will conflict with your own metadata. The remainder of this chapter identifies areas of conflict you should review prior to functional testing.

## Verify Security

Application updates include new features and functionality. These new features require security changes. Performing an upgrade may overwrite changes you have made to delivered permission lists and roles. Compare permission lists your organization has modified with your production instance and adjust the permission lists as necessary.

## Integration Broker Configurations

PeopleTools upgrades often include node and integration changes. The WSDL_NODE and ANONYMOUS nodes are examples of delivered nodes that Oracle preconfigures for internal and external integrations. Open these nodes and confirm that the node's default user ID exists within your database.

Application upgrades often replace Integration Broker service operations, handlers, and routings. Be sure to reactivate all service operations your organization uses, including PeopleSoft-to-PeopleSoft integration points.

## URL Definitions

Some application processes require URL definitions. An application upgrade will reset these URLs to generic values. Be sure to update them with values appropriate for your environment.

# Conclusion

Upgrades are difficult. They require tremendous attention to detail and a significant investment in functional testing. Several factors contribute to the complexity of an upgrade:

- Amount and complexity of modifications
- Integrations with other applications
- Architecture changes, such as hardware and database upgrades

In this chapter, you learned about many of the difficulties encountered during an upgrade as well as tips to help you successfully navigate the upgrade highway.

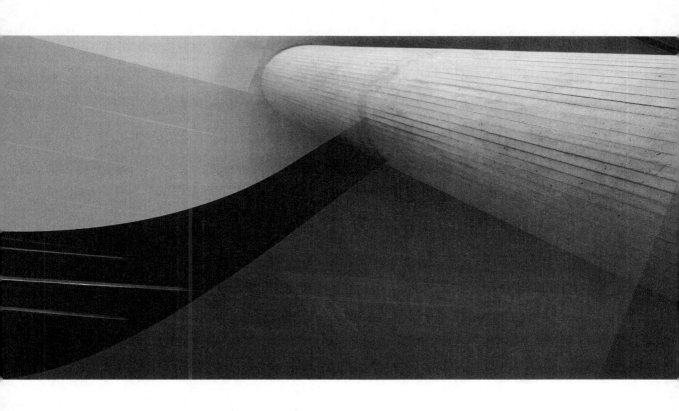

# PART
## IV
### Appendixes

# APPENDIX
## A

# Manually Applying
# Patches and Bundles

n Chapters 6 and 7 you learned how to use the Environment Management Framework (EMF) and Change Assistant to apply patches, bundles, and maintenance packs. If you are not able to use these tools within your organization, you will have to apply maintenance manually. In this appendix you will learn tips to guide you through the change package application process so you can feel comfortable applying maintenance without Change Assistant and the EMF. For smaller bundles and updates, applying maintenance manually can be faster than using Change Assistant.

# Download the Update

As you learned in Chapter 7, PeopleSoft delivers periodic maintenance updates as Zip files. Follow the manual discovery steps in Chapter 7 to identify and download updates required for your system. The download location is not important; just remember where you place them. You will run all commands yourself and will have the opportunity to update file locations accordingly.

# Extract the Update Archive

After downloading updates, unzip each file into its own directory. Since I am usually performing updates from my local workstation and have no desire to maintain those updates in my file system, I usually unzip maintenance files into subdirectories of my `c:\temp` folder. After applying maintenance, you can copy these files into a permanent storage location.

# Apply the Update

Oracle delivers everything you need, including a document detailing the steps required to apply the selected maintenance; you just have to know where to find the document.

## Identify Maintenance Documentation

All PeopleSoft maintenance archives have the prefix *upd* followed by the update ID. After expanding the archive, open the upd*xxxxxx* folder and then look for the upd*xxxxxx*_install folder. Inside that folder, you will find an HTML document named  upd*xxxxxx*_install.htm. This HTML document contains step-by-step instructions for applying the downloaded maintenance to your PeopleSoft system. For example, in Chapter 7, we applied upd860101. Inside the upd860101\upd860101_install folder is an HTML document named upd860101_install.htm containing step-by-step instructions.

## Follow the Instructions

The HTML documentation contains every step required to apply maintenance as well as many generic steps. Due to the generic nature of the documentation, some steps may not apply to your environment. Most of the documented steps describe the action Change Assistant would perform if the step was required. For example, upd860101 from Chapter 7 contains the instruction, "Step: Run Create Triggers Script," regardless of whether that applies to your maintenance on your system.

Perform each task in the order specified within the HTML documentation. I often print a copy so I can check off each step as I finish.

**CAUTION**
*Perform tasks in the order identified in the documentation. Bundles and other maintenance may include data structure changes and conversion routines. Running those conversion routines before applying data structure changes may result in database corruption.*

Unfortunately, the documentation is written from Change Assistant's perspective, telling you what Change Assistant will accomplish when performing each task. When reading the documentation, just convert the phrase "Change Assistant will" to "I will."

Pay special attention to instructions in blue text. The main text of the change package's instructions may contain several irrelevant steps. Anything in blue was intentionally inserted and requires action.

## Change Projects

Downloaded maintenance archives often include Application Designer change projects. Prior to applying a change project, run a file compare as described in Chapter 11. This will identify any modifications your site has made to delivered definitions. Note these changes so you can reapply them after importing the change project.

## Files

Most of the steps involve files: deploying files and running files. The instructions are rather generic regarding deployment locations. It is not possible for Oracle to document exact deployment locations given PeopleSoft's flexible deployment options. Change Assistant knows where to deploy files based on EMF and Change Assistant configurations. Since you are not using these tools, you will need to identify your application server, web server, file server, and process scheduler file systems including `PS_HOME`, `PS_CFG_HOME`, and `PS_APP_HOME`.

Before running Data Mover scripts, review their contents and look for file references. Often Data Mover scripts include `INPUT` and `LOG` directives as relative file paths and assume that files exist in the Data Mover input, output, and log directories (see Chapter 3 for more information). If your maintenance input files exist in a different location, be sure to update the Data Mover script accordingly.

## Binary File Considerations

Some PeopleSoft maintenance items include Java and other binary files. Deploying these files may require you to restart your web server, application server, or batch server. Be sure to make note of this and schedule maintenance accordingly.

# Conclusion

Because each change package is a little different, it is not possible to document fully the steps required to apply every change package manually. In this appendix you learned tips to guide you through the change package application process so you can feel comfortable applying maintenance without the assistance of Change Assistant and the EMF.

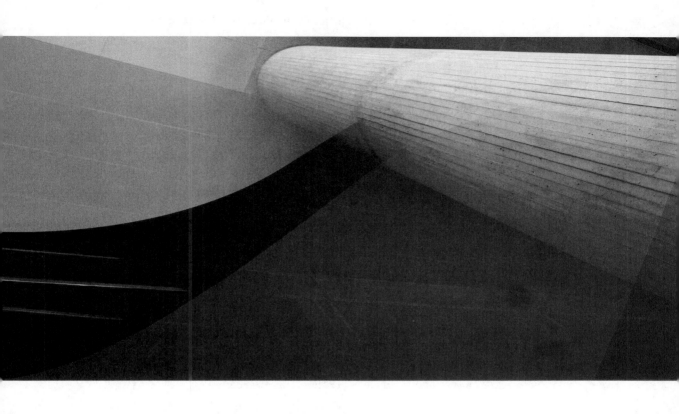

# APPENDIX B

## Data Mover Commands and Syntax

his appendix contains a listing of common Data Mover commands and command syntax. In the syntax and example sections, the combination { | } represent a choice. For example, {record_name | *} means either record_name or *, but not both. Text inside [] represents an optional parameter. For example, [WHERE SQL] means the WHERE parameter is optional.

# CHANGE_ACCESS_PASSWORD

Change the password associated with a Symbolic ID. For Oracle, Microsoft SQL Server, and Sybase, this command updates the Symbolic ID's database password. All other databases require you to change the database password from within your database's management tool. For all databases, this command updates the password in PeopleSoft's metadata (the PSACCESSPRFL record).

## Syntax

```
CHANGE_ACCESS_PASSWORD symbolic_id new_password;
```

## Parameters

- `symbolic_id`  The symbolic ID you want to update.
- `new_password`  The new password value for the database symbolic ID.

# CREATE_TEMP_TABLE

This command creates temporary table instances for an Application Engine temporary table based on the number of instances requested in the Application Engine's properties as well as the number of instances specified in the PeopleTools Options page.

## Syntax

```
CREATE_TEMP_TABLE {record_name | *};
```

## Parameter

■ `record_name`   Either an Application Engine record name (usually suffixed with *TAO*) to build temporary table instances for a single record definition or the wildcard * to build all temporary Application Engine tables.

# CREATE_TRIGGER

This command creates database triggers.

## Syntax

```
CREATE_TRIGGER {record_name | *};
```

## Parameter

■ `record_name`   Either the name of a record definition or the wildcard * to build triggers for all record definitions.

# ENCRYPT_PASSWORD

This command encrypts the password for a user (or all users) within the PeopleSoft user profile (PSOPRDEFN).

## Syntax

```
ENCRYPT_PASSWORD {OPRID | *};
```

## Parameter

■ `OPRID`   The PeopleSoft operator ID whose password will be encrypted. Specify the wildcard * to encrypt all PSOPRDEFN passwords.

# EXPORT

This command exports the contents of a table (or all tables) to a file. Prior to using the EXPORT command, use the SET OUTPUT command to specify a destination file.

## Syntax

```
EXPORT {record_name | *} [WHERE SQL];
```

## Parameters

- `record_name`  Either a record definition name or SQL table name to export a single table, or the wildcard * to export all tables.

- `WHERE SQL`  Optional selection criteria identifying which rows to export from `record_name`. This parameter is not valid when using the wildcard * to export all tables.

# IMPORT

This command imports data contained in a previously created export file. The target tables do not have to exist, because the `IMPORT` command will create missing tables and indexes based on metadata stored in the export file. When you're copying data between two databases, however, the record definitions must be identical.

## Syntax

```
IMPORT {record_name | *} [IGNORE_DUPS]
   [AS new_table_name] [WHERE SQL];
```

## Parameters

- `record_name`  The name of a specific record contained in the export file or the wildcard * to import all record definitions contained in the export file.

- `IGNORE_DUPS`  Optional modifier that tells Data Mover to ignore error messages when inserting duplicate rows as identified by a record's unique index.

- `AS new_table_name`  Optional parameter that requests Data Mover to import data into a table with a different name than the original table name. This parameter cannot be used with the wildcard *.

- `WHERE SQL`  Optional parameter to import a subset of the rows contained in the export file. This parameter cannot be used with the wildcard *.

# RENAME

This command renames a record or a field within the PeopleSoft metadata tables. It does not change the database structure. After using Data Mover to change the definition's name, use Application Designer to rebuild the definition and all related dependencies.

## Syntax

```
RENAME {RECORD record_name |
       FIELD {field_name | record_name.field_name}}
  AS new_name;
```

## Parameters

- `RECORD record_name`  The name of a record to rename.

- `FIELD field_name`  The name of a field to rename, causing an update to all records that use this field.

- `FIELD record_name.field_name`  Rename the field and update only one record definition.

- `AS new_name`  The new name for the record or field.

# REPLACE_ALL

This command is a variant of `IMPORT` that drops the target table before performing the import. The `REPLACE_ALL` command will re-create the target table and its indexes.

## Syntax

```
REPLACE_ALL {record_name | *}
    [AS new_table_name);
```

## Parameters

- `record_name` The name of a specific record contained in the input file or the wildcard * to import all record definitions contained in the input file.

- `AS new_table_name` Optional parameter that requests that Data Mover import data into a table with a name different from the original table name. This parameter cannot be used with the wildcard *.

# REPLACE_DATA

This command is a variant of the `IMPORT` command. It deletes all data from the target table prior to import. It differs from the `REPLACE_ALL` command in that it does not change the structure of the target table.

## Syntax

```
REPLACE_DATA {record_name | *};
```

## Parameter

- `record_name` The name of a specific record contained in the input file or the wildcard * to import all record definitions contained in the input file.

# REPLACE_VIEW

This command drops and re-creates one or all views defined in the PeopleSoft record metadata.

## Syntax

```
REPLACE_VIEW {record_name | *};
```

### Parameter

- `record_name`   The name of a specific view record or the wildcard * to re-create all views.

# RUN

This command runs another Data Mover script from within the current Data Mover script. The requested Data Mover script must reside in the same file directory as the currently running Data Mover script.

### Syntax

```
RUN data_mover_file_name.dms;
```

### Parameter

- `data_mover_file_name.dms`   The name of the Data Mover file to execute.

# SWAP_BASE_LANGUAGE

This command changes the base language and updates the appropriate PeopleSoft metadata.

### Syntax

```
SWAP BASE_LANGUAGE language_cd;
```

### Parameter

- `language_cd`   Three-letter target language code.

# SET Statements

The `SET` statement alters Data Mover's default behavior and provides Data Mover with additional information where necessary. `SET` statements grouped together before a command alter the way Data Mover executes the following commands. A `SET` statement following a command invalidates all prior `SET` statements.

# SET BASE_LANGUAGE

Use this `SET` statement prior to the command `SWAP_BASE_LANGUAGE record_name` to swap the base language of a specific record definition only if a standard `SWAP_BASE_LANGUAGE` command failed.

**Example**

```
SET BASE_LANGUAGE CFR;
```

# SET COMMIT

Use this `SET` statement to specify the commit interval when inserting rows into the database. Managing the commit interval is important for performance. A commit interval that is too large may cause large updates to fail due to temporary space constraints. A commit interval that is too small may reduce performance. A commit interval of 0 will commit after processing all of the rows for a record definition. Be aware that some database platforms will perform an implicit commit when executing data definition language (DDL) statements.

**Example**

```
SET COMMIT 1000;
```

# SET CREATE_INDEX_BEFORE_DATA

When importing data using the `REPLACE_ALL` command, Data Mover's default is to import data and then create indexes. This `SET` statement directs Data Mover to create indexes before importing data. Creating indexes first may reduce performance as the database alters index metadata for each row.

**Example**

```
SET CREATE_INDEX_BEFORE_DATA;
```

# SET DDL

This SET statement allows you to import definitions into containers that differ from the input file. For example, use this SET statement to import all indexes from the input file into a different tablespace.

**Example**

```
SET DDL INDEX * INPUT PTTLRG AS PTTLRG_IDX;
```

# SET EXECUTE_SQL

Use this SET statement to execute an SQL statement prior to performing an IMPORT command. This statement was used with Oracle versions prior to 10*g* to manage rollback segments. It is not necessary with 10*g* and later versions when using undo segments.

**Example**

```
SET EXECUTE_SQL sql_statement;
```

# SET EXTRACT

Use this SET statement to extract DDL information from an input file.

**Example**

```
SET EXTRACT OUTPUT c:\temp\ddl.sql;
SET EXTRACT DDL;
```

# SET IGNORE_DUPS

This SET statement tells Data Mover to ignore duplicate row warnings. Duplicate row errors are thrown by the database on insert when a row has a unique index and a Data Mover import attempts to insert a new row that violates the unique index constraint. This statement turns off bulk imports, causing a row-by-row insert.

**Example**

```
SET IGNORE_DUPS;
```

## SET IGNORE_ERRORS

Use this `SET` statement with the `SWAP_BASE_LANGUAGE` command to allow the command to continue even if it encounters errors. If you use this `SET` statement, review the log, resolve errors, and then run the `SET BASE_LANGUAGE; SWAP_BASE_LANGUAGE record_name;` combination.

**Example**

```
SET IGNORE_ERRORS;
```

## SET INPUT

Use this `SET` statement to specify the name of an export file for `IMPORT` commands or `EXTRACT` statements.

**Example**

```
SET INPUT C:\TEMP\my_exported_file.dat;
```

## SET INSERT_DATA_ONCE

This `SET` statement tells Data Mover to execute an `IMPORT` only if the target table is empty.

**Example**

```
SET INSERT_DATA_ONCE INSTALLATION;
```

## SET LOG

Use this `SET` statement to specify the name and location of the Data Mover log file.

**Example**

```
SET LOG c:\temp\my_datamover.log;
```

## SET NO DATA

Use this `SET` statement to prevent data from being imported or exported.

**Example**

```
SET NO DATA;
```

# SET NO INDEX

Use this SET statement to prevent Data Mover from creating indexes during an IMPORT operation.

**Example**

```
SET NO INDEX;
```

# SET NO RECORD

Use this SET statement to tell Data Mover to skip creating records when importing data.

**Example**

```
SET NO RECORD;
```

# SET NO SPACE

Use this SET statement to prevent Data Mover from creating tablespaces when importing data.

**Example**

```
SET NO SPACE;
```

# SET NO TRACE

Use this SET statement to turn off tracing options that were previously set in Configuration Manager.

**Example**

```
SET NO TRACE;
```

# SET NO VIEW

Use this SET statement to keep Data Mover from creating views.

**Example**

```
SET NO VIEW;
```

## SET OUTPUT

Use this SET statement to identify the output file for EXPORT commands. You need to use this SET statement only once. Multiple definitions can be added to the same output file.

**Example**

```
SET OUTPUT c:\temp\my_export_file.dat;
```

## SET SPACE/DBSPACE

Use this SET command to import data into a different tablespace than what was specified in the input file. Use the DBSPACE statement with DB2 for z/OS. Use the SPACE statement for all other database platforms.

**Example**

```
SET SPACE old_tbs AS new_tbs;

SET DBSPACE old_db.old_tbs AS new_db.new_tbs;
```

## SET START

Use this SET statement to restart an import when a prior import failed. This statement tells Data Mover where to restart the import. This statement may also be used with the REPLACE_VIEW command to restart a failed REPLACE_VIEW command.

**Example**

```
SET START AFTER PSOPRDEFN;
```

## SET STATISTICS

When running an IMPORT command in bootstrap mode, use this SET statement to tell Data Mover whether or not to update database statistics.

**Example**

```
SET STATISTICS OFF;
```

# SET UNICODE
Use this SET statement in bootstrap mode for the initial database load.

**Example**

```
SET UNICODE ON;
```

# SET UPDATE_DUPS
Use this SET statement to cause Data Mover to import new rows only, updating rows that already exist.

**Example**

```
SET UPDATE_DUPS;
```

# Standard SQL Commands
You can use the following standard SQL commands within any Data Mover file:

- ALTER
- COMMIT
- CREATE
- DELETE
- DROP
- GRANT
- INSERT
- ROLLBACK
- TRUNCATE
- UPDATE

# Nonstandard SQL Commands

PeopleSoft uses the following nonstandard SQL commands to manipulate COBOL SQL statements.

## STORE

The `STORE` command inserts COBOL SQL statements into the `PS_SQLSTMT_TBL` table, deleting duplicates prior to insertion.

### Syntax

```
STORE programname_type_statementname
SELECT ...
```

The parameter is a concatenation of the program name, SQL type, and the statement name.

### Example

```
STORE MYPGM_S_OPRQRY
SELECT SETID, OPERID
  FROM PS_TABLE_NAME
 WHERE SOME_FIELD != ' ';
```

## ERASE

Use the `ERASE` command to delete a stored COBOL SQL statement or to delete all stored SQL statements for a specific COBOL program.

### Syntax

```
ERASE programname_type_statementname
```

### Example

```
ERASE MYPGM_S_OPRQRY;

ERASE MYPGM;
```

# Meta-SQL Statements

Data Mover supports the following Meta-SQL statements.

## CURRENTDATEOUT

Use this Meta-SQL statement anywhere that you require the database date as an output value—for example, in a SELECT list or column UPDATE statement.

**Example**

```
SELECT OPRID, OPRDEFNDESC, %CURRENTDATEOUT
   FROM PSOPRDEFN;
```

## CURRENTTIMEOUT

Use this Meta-SQL statement anywhere that you require the database time as an output value—for example, in a SELECT list or column UPDATE statement.

**Example**

```
SELECT OPRID, OPRDEFNDESC, %CURRENTTIMEOUT
   FROM PSOPRDEFN;
```

## CURRENTDATETIMEOUT

Use this Meta-SQL statement anywhere that you require the database date/time as an output value—for example, in a SELECT list or column UPDATE statement.

**Example**

```
SELECT OPRID, OPRDEFNDESC, %CURRENTDATETIMEOUT
   FROM PSOPRDEFN;
```

## DATEIN

Use this Meta-SQL statement in a WHERE clause when specifying a plain text date.

**Example**

```
UPDATE PSOPRDEFN
    SET ACCTLOCK = 1
 WHERE LASTSIGNONDTTM < %DATEIN('2011-12-31');
```

## TIMEIN

Use this Meta-SQL statement in a WHERE clause when specifying a plain text time.

**Example**

```
UPDATE PSOPRDEFN
    SET ACCTLOCK = 1
 WHERE LASTSIGNONDTTM < %TIMEIN('23.34.55.144267');
```

# Conclusion

In this appendix, you learned how to use Data Mover's commands and statements to write Data Mover scripts.

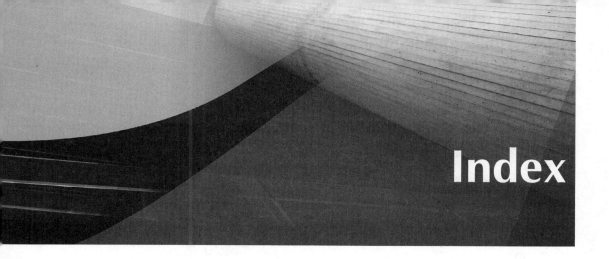

# Index

3 1170 00924 3720

# GET YOUR FREE SUBSCRIPTION
# TO *ORACLE MAGAZINE*

*Oracle Magazine* is essential gear for today's information technology professionals. Stay informed and increase your productivity with every issue of *Oracle Magazine*. Inside each free bimonthly issue you'll get:

- Up-to-date information on Oracle Database, Oracle Application Server, Web development, enterprise grid computing, database technology, and business trends
- Third-party news and announcements
- Technical articles on Oracle and partner products, technologies, and operating environments
- Development and administration tips
- Real-world customer stories

If there are other Oracle users at your location who would like to receive their own subscription to *Oracle Magazine*, please photo-copy this form and pass it along.

## Three easy ways to subscribe:

**① Web**
Visit our Web site at **oracle.com/oraclemagazine**
You'll find a subscription form there, plus much more

**② Fax**
Complete the questionnaire on the back of this card
and fax the questionnaire side only to **+1.847.763.9638**

**③ Mail**
Complete the questionnaire on the back of this card
and mail it to **P.O. Box 1263, Skokie, IL 60076-8263**

ORACLE®

# Want your own FREE subscription?

To receive a free subscription to *Oracle Magazine*, you must fill out the entire card, sign it, and date it (incomplete cards cannot be processed or acknowledged). You can also fax your application to +1.847.763.9638. **Or subscribe at our Web site at oracle.com/oraclemagazine**

○ **Yes, please send me a FREE subscription** *Oracle Magazine.*     ○ No.

○ From time to time, Oracle Publishing allows our partners exclusive access to our e-mail addresses for special promotions and announcements. To be included in this program, please check this circle. If you do not wish to be included, you will only receive notices about your subscription via e-mail.

○ Oracle Publishing allows sharing of our postal mailing list with selected third parties. If you prefer your mailing address not to be included in this program, please check this circle.

If at any time you would like to be removed from either mailing list, please contact Customer Service at +1.847.763.9635 or send an e-mail to oracle@halldata.com. If you opt in to the sharing of information, Oracle may also provide you with e-mail related to Oracle products, services, and events. If you want to completely unsubscribe from any e-mail communication from Oracle, please send an e-mail to: unsubscribe@oracle-mail.com with the following in the subject line: REMOVE [your e-mail address]. For complete information on Oracle Publishing's privacy practices, please visit oracle.com/html/privacy/html

**X** _____  date _____
signature (required)

name _____  title _____

company _____  e-mail address _____

street/p.o. box _____

city/state/zip or postal code _____  telephone _____

country _____  fax _____

**Would you like to receive your free subscription in digital format instead of print if it becomes available?** ○ Yes  ○ No

---

## YOU MUST ANSWER ALL 10 QUESTIONS BELOW.

**① WHAT IS THE PRIMARY BUSINESS ACTIVITY OF YOUR FIRM AT THIS LOCATION? (check one only)**
- ☐ 01 Aerospace and Defense Manufacturing
- ☐ 02 Application Service Provider
- ☐ 03 Automotive Manufacturing
- ☐ 04 Chemicals
- ☐ 05 Media and Entertainment
- ☐ 06 Construction/Engineering
- ☐ 07 Consumer Sector/Consumer Packaged Goods
- ☐ 08 Education
- ☐ 09 Financial Services/Insurance
- ☐ 10 Health Care
- ☐ 11 High Technology Manufacturing, OEM
- ☐ 12 Industrial Manufacturing
- ☐ 13 Independent Software Vendor
- ☐ 14 Life Sciences (biotech, pharmaceuticals)
- ☐ 15 Natural Resources
- ☐ 16 Oil and Gas
- ☐ 17 Professional Services
- ☐ 18 Public Sector (government)
- ☐ 19 Research
- ☐ 20 Retail/Wholesale/Distribution
- ☐ 21 Systems Integrator, VAR/VAD
- ☐ 22 Telecommunications
- ☐ 23 Travel and Transportation
- ☐ 24 Utilities (electric, gas, sanitation, water)
- ☐ 98 Other Business and Services _____

**② WHICH OF THE FOLLOWING BEST DESCRIBES YOUR PRIMARY JOB FUNCTION? (check one only)**

CORPORATE MANAGEMENT/STAFF
- ☐ 01 Executive Management (President, Chair, CEO, CFO, Owner, Partner, Principal)
- ☐ 02 Finance/Administrative Management (VP/Director/ Manager/Controller, Purchasing, Administration)
- ☐ 03 Sales/Marketing Management (VP/Director/Manager)
- ☐ 04 Computer Systems/Operations Management (CIO/VP/Director/Manager MIS/IS/IT, Ops)

IS/IT STAFF
- ☐ 05 Application Development/Programming Management
- ☐ 06 Application Development/Programming Staff
- ☐ 07 Consulting
- ☐ 08 DBA/Systems Administrator
- ☐ 09 Education/Training
- ☐ 10 Technical Support Director/Manager
- ☐ 11 Other Technical Management/Staff
- ☐ 98 Other

**③ WHAT IS YOUR CURRENT PRIMARY OPERATING PLATFORM (check all that apply)**
- ☐ 01 Digital Equipment Corp UNIX/VAX/VMS
- ☐ 02 HP UNIX
- ☐ 03 IBM AIX
- ☐ 04 IBM UNIX
- ☐ 05 Linux (Red Hat)
- ☐ 06 Linux (SUSE)
- ☐ 07 Linux (Oracle Enterprise)
- ☐ 08 Linux (other)
- ☐ 09 Macintosh
- ☐ 10 MVS
- ☐ 11 Netware
- ☐ 12 Network Computing
- ☐ 13 SCO UNIX
- ☐ 14 Sun Solaris/SunOS
- ☐ 15 Windows
- ☐ 16 Other UNIX
- ☐ 98 Other
- 99 ☐ None of the Above

**④ DO YOU EVALUATE, SPECIFY, RECOMMEND, OR AUTHORIZE THE PURCHASE OF ANY OF THE FOLLOWING? (check all that apply)**
- ☐ 01 Hardware
- ☐ 02 Business Applications (ERP, CRM, etc.)
- ☐ 03 Application Development Tools
- ☐ 04 Database Products
- ☐ 05 Internet or Intranet Products
- ☐ 06 Other Software
- ☐ 07 Middleware Products
- 99 ☐ None of the Above

**⑤ IN YOUR JOB, DO YOU USE OR PLAN TO PURCHASE ANY OF THE FOLLOWING PRODUCTS? (check all that apply)**

SOFTWARE
- ☐ 01 CAD/CAE/CAM
- ☐ 02 Collaboration Software
- ☐ 03 Communications
- ☐ 04 Database Management
- ☐ 05 File Management
- ☐ 06 Finance
- ☐ 07 Java
- ☐ 08 Multimedia Authoring
- ☐ 09 Networking
- ☐ 10 Programming
- ☐ 11 Project Management
- ☐ 12 Scientific and Engineering
- ☐ 13 Systems Management
- ☐ 14 Workflow

HARDWARE
- ☐ 15 Macintosh
- ☐ 16 Mainframe
- ☐ 17 Massively Parallel Processing
- ☐ 18 Minicomputer
- ☐ 19 Intel x86(32)
- ☐ 20 Intel x86(64)
- ☐ 21 Network Computer
- ☐ 22 Symmetric Multiprocessing
- ☐ 23 Workstation Services

SERVICES
- ☐ 24 Consulting
- ☐ 25 Education/Training
- ☐ 26 Maintenance
- ☐ 27 Online Database
- ☐ 28 Support
- ☐ 29 Technology-Based Training
- ☐ 30 Other
- 99 ☐ None of the Above

**⑥ WHAT IS YOUR COMPANY'S SIZE? (check one only)**
- ☐ 01 More than 25,000 Employees
- ☐ 02 10,001 to 25,000 Employees
- ☐ 03 5,001 to 10,000 Employees
- ☐ 04 1,001 to 5,000 Employees
- ☐ 05 101 to 1,000 Employees
- ☐ 06 Fewer than 100 Employees

**⑦ DURING THE NEXT 12 MONTHS, HOW MUCH DO YOU ANTICIPATE YOUR ORGANIZATION WILL SPEND ON COMPUTER HARDWARE, SOFTWARE, PERIPHERALS, AND SERVICES FOR YOUR LOCATION? (check one only)**
- ☐ 01 Less than $10,000
- ☐ 02 $10,000 to $49,999
- ☐ 03 $50,000 to $99,999
- ☐ 04 $100,000 to $499,999
- ☐ 05 $500,000 to $999,999
- ☐ 06 $1,000,000 and Over

**⑧ WHAT IS YOUR COMPANY'S YEARLY SALES REVENUE? (check one only)**
- ☐ 01 $500, 000, 000 and above
- ☐ 02 $100, 000, 000 to $500, 000, 000
- ☐ 03 $50, 000, 000 to $100, 000, 000
- ☐ 04 $5, 000, 000 to $50, 000, 000
- ☐ 05 $1, 000, 000 to $5, 000, 000

**⑨ WHAT LANGUAGES AND FRAMEWORKS DO YOU USE? (check all that apply)**
- ☐ 01 Ajax
- ☐ 02 C
- ☐ 03 C++
- ☐ 04 C#
- ☐ 05 Hibernate
- ☐ 06 J++/J#
- ☐ 07 Java
- ☐ 08 JSP
- ☐ 09 .NET
- ☐ 10 Perl
- ☐ 11 PHP
- ☐ 12 PL/SQL
- ☐ 13 Python
- ☐ 14 Ruby/Rails
- ☐ 15 Spring
- ☐ 16 Struts
- ☐ 17 SQL
- ☐ 18 Visual Basic
- ☐ 98 Other

**⑩ WHAT ORACLE PRODUCTS ARE IN USE AT YOUR SITE? (check all that apply)**

ORACLE DATABASE
- ☐ 01 Oracle Database 11*g*
- ☐ 02 Oracle Database 10*g*
- ☐ 03 Oracle9*i* Database
- ☐ 04 Oracle Embedded Database (Oracle Lite, Times Ten, Berkeley DB)
- ☐ 05 Other Oracle Database Release

ORACLE FUSION MIDDLEWARE
- ☐ 06 Oracle Application Server
- ☐ 07 Oracle Portal
- ☐ 08 Oracle Enterprise Manager
- ☐ 09 Oracle BPEL Process Manager
- ☐ 10 Oracle Identity Management
- ☐ 11 Oracle SOA Suite
- ☐ 12 Oracle Data Hubs

ORACLE DEVELOPMENT TOOLS
- ☐ 13 Oracle JDeveloper
- ☐ 14 Oracle Forms
- ☐ 15 Oracle Reports
- ☐ 16 Oracle Designer
- ☐ 17 Oracle Discoverer
- ☐ 18 Oracle BI Beans
- ☐ 19 Oracle Warehouse Builder
- ☐ 20 Oracle WebCenter
- ☐ 21 Oracle Application Express

ORACLE APPLICATIONS
- ☐ 22 Oracle E-Business Suite
- ☐ 23 PeopleSoft Enterprise
- ☐ 24 JD Edwards EnterpriseOne
- ☐ 25 JD Edwards World
- ☐ 26 Oracle Fusion
- ☐ 27 Hyperion
- ☐ 28 Siebel CRM

ORACLE SERVICES
- ☐ 28 Oracle E-Business Suite On Demand
- ☐ 29 Oracle Technology On Demand
- ☐ 30 Siebel CRM On Demand
- ☐ 31 Oracle Consulting
- ☐ 32 Oracle Education
- ☐ 33 Oracle Support
- ☐ 98 Other
- 99 ☐ None of the Above